MARINE
BADGES
&
INSIGNIA
OF THE WORLD

BERT L. CAMPBELL · RON REYNOLDS

MARINE BADGES

&

INSIGNIA

OF THE WORLD

Including Marines, Commandos and Naval Infantrymen

BLANDFORD PRESS
POOLE · DORSET

First published in the U.K. 1983 by Blandford Press,
Link House, West Street, Poole, Dorset, BH15 1LL

Copyright © 1983 Blandford Books Ltd.

Distributed in the United States by
Sterling Publishing Co., Inc.,
2 Park Avenue, New York, N.Y. 10016.

British Library Cataloguing in Publication Data

Campbell, Bert L.
  Marine badges & insignia of the world including
  marines, commandos and naval infantrymen.
  1. Navies—Insignia
  I. Title
  359.1'4   VC345

ISBN 0 7137 1138 8

Typeset in 10/11pt Plantin Light by
Asco Trade Typesetting Ltd., Hong Kong.

Printed and Bound in Great Britain by
Shenval Marketing Ltd, Harlow, Essex.

CONTENTS

LIST OF PLATES

ACKNOWLEDGEMENTS

A book of this type is necessarily a mosaic, and many have contributed time, energy, knowledge, and material toward the completed work. Staff Sergeant Leo P. Cabal, Jr, USMC, a prime mover in this project; Colonel B. Heiberg-Iurgensen, Commandant, the Marine Regiment, Royal Danish Army; Captain Bent Sohnemann, the Marine Regiment, Royal Danish Army; Captain Helge Nielsen, Royal Danish Navy; Commander Eduardo P. Alimonda, Assistant Naval Attaché, Argentine Embassy, Washington, D.C.; Commander Giuseppe Mazzoli, Italian Navy, Assistant Naval Attaché, Italian Embassy, Washington, D.C.; Lieutenant Colonel M. F. Murray, Royal Marines; Major A. G. Brown, MBE, Royal Marines, Director of Royal Marines Museum; Commander J. J. W. van Waning, Royal Netherlands Navy, Assistant Naval Attaché, Royal Netherlands Embassy, Washington, D.C.; Colonel J. C. Hardy, MVO, British Defence Staff, British Embassy, Washington, D.C.; Rear Admiral Le Cloerec, Naval Attache, Embassy of France, Washington, D.C.; Bruna Gay Pecciarini, Rome, Italy; Colonel Henryk Krezeszowski, Embassy of the Polish People's Republic, Washington, D.C.; Rear Admiral Peixoto Faria Lima, Brazilian Navy; Captain José L. Fauste, Spanish Navy, Naval Attaché, Spanish Embassy, Washington, D.C.; Major Timo Apajakari, Finnish Army, Helsinki, Finland; Admiral Julio C. Lanz C., Commandant, del Cuerpo de la Infanteria de Marina, Republic of Venezuela; Captain Raul A. Canizares, Naval Attaché, Embassy of Ecuador, Washington, D.C.; Major C. D. Espinoza, USMC, Marine Advisor to the Venezuelan Marines; Master Gunnery Sergeant Chuck Gaustein, USMC (Ret.), Quartermaster, Marine Military Academy, Harlingen, Texas; Master Sergeant Matthew C. Thompson, USMC, Military Instructor, Des Moines Technical High School, Des Moines, Iowa; Ralph W. Donnelly, Historian, Washington, North Carolina; Ken L. Smith-Christmas, Registrar, History and Museum Division, USMC; Gunnery Sergeant William K. Judge, DAVA, U.S. Marine Corps Historical Center; First Lieutenant Pepper Guthrie, USMC; Tom Bartlett, Managing Editor, Leatherneck magazine; Mark Beveridge, Curator, and Elizabeth Pessek, Archivist, the Liberty Memorial World War I Museum; Chip Minx, authority on Imperial German Units and Militaria; Major Donald F. Bittner, Ph.D., USMC; Lieutenant Colonel R. K. Young, Major John Hudson and Sergeant Major J. T. Barnes, Headquarters Company, 24th (U.S.) Marines; Fire Chief Patrick G. Clark, a former Marine and authority on Marine insignia; Loren Taylor, Lawyer, U.S. Army officer and former Marine; Robert L. Serra, Italian Vice-Consul, Kansas City, Kansas; Eugene F. Gray, Spanish Consul, Kansas City, Missouri; Craig Murray, Latin Scholar; Sergeant Major Charles W. Gamm, USMC (Ret.); Master Sergeant Michael Senkas, USMC, Marine Corps Recruiting Station, Kansas City, Mo.; Tom Shutt, The King's Crown Militaria, Overland Park, Kansas; Staff Sergeant H. E. Rogers, USMC, (Ret.); Sergeant Frank Clair and Officer Randy Murphy, Laboratory Technician, both Kansas City, Kansas Police Dept; The Atlanta Historical Society; Ron Manion; Major A. J. Donald, Royal Marines, Corps Historical Records Officer; Emanuel Scoulas, Illinois; and Barry Gregory, Blandford Press, and several dozen collectors, Marines, former Marines, veterans of World War I and II, Korea and Vietnam. If 'thank you' will suffice, consider it said.

Bert Campbell
Kansas City, Mo.
USA

INTRODUCTION

At some unrecorded place centuries ago, a warrior stood up in a boat and prepared to go ashore to join the battle. No ancient scribe was present to set down whether the man won or lost, lived or died, and yet, as he ran through the surf toward the unnamed shore, primitively armed and equipped, he was blazing a trail that thousands would follow in the ages to come. By the most basic definition, he was a marine.

As early as 500 B.C., the Greeks were using *epibatae*, a term that translates roughly as 'heavily armed sea-soldiers'. In later times, the Romans also had sea-going soldiers in the fleet.

But Marines, as we know them today, probably were born on 28 October 1664, when England's Lord High Admiral, the Duke of York and Albany, was ordered to raise a body of 1200 'land souljers' to be distributed throughout His Majesty's Fleets prepared for sea service. It was to be known as the Lord High Admiral's Regiment, and its members would be cloaked in coats of yellow cloth, which was the favorite color of the Lord High Admiral.

This volume, in a sense, will concentrate more on the color of the coats than the exploits of the men who wore them. It is not intended to be a history, although it will unavoidably be intertwined with history. It will also skip back and forth in time in dealing with the badges and insignia of some of the nations covered, because of the longevity of their Marine or Naval Infantry units and the relatively high visibility of their emblems from times long past.

Since the emergence of the modern-day Marine in the seventeenth century, their uniforms and insignia have been among the most colorful and distinctive of any military units in the world.

The Marine is clearly a 'sea-soldier', although his duties in the late twentieth century go far beyond that definition. His uniforms and insignia usually reflect the dual nature of his role, particularly the dress uniforms, which commonly, through coloring, show the naval link, while the military connection is evident in the cut, the accessories and the frequent use of army rank structure and insignia.

The existence of a Marine Corps is often a clear sign that a nation is or was a strong naval power with colonial interests. Some nations, such as Austria and Sweden, once had Marine formations in their forces but abolished them. It is estimated that about twenty-nine nations currently have units that can be counted as Marine or Naval Infantry. The latter is more difficult to define than the former. Obviously, a naval infantryman has to be something of a specialist, not just a sailor who has been handed a rifle and told to join the battle on land.

Naval brigades, battalions or divisions are often formed when a nation is in its death throes, and its beached sailors are utilized in the only places left for them to fight – on land. There is usually an attempt or two made to legitimatize such formations, such as in the case of the American Confederacy, when an admiral was redesignated a general and told to press on with his gaunt columns of seafarers to try to reinforce Lee near Appomattox; or in the twilight of Germany's Third Reich, when the shipless naval personnel were issued Army-type uniforms and herded to battles that could never be won for a cause that was long since lost. Whatever their valor, and even though many died without a deck beneath their feet, they were still sailors, not Marines or specialized Naval Infantry and, for the most part, will not be covered in this volume.

Throughout this book, except in the Royal Marines section, American terms will generally, but not always, be used. The American term 'enlisted men', instead of the British 'other ranks' is one example, and 'shoulder patch' instead of 'formation sign' is another. Most such terms are universally understood.

1

UNITED STATES MARINE CORPS

Second Lt G. Greeley Wells had brought the first flag with him in his map case, but once raised, it was obviously too small, so he went back down the steep hillside to the shore below to get a larger one from LST (Landing Ship, Tank) 779, and it was the one everyone would remember. It was put on a length of pipe, and as it was being thrust into the soft, volcanic soil, a news service photographer snapped a picture that would become one of the most famous news photographs of World War II.

There were six of them raising the Stars and Stripes that February day in 1945, all members of E Company, 28th Marines. They were all clustered together so closely that only four can clearly be seen on the news photograph. At the very back of the group Pfc. Ira H. Hayes, an American Indian from Bapchule, Arizona, strains with arms outstretched as if he had just released his grip on the pipe. Like the others, he was wearing the standard Marine Corps combat fatigues with a camouflaged cover over his steel helmet, but also seems to have a poncho or shelter half hanging from the back of his belt. In front of him, hands closed firmly around the pipe, was Pfc. Franklin R. Sousely of Flemingsburg, Kentucky. Sgt Michael Strank, Conemaugh, Pennsylvania; Navy Pharmacist's Mate 2nd Class John H. Bradley, then of Appleton, Wisconsin; Pfc. Rene A. Gagnon, Manchester, New Hampshire, and Cpl Harlon H. Block, Weslaco, Texas, completed the tableau of the American flag being raised atop Mount Suribachi, an extinct 550-foot volcano on a 5-mile long, $2\frac{1}{2}$-mile wide island called Iwo Jima, 670 miles from Tokyo and the Japanese heartland.

Block, Strank and Sousely would not leave Iwo Jima alive. As the years passed, the remaining Marines from that historic flag raising would die, one by one, all much too young. Gagnon died at 53 during the 1970s, leaving Bradley, now of Antigo, Wisconsin, who was the only Navy man (a corpsman attached to the Marines) in the group, as the sole survivor.

It had taken Easy Company's Marines about 30 minutes to clamber up the side of Suribachi, but the road leading to it had started 170 years before and half-a-world away in Philadelphia, Pennsylvania. It was there that the tavernkeeper of the Tun Tavern, Robert Mullan, signed up men for the newly authorized Continental Marines with such success that he was soon commissioned a captain and was the Corps' first recruiting specialist.

The men recruited for the Marines (not yet officially a Corps) went into battle wearing green coats with white facings, white breeches and black hats with the brim edged in white. The left side of the brim was turned up against the crown. The raising of two battalions of Marines had been approved by the Continental Congress on 10 November 1775, the date the United States Marine Corps celebrates as its birthday. Less than four months later, at New Providence Island in the Bahamas, the American Marines landed for the first time. They captured Fort Montagu and Fort Nassau and took cannon, mortars and gunpowder before sailing away two weeks later, taking along three American ships recaptured from the British.

The green-coated 'leathernecks', so nicknamed because of leather stocks or neckpieces which legend has it were supposed to deflect cutlass slashes in battle, fought in many important engagements during the War for Independence, although their estimated strength never exceeded 2100. Their senior officer was Major Samuel Nicholas, often referred to as the first commandant, although that office was not established until 1800. Their last battle of that war, at Charleston, S.C., in 1780, turned into a defeat as the British recaptured the city and routed the defenders. In the long run, however, the Revolution was successful, peace came, and, in September 1783, the last officer of the Continental Marines was discharged. There would be no more American Marines until 1797, when detachments for three new naval frigates were authorized. One year after that, Congress passed a law establishing a Marine Corps.

The new Marines were not exactly decked out in the latest military fashions. In fact, they were given surplus Army uniforms, consisting of dark blue coats and trousers and red waistcoats. The hat still looked much like the one worn by Continental Marines and was still worn turned up on the left side. The Marines would make do with this outfit for several years.

By 1800 the Marine Corps had its first official commandant, Lt Col. William Ward Burrows, a new headquarters at 8th and 'I' Streets in Washington, D.C., and a new uniform. This one was a little more special than the Army hand-me-downs they had been wearing. The coat was dark blue with scarlet facings and gold trim. The trousers were white and the tall black shakos had red plumes, gold cords and square, brass front plates that left no doubt as to who the wearers were. The word 'MARINES' was inscribed in half-inch capital letters across the bottom of the plate.

It was during this period that the Marines went to 'the shores of Tripoli' – famed in the 'Marine Hymn' – where they fought the pirates of the Barbary States of North Africa, and sniped at the French in an undeclared war that ran on for several years. It was at the end of the conflict in Tripoli that the Marine Corps gained a uniform item that is still in use today. Legend has it that Marine Lt Presley Neville O'Bannon, whose Marines were part of a 500-man force that attempted to attack Tripoli after an across-the-desert march, was presented the sword of a native leader. The sword, with a jeweled ivory hilt and a 32-inch blade, was the model for the so-called

Above: An enlisted Marine of the early 1870s who still wears the Civil War-type kepi, but has the new Corps badge on both cap and belt buckle. The chevrons on the lower cuffs may be just ornamentation since the archive caption states that the man is a private.

Left: U.S. Marine officer of the Civil War period strikes a popular pose of that era. The kepi badge of hunter's horn with an encircled 'M' is a modification of the U.S. infantry badge of that day. The Corps did not adopt its famous eagle, globe and anchor badge until 1868, four years after the Civil War's end. The double-breasted frock coat shown here was dark blue. The trousers were light blue with a thin red stripe. The officer is carrying the sword used by USMC officers in that period; later, the famous 'mameluke' sword was officially adopted. The shoulder knot indicates that the man is a second lieutenant.

Mameluke sword carried by Marine officers today.

On 18 June 1812, the Americans went to war with England once again, ostensibly over the impressment of American sailors into the Royal Navy, although attempting to bring Canada into the Union has always been considered at least a secondary motive. The Corps, 1565-men strong, including 42 officers, marched into that war clad in the same uniforms adopted twelve years earlier. The uniforms worn by the officers were a little more ornate. The high, scarlet collars of the officers' coats were trimmed with gold welts. Fringed gold epaulets and a red sash were worn. Instead of a shako, officers wore a fore-and-aft cocked hat with a gold (or brass) American eagle badge high on the left side. Sea battles, such as aboard the *Constitution*, and land battles, such as those at Bladensburg and New Orleans, helped build the legend of the fighting prowess of the U.S. Marines.

In 1820 Lt Col. Archibald Henderson became commandant of the Corps, a post he was to hold for 38 years – longer than any other man. Nearly twelve years of peace followed his appointment, broken finally by a battle with pirates in far-off Sumatra. In 1836, Henderson, now a colonel, volunteered his Marines to help the Army fight Indians in the Southern United States. The Marines had new uniforms for this conflict, including a fatigue outfit. The dress uniform consisted of a dark blue, bell-crowned shako with a brass eagle plate and a yellow pom-pom, a dark blue coat with a gold high collar and epaulets and white trousers. The tropical fatigue uniform employed the shako without ornamentation and had a white jacket and trousers. This war lasted until 1842 and cost the Marine Corps a total of 61 men. Only four years would pass this time before the Corps found itself once again embroiled in war.

California was probably the key to the Mexican War, since the United States wanted it and it became so swollen with American settlers that it became obvious that the Mexicans were not able to hold it. Although the Marine Corps had only 63 officers and 1200 men, it would gain new glory in what would become the 'Halls of Montezuma' in their hymn.

There had been some uniform changes since the Indian Wars. The Marine Band, founded in 1800 by Commandant Burrows, was now wearing red coats. The rest of the Corps wore dark blue coats, but both the red and blue coats had the same trim – gold strips on the high, standing collar and gold, fringed epaulets. Whereas the coat of the Indian Wars days had had two rows of brass buttons down the front, there was now a single row of buttons. White cross belts with a center brass buckle were worn, attaching to a white belt at the waist. White trousers were worn. The shako remained essentially the same as before except the plume was now red. In Mexico, many of the Marines wore the blue, flat-topped peaked cap as worn by the Army. The white tropical fatigues were also used as well as a blue shell jacket. After the Mexican War ended, a red trouser stripe was added for officers and enlisted men to commemorate the Marine blood shed at the battle of Chapultepec.

Less than two years before the outbreak of the American Civil War, an abolitionist named John Brown seized an engine house at Harper's Ferry, Va., about 55 miles from Washington, and, with a small band of followers, apparently tried to touch off an uprising of black slaves in the Southern states. It was an abortive and short-lived attempt. In the first place, few knew he was there. Among the first to know was a Marine detachment from the Washington Navy Yard commanded by 1st Lt Israel Greene. It was ordered to Harper's Ferry, where it was placed under the command of Army Lt Col. Robert E. Lee, whose date with destiny was drawing near. Brown was captured and later hanged.

The Marines, according to drawings of that period, were wearing the blue, flat-topped peaked caps of the Mexican War, but one written account described their headgear as 'French fatigue caps' which probably referred to the képis favored by both sides in the Civil War.

The Civil War cannot be claimed by the Marine Corps as one of its most distinguished periods. Led by aging senior officers and deserted by many junior officers of Southern birth, the Corps saw scattered action both afloat and ashore that did little to enhance its image as a fighting force.

Dressed in long, navy blue frock coats and light blue trousers, the Marines had little to distinguish them from their Army counterparts. Even the badge worn at the front of the dark blue képi – a stringed bugle or hunter's horn – was the badge of the Army's infantry. The Marines, however, added the letter 'M' to the center of the horn's handle. Officers wore shoulder knots of gold on red with rank devices, the same as the Army, affixed near the center. For field service, the smaller, French-type shoulder strap was worn. Chevrons were now in use by NCOs, but, unlike those of the Army, were worn point up. At that time the Corps had only one sergeant major and

Above: An enlisted Marine in the full-dress uniform worn from 1876 to 1891. Both the Marine Corps emblem and U.S. shield on the shako were in brass. The pom-pom was red.

one quartermaster sergeant. The rank of 'orderly sergeant' was the next non-com grade, but it was becoming popularly known as 'first sergeant'. By the Civil War's end, this rank had become the second pay grade, sandwiched between the sergeant major and the quartermaster sergeant.

If the Civil War Marine Corps added little to its glory, it also added few to the casualty list. Out of a strength that never exceeded 3900, the Marines had 77 killed and 131 wounded between 1861 and the war's end in 1865. During a conflict that sometimes pitted brother against brother on the battlefield, Yankee Marine never met Rebel Marine in head-on combat in any numbers throughout the four years, a fact mourned by war gamers more than a century later.

In the years between the end of the Civil War and the start of the Spanish-American War, the Marine Corps made several dozen landings to protect American lives and property at various points around the globe, principally in the Far East, South America and Africa, but the landing parties were usually shipboard detachments, small in number, that dashed in to do their job, then were gone. For 33 years, otherwise, the United States was at peace. The Marines were almost abolished or merged with the Army, but Congress thought better of such proposals and the Corps survived.

A few uniform changes gradually took place during this time, the most notable being the adoption of a Corps emblem to replace the infantry-horn as the headgear badge in 1868. Borrowing from their British cousins, the Royal Marines, the United States Marine Corps' new badge featured a globe (with the Western not the Eastern Hemisphere, however) topped by an American eagle and with a diagonal foul anchor behind the globe. This was worn at the front of the blue, Civil War-type képis still in use, and in the center of the brass shield worn as a shako plate above a laurel wreath. The shako itself was shorter than before and no longer had a bell crown. The red plume at the top was also shorter. Big gold on red chevrons were now being worn by the non-coms.

During the 1870s, Prussian influence replaced French in uniform fashions, and the United States Marines adopted a spiked cork helmet with a large eagle, globe and anchor in brass on the front. The helmets came in both white and dark blue. The coats were dark blue and were worn with either white or light blue trousers. So

Above: This Marine sergeant is wearing the khaki uniform worn from 1892 to 1900. Although the chevrons appear to be white, they were probably gold on red. Marine chevrons were always worn point up. The wide brimmed campaign hat was usually worn with a center crease during the Spanish-American War period, with the Corps badge in the center. Later, during the Boxer Rebellion, it was worn with the brim turned up on the left side, and held in place by the badge. By the start of World War I, the campaign hat was worn with the four-dent 'Montana crease'.

Left: From the size of the helmet ornament, there would be no mistaking from a block away that this officer was a U.S. Marine. Spiked helmets in both dark blue and white were worn by U.S. Marines in the 1880s and 1890s, but were never very popular with the wearers. This man was probably a senior officer since the medal at the far left is not actually a decoration, but the badge of the Grand Army of the Republic, a Civil War veterans' association.

called 'banjo' epaulets, brass-trimmed and with the Corps emblem centered in the round end were now worn with dress uniforms. Service dress coats had a single row of metal buttons, while full dress coats were double-breasted and had two rows of buttons.

At 9.40 pm, on 15 February 1898, two blasts – one short and the other deep and rolling – rocked the battleship U.S.S. *Maine* in the harbor of Havana, Cuba. The ship's bow had been blown away and 250 men, including 28 members of the *Maine*'s Marine detachment were dead.

Capt. Charles D. Sigsbee, commander of the *Maine*, bumped into his Marine orderly, Pvt. William Anthony, in a smoked-filled corridor. 'I beg to report the Captain's ship is sinking', Anthony said as he threw a smart salute. History did not record what Sigsbee replied, but the cry 'Remember the *Maine*' was raised throughout the United States and, despite the lack of proof that Spain was responsible for the sinking, Congress quickly declared war on the once formidable European power. It was to be a short war with few casualties for the Americans, but a costly one for Spain, which lost an empire which the United States gained.

The 1st Marine Battalion, under the command of Lt Col. Robert W. Huntington, went to fight in Cuba wearing blue shirts, light khaki trousers and a khaki hat that would become, in one form or another, a Marine trademark. Generally called a 'campaign' hat, the headgear was broad-brimmed, and during the Spanish-American War, at least, was worn with a center crease.

Officers wore a dark blue coat with elaborate braided frogging across the front. Insignia of rank was worn on the standing collars forward of the Corps insignia. Photographs from that era show some officers wearing dark blue trousers and others light blue with a scarlet stripe. It also appears that some of the enlisted men also wore the light blue trousers in the field with khaki canvas leggings. Khaki for tropical wear was just appearing in the United States Armed Forces when the war broke out, so it may have been in short supply at the onset of hostilities.

Marines landed at Guantanamo Bay – a base they still man – and during the operation supporting shellfire from ships off-shore began falling short. Sgt John H. Quick became the first hero of that war when he calmly picked up semaphore flags, walked to the top of a ridge and wigwagged a message re-directing the ships'

gunfire as Spanish bullets buzzed about him. He was awarded the Congressional Medal of Honor for this action. Quick is shown in a photograph made sometime after the award wearing dress blues with the dark blue, bell-crowned visored cap and the gold on red chevrons of a quarter-master sergeant with 'three up and three bars down'.

The war ended after 114 days and America found itself with control over the Philippine Islands, Puerto Rico, Guam and Wake Island as

---

All the braid and other ornamentation would lead some to think that this man was a high-ranking officer, but he is just a second lieutenant in the full-dress uniform of 1904. His rank is indicated by both the sleeve braid and the gold bars on shoulder knots. An expert rifleman badge is on his left chest and he is holding the traditional Marine officer's 'mameluke' sword. The quatre-foil braid on the crown of the cap he is holding is still worn by U.S. Marine officers and is supposed to commemorate when Marines on sailing ships put pieces of rope in a cross pattern on the tops of their shakos so that their comrades in the rigging could tell them apart from the enemy, similar to that on the caps of French army officers.

a result of the Spanish surrender, as well as the Hawaiian Islands as a result of the momentum gained during the conflict.

Photographs of the Spanish-American War seem to indicate there was no widespread wearing of the Marine cap badge on the new campaign hats. In the Philippines, however, where the Americans had inherited a native uprising from the Spanish, Marines are shown wearing the badge affixed at the center of the crown. However, within two years the Marines sent to China, as part of an international force to put down the Boxer Rebellion, are shown wearing the badge high on the left side of the crown. At one point during this action, the Marines were on the left flank of an attacking group, while the 2nd Battalion, Royal Welch Fusiliers were on the right. The comradeship has never been forgotten. For the past 81 years on 1 March, which is

St David's Day, and 10 November, the Marine Corps birthday, the commanders of these respective units exchange the watchword, '. . . and Saint David.'

During the early 1900s the Marines wore a service dress that was all khaki. The coat had a standing collar, four pockets with pointed flaps that became a standard Marine design and bronze buttons. The Marine collar ornaments, worn only by officers at that time, were also bronze. The campaign hat was now worn with a sharp center crease, and the bronze emblem once again affixed at the front center. When no coat was worn, a shirt in the same khaki color as the rest of the uniform was worn. It had a soft roll collar on which officers wore rank badges. Judging from photographs of that era, neckties (or 'field scarves' as the Corps called them) were never worn with this shirt.

This was the uniform worn by members of the Corps as they were called to intervene in Nicaragua, Mexico, Haiti, and the Dominican Republic during the early years of the twentieth century. Officers wore black and gold Army-style cords with 'acorn' tips at the base of the crowns of their campaign hats. Some of the officers wearing them – such as Smedley D. Butler and John A. Lejeune – would become Corps legends. Both had participated in actions with relatively small units, for which the Marines had become famed. There were bigger things ahead for these men, both in the size of the units and the actions.

In 1912 new uniform regulations introduced the winter field service uniform, often called 'field green' and later referred to as forestry green. It had a stand collar and four flap pockets with the flaps having a rounded 'point'. Epaulets were rounded rather than pointed on the ends where they were fastened by a small regulation Marine Corps button. All buttons were in bronze, as was the hat ornament. Officers also wore collar ornaments in dark bronze. A summer service uniform in the same cut, but of light colored khaki twill was also introduced at this time. A 'wear-out' period of two years was authorized to use up existing stocks of uniforms. Thus the Marines were to be in their new dress in 1914. In that year, the campaign hat, officially called a 'field' hat, was issued with the 'Montana peak', rather than a center crease. It was similar to what the New Zealanders called a 'lemon squeezer' shape for their broad-brimmed hats. The white spiked helmet worn by all ranks since 1881 for

This Marine gunner is wearing the tropical khakis adopted after the turn of the century. His rank device, the bursting bomb, can be seen on the epaulets. Gunners are warrant officers.

full-dress occasions was discontinued, and the forerunner of the present-day 'dress blues' made their bow for enlisted men.

In 1914, Marines landed in what was called 'the second intervention' in Cuba and at Vera Cruz, Mexico, in April because of 'disorders' brought about by the Mexican Revolution. Two Marine regiments stayed there until November. Four months before, a war had broken out in Europe, one that would be known as the Great War or the World War before it was over. Also, before it was over, many of the Marines at Vera Cruz and in Cuba would be in it.

On 16 April 1917, the United States declared war on Germany and the Central Powers. Maj. Gen. Commandant George Barnett pushed for a major role for his Marines in this new war, and over Army objections, the 5th Marine Regiment was included in the first contingents of the American Expeditionary Force to embark for Europe on 14 June. It landed at Saint Nazaire, France fourteen days later.

The Marines that stepped on to French soil that day were wearing their forestry green uniforms. Some Allied forces veterans on the docks noticed the similarity in the shade to the 'field gray' worn by the Germans. That, however, was not the problem the uniform presented. Before the unit – later joined by the 6th Marine Regiment to form the 4th Marine Brigade – would go into action nearly ten months later, a directive came down from AEF headquarters on 10 January 1918, that stated in part: 'During the present war, the regulation Army uniform will be regularly issued to Marines of the AEF, thereby gradually replacing the Marine uniform.'

The directive, of course, was resisted, particularly by officers who had to buy their own uniforms, and it is doubtful if the Army ever got close to 100 percent cooperation from the 4th Brigade, now part of the Army's 2nd Division, or the members of the 5th Marine Brigade, which arrived in September 1918 but did not see combat as a unit.

The 4th Marine Brigade was blooded near Verdun in April 1918. There were other battles, but the one that brought them the most fame during World War I came in June, and cost them some of the heaviest casualties of the war.

Newspapermen helped to spread the fame of the Marines from around the time of the Spanish-American War. A correspondent for the Hearst Chain, William Harding Davis, made 'the

Marines have landed and have the situation well in hand' a catch phrase in America during the early years of this century. Another reporter, Floyd Gibbons of the *Chicago Tribune*, cabled a story back to his newspaper on 6 June 1918 that contained a quote that also became a catch phrase as it was repeated the length and breadth of the U.S.A.: 'Come on, you sons-o'-bitches! Do you want to live forever?' The speaker was First Sgt Dan Daly who had won his first Congressional Medal of Honor in the Boxer Rebellion and his second in Haiti. The place was Belleau Wood. Those being addressed were the men of Daly's platoon, which he now commanded because the lieutenant had been shot and was out of action.

This photograph was probably taken in 1918 and shows Franklin D. Roosevelt, then Assistant Secretary of the Navy, flanked by Marine Brigadier General Wendall C. Neville and Marine Major General John A. Lejeune, somewhere in France. Major General Lejeune commanded 2nd

Daly's men were wearing the 'dishpan' steel helmet developed by the British. Many of the Marines had affixed the Corps emblem at the front of this headgear that American veterans would come to call the 'tin hat'. It was to take twenty days to secure Belleau Wood and the cost was high – 5183 U.S. Marines were killed or wounded during the battle. The commander of the French Sixth Army, Gen. Degoutte, issued a decree on 30 June declaring, 'Henceforth in all official papers, Belleau Wood shall bear the name, "Bois de la Brigade de Marine."'

The Marines had done their job and so had the newspapers back in the States. They reported such morale boosting tidbits as Marine Capt.

Division, an Army unit which contained the 4th Marine Brigade. He is wearing the 2nd Division patch, also worn by the 4th Marine Brigade at this time, on his left shoulder. The single inverted chevron on his lower left sleeve indicates six months overseas service.

Lloyd Williams, after being told by a French officer that he should fall back with his 51st Company, saying, 'Retreat, hell. We just got here', and the fact that the Germans had dubbed them *Teufelhunden*, or 'Devildogs'. The Marines were the glory boys of the folks on the home front, but this created a problem. The Marines were not winning the war by themselves; the Army was also winning fights and taking heavy casualties. The jealousy over the publicity given the Marines stretched from the AEF Headquarters of Army Gen. John J. Pershing down to the ranks of the junior officers who, in less than a quarter of a century, would be the Army's top brass and would remember the Marines and keep them from playing any major role in the European Theater of Operations in World War II. A cocky little National Guard Artillery captain with a long memory wrote some 33 years later: 'For your information, the Marine Corps is the Navy's police force, and as long as I am President, that is what it will remain. They have a propaganda machine that is almost equal to Stalin's.' This was in a note to Rep. Gordon L. McDonough of California who had written to the President suggesting the Marine commandant be given a voice on the joint chiefs of staff. The note was signed 'Harry S. Truman'.

Although Belleau Wood was behind them, there was still a lot of war left ahead for the Marines. So many had been wounded that a new insignia appeared with increasing frequency on the right cuffs of their uniforms. It was the 'wound stripe', a gold inverted chevron awarded for each wound. The identical type chevron worn on the left sleeve signified six months of overseas service for each one worn. These were primarily army insignias, but were worn by Marines for many years after the war. Reference works never seem to indicate if the Marine non-coms in Army uniforms during World War I wore Marine Corps or Army chevrons. The Marine chevrons for winter field service were forestry green on a red background, and the Army's were a medium khaki on an olive drab background.

Marines of both the 4th and 5th Brigades wore shoulder patches, which are discussed in detail in the text for the World War I shoulder patch plate. As part of the 2nd Division, the Marines of the 4th Brigade wore the 2nd Division patch with square or diamond-shaped backgrounds and different colors to indicate units in the division.

The 2nd Division consisted of the Marine

Brigade and the Army's 3rd Infantry Brigade. It had several commanders, the first being Marine Col. Charles A. Doyen who held the post temporarily for two weeks at the formation of the unit. During the course of its overseas history in World War I the division was also commanded by Army Maj. Gen. Omar Bundy, Army Maj. Gen. James G. Harbord (who, as a brigadier general, led the Marine Brigade for a short time) and, finally, Marine Gen. John A. Lejenue. Lejenue had come to France with the hope of commanding a Marine Division, a hope also fostered by the commandant, Maj. Gen. Barnett, but Pershing dashed these hopes by crankily turning down the suggestion for a Marine Division, although he accepted the additional Marine Brigade (the 5th) brought over by Brig. Gen. Eli Cole, who then passed command to Brig. Gen. Smedley Butler.

Another Marine unit to reach France was the First Marine Aviation Force, but it arrived late in the war and served primarily with Royal Air Force squadrons because it lacked its own aircraft. Still, the unit sustained losses of four dead and eight wounded, and two of its members won the Congressional Medal of Honor.

The last battle for the 4th Marine Brigade was in the Meuse-Argonne, where it took Blanc Mont. For this, the French government awarded the 5th and 6th Marine Regiments the Croix de

Above left: This Marine lieutenant is wearing the Marine 'greens' which were supposed to be replaced by Army khakis in France during World War I, so the photograph was probably taken about 1919. He is wearing the 2nd Division patch on left shoulder. Its shape indicates that he was a member of the 5th Marine Regiment, one of two Marine regiments in the Division. Its color would indicate his battalion or company. It is probably dark blue, the color for the 3rd Battalion, or black, for Headquarters Company. The three inverted chevrons on his lower left sleeve indicate eighteen months of service overseas in World War I. The single chevron on the right sleeve indicates that he had been wounded in action.

Below left: A sergeant in dress blues of the 1920s period wearing the yellow gun barrel insignia beneath his rank chevrons indicating that he was qualified as a gun captain. The diagonal stripes below the gun captain badge each indicate a four-year enlistment, thus he had served at least twenty years. The first medal on his chest is the Marine Good Conduct Medal with three clasps to indicate four awards. The shooting badges worn last in the second row show that he was an expert with both rifle and pistol. The sergeant is wearing collar ornaments which were not authorized for Marine enlisted men until late in 1918.

Guerre, which entitled every man in these units to wear the green and red shoulder cords called a fourragère. The Marines serving in the units could wear it as an individual decoration no matter what other unit they were in while in the Corps. Men serving in those regiments to this day wear the fourragère as a regimental decoration.

In addition to acquiring Army uniforms while in Europe, the Marines also got a new style of headgear which the Americans had borrowed from the British. Officially called a 'Glengarry cap' in early regulations, it was commonly called an 'overseas cap' by the Americans.

With the war over, the Marines spent a tour of duty in the 'Watch on the Rhine' occupation forces in Germany, then headed home to parades and accolades and, finally, return to the jurisdiction of the Navy Department. As they got back into their 'greens', the enlisted men usually transferred one item from their Army uniforms: the bronze collar discs with the Marine emblem authorized for wear on the collars in August 1918. They were soon replaced by smaller versions of the cap badge but, as with the officers' collar badges, the anchors pointed inward.

The two decades following World War I found the United States Marines serving in a variety of trouble spots. Russia, the Dominican Republic, Haiti, Nicaragua, Honduras, and China all became familiar places to the shrinking peace-time Corps. During the war its strength had grown to more than 75,000. It dropped to a low of 15,000 in 1933 before it started an upward climb again.

The uniforms underwent some changes during this period. The one most noticeable was the change in the collars of the winter and summer (greens and khakis) field uniforms. Both of these uniforms had stand collars, as prescribed by the regulations of 1912, but, in April 1926, new

Above right: A Marine captain of the 1930s wearing the Paymaster's Department insignia behind his Corps collar ornaments. Departmental insignia were abolished in the 1940s.

Below right: The star centered between chevrons and arc show that this Marine NCO is a platoon sergeant. The stripes on his lower sleeves show that he has completed three four-year enlistments. This photograph was taken in 1938, near the end of the period when a wide variety of speciality marks, such as the star, were worn with Marine chevrons.

orders prescribed 'roll' collars for these uniforms. This meant the coats would have lapels. This also meant smaller collar ornaments would be needed and they were ordered to be in use no later than 1 January 1928. The stand collars on the dress blue (called 'undress' for some illogical reason) uniform remained as before for both officers and enlisted men.

The peaked caps began to undergo changes, too. During the war and into the early 1920s, the cap had a narrow 'bell' crown. This began to get larger by degrees, judging from photographs. The color of the visors and chin straps on these caps were a very deep reddish-brown, usually called 'cordovan color' in the Corps. Belts and shoes, except white dress belts, were of the same color. The theory behind the use of this color apparently was that brown leather looked better with greens and khakis, while black looked better with blue. Since cordovan was so dark, it seemed to go well with all three uniform colors. This color continued to be used until a change to black was ordered in June 1963. The service dress cap and collar ornaments that had been bronze were also changed to black as a result of that order.

The 1920s and 1930s were the period of the 'China Marines' when Marine detachments up to brigade strength were sent there for one reason or another. The most long-lasting was the 4th Regiment, which was stationed there for fifteen years.

The most unique uniform worn by Marines stationed in China was that of the 'Horse Marines'. A 22-man mounted detachment was included in the legation guard at Peking. These men, who were mounted on Mongolian ponies, had to have special uniform trousers for both greens and blues made in the breeches style of the United States Cavalry. Standard cavalry equipment was supplied by the Army for these mounts. The mounted Marines wore standard cavalry boots and, during cooler weather, a fur cap with the Marine emblem affixed at the front. The emblem, also, generally seems to have been placed on the front of the steel helmets (still the World War I British type) by the China Marines, although a general order in January 1919 directed that this unauthorized practice be discontinued until 'further orders'.

The Far East and Central and South America were not the only foreign shores to echo to the tramp of U.S. Marine boots. In September of 1939 what would be called World War II had broken out in Europe, and before a year had passed, Allied armies were being chewed up before the Nazi juggernaut. America's sympa-

---

These members of the First Provisional Marine Brigade in Iceland are wearing the fur caps that were usually associated with U.S. Marines serving with the mounted detachment in China during the 1930s. The First Brigade served in Iceland during part of 1941–42 and was the largest Marine unit to serve in any theater of war except the Pacific during World War II. These troops are wearing the polar bear formation sign of the West Riding Division, given to them by the troops they relieved. The patch was worn on both shoulders in British fashion, but was never authorized by the Corps. Later in the war, Marine shoulder patches were authorized, but were worn on the left shoulder only. Their use by U.S. Marines was discontinued in 1947.

thies were clearly with the Allies, and various steps short of entering the war were taken to aid them, particularly Britain.

In what was said to be an extension of the Monroe Doctrine, 4095 U.S. Marines landed at Reykjavik, Iceland, on 7 July 1941, in a step that would relieve British troops who were 'protecting' the somewhat reluctant Icelanders. The Marines who landed there brought along their dress blues to wear when the rare occasion arose that did not require wearing greens. A formula for the blues had been worked out some years before. All officers, warrant officers, and sergeants wore the scarlet stripes on both legs of the light blue trousers. Corporals wore the stripe on the left leg only and privates first class and privates did not wear them at all.

The Marines in Iceland, designated the 1st Provisional Brigade, were not wearing blues when they were reviewed by the British Prime Minister, Winston Churchill, that August. They marched past in greens with khaki leggings and web equipment and 'dishpan' steel helmets without the Marine emblem. They also wore, on both sleeves, the polar bear shoulder patch of the 49th West Riding Division that had been presented to them. As the Marines marched past Churchill, their band blared 'The Marines Hymn' chorus after chorus until Churchill was to say later he could not get it out of his head.

The music itself is from the Offenbach opera, *Genevieve de Brabant*, written in 1859, but the words for the Marine march were written during the nineteenth century by an unknown author. Its third chorus contains the line '. . . if the Army and the Navy ever look on Heaven's scenes, they will find the streets are guarded by the United States Marines,' which Marines sing with relish at inter-service functions.

Another relatively famous Marine march, 'Semper Fidelis', was written by John Philip Sousa, the most famous of all leaders of the Marine band – called the President's own – who went on to gain world-wide fame as the 'March King'.

While the Marines in Iceland huddled in their double-breasted green overcoats against the Arctic cold in December 1941, the men of the 1st Defense Battalion on Wake Island got a rare Saturday afternoon off on 6 December and splashed in the crowded pool, went fishing or just loafed around enjoying their leisure. For 49 of them, it would be the last time.

At the time the United States entered World War II, there were about 25,000 Marines on active duty. Of that number, 449 of them were on Wake Island, part of a coral atoll in the mid-Pacific that included Peale and Wilkes Islands. Marines had been stationed there only since 19 August 1941, when five officers and 173 enlisted men – the advance party of the 1st Defense Battalion – landed there to begin defensive preparations. The staff of the Walt Disney Studios had been called upon to design special unit insignia (for novelty use, not for wear on uniforms) for a number of armed forces units, and the 1st Defense Battalion, Fleet Marine Force was one of them. There is no indication that the men on Wake ever saw what Disney's artists had wrought. It featured an anthropomorphic gorilla

A lieutenant colonel wearing insignia behind the Corps badge on his collar showing that he is an aide-de-camp to a full general. The red and gold shoulder cords, called aiguillettes, indicate the same function. The aide collar badges are no longer in use. So-called 'scrambled eggs' ornamentation on the cap visor show that he is a field grade officer. Oak leaves on epaulets are silver for his rank, but would be gold for major. Among ribbons are a bronze star medal, presidential unit citation, American Defense Medal, with a star showing that the wearer served overseas, and the Pacific Theater of War Medal with combat stars.

The drum major of the United States Marine Corps band is shown in his 'one-of-a-kind' uniform, which includes bearskin hat with special plate based on an historical Marine cap plate. The red-coated Marine band is the oldest musical organization in the U.S.A. and dates its founding to 10 November 1775, the birthday of the Corps itself. By virtue of its long association with the Presidency and the White House, the USMC band is known as 'the President's own'.

in dishpan helmet, khaki shirt and green trousers striding through the surf with a cannon under his left arm and a rifle clutched in his left hand. A critic of military cartoon art might say it was not one of Disney's better works. His design for the shivering Marines in Iceland carried a more definite Disney stamp. It featured a penguin with a Donald Duck face in a snow-encrusted rowboat

getting ready to load a shell into a snow-covered cannon that was obviously designed for cannon balls. The penguin was wearing a scarf wrapped around his neck and, like Wake's gorilla, the old British-type dishpan steel helmet. There was a new American steel helmet out, but neither the Marines in Iceland nor on Wake had it.

The Marines on Wake had been issued the light olive green herringbone twill dungarees with the letters 'USMC' and the Marine emblem stenciled in black on the left pocket. This apparently was thought of at that time as 'dirty work' attire and did not seem to be utilized by Marines in combat until late the next summer. Khaki twill was to be the combat clothing on Wake.

The Marines on Wake were not the only members of the Corps at scattered outposts throughout the Pacific who were in harm's way as that first week in December 1941 moved toward its close. They would, however, get one more calendar day of peace since the atoll is west of the international dateline and 22 hours ahead of Hawaii, where it was Sunday, 7 December at the same time it was Monday, 8 December on Wake.

At Pearl Harbor, Hawaii at several minutes before 8 am (accounts differ as to the exact time). Japanese bombs blasted the United States into World War II. One of the first of those bombs fell on the deck of the battleship U.S.S. *Arizona*, throwing Marine Maj. Alan Shapley, of the ship's detachment, 100 feet into the water. He managed to swim to safety. Before the raid ended, 112 Marines at or near Pearl Harbor would be counted among the 2280 Americans killed that day.

In the six months to follow, much of what the Marines called 'the old Corps' died or went into captivity at places like Wake and Guam and in the scattered Marine outposts still left in China. The 4th Marine Regiment had been transferred from China to the Philippines just ten days before the Japanese drew America into World War II, but for them it would be a reprieve rather than an escape. They would help make a last ditch stand on the fortress island of Corregidor, then, on 5 May 1942, they burnt their colors and became members of the only Marine regiment in history to surrender.

Maj. Jimmy Devereux's Wake Marines would hold on against overwhelming odds for sixteen days, taking a heavy toll of the attackers in ships, planes and men, and earning a lump-in-the throat admiration from the American public, who believed the Wake defenders had responded 'Send us more Japs' when asked what they needed. Actually, words taken out of context in a padded, coded message from Wake were seized upon by the press and expanded into a wartime legend. When the battered Marines on the atoll heard about it, it just made them angry. Few of them knew, until after the war, that a rescue mission had been launched from Pearl Harbor on 15 December. But the Admiral in charge, Frank Jack Fletcher, was concerned that his cruiser, the aircraft carrier *Saratoga*, and nine destroyers would only be added to the frightful toll of ships destroyed at Pearl Harbor and did not press his speed. The Task Force was scheduled to reach Wake on 24 December. A Japanese task force reached the atoll first, and Fletcher turned back on 22 December. Wake fell the next day.

Drawn up on the flight deck of the *Saratoga*, VMF (Marine Fighter Squadron) 221, which had been part of the relief force for Wake, took off for another island where Marines of the 3rd, 4th and 6th Defense Battalions, the 2nd Raider Battalion, and Marine Scout-Bomber Squadron 231, were digging in to resist the expected Japanese invasion attempt. The island was Midway, northwest of Hawaii and high on the Japanese list of expected conquests. The Marines were still wearing the old-style steel helmets and tropical khakis as the battle of Midway began. This time, the Americans did not lose, and the Japanese took the first step toward losing the war by having four carriers sunk, 332 planes destroyed and hundreds of skilled men killed. It was a naval victory, but the Marines played a role and suffered 49 killed and 53 wounded.

The last of the Marines in Iceland left in March 1942. Although there would later be a Marine barracks in Londonderry, Northern Ireland, further Marine Corps participation in the Atlantic theater of war would be largely peripheral, consisting of brief, small-unit actions or assignments carried out by individuals.

In 1941, the man who had been Assistant Secretary of the Navy in 1918 and had recommended that Marine enlisted men be authorized to wear the Corps emblem on their uniform collars was President. What Generals Barnett and Lejeune could not persuade Gen. Pershing to do in 1918, President Franklin D. Roosevelt approved in February 1941. The 1st and 2nd Marine Brigades became, respectively, the 1st

This Marine captain wears his rank insignia on the collar of his summer khaki tropicals, which were phased out in favor of light-weight greens during the 1970s. Shirts, however, are still khaki. This officer, holding his battalion's colors, is qualified as a Naval Aviator, indicated by the gold wings badge worn above the ribbons on the left chest; they are the same as worn by U.S. Navy aviators.

and 2nd Marine Divisions, the first units of that size so officially designated in the history of the Corps.

Two months before the last of the Iceland Marines headed back to the States, elements of 2nd Marine Division were already headed for the Pacific. A brigade of the 1st Marine Division was sent to join them two months later.

Roosevelt, fascinated by the exploits of the British Commandos, had sent two young Marine officers, Capt. Wallace M. Greene, Jr, a future commandant of the Corps, and Capt. Samuel B. Griffith II, to England to study Commando techniques. The result was the Marine Raiders, formed before the United States entered the war.

The 1st Raider Battalion was commanded by Lt Col. Merritt A. Edson, the 2nd by Lt Col. Evans F. Carlson. Marine Raiders came to wear the death's head as their shoulder patch, but, at this time, there were no such insignia authorized for Marines, and the polar bear worn by the Marines in Iceland was never officially approved.

It was Carlson's unit that supplied two rifle companies to the hastily assembled defense force on Midway, but they were not performing their specialty there. It would be Edson's 1st Raiders who would go into action first in the Corps' first amphibious offensive operation of the war on

7 August 1942 in the Solomon Islands. But it was Carlson's Raiders who made the first Commando-type raid ten days later on the Makin Atoll in the Gilbert Island.

The Marines in the Pacific were now dressed in essentially the way combat Marines would be dressed for the rest of the war. The new M-1941 steel helmet had been issued to all hands. It was much deeper than the old-style 'tin hat' and had no brim. The steel shell was worn over a hard plastic liner of identical shape that was worn separately as a field hat when out of immediate combat zones. The liner had an eyelet as a ventilating hole at the front, and some Marines affixed the Corps emblem there. Others followed the World War I practice of soldering it to the front of the steel helmet. This was a fashion that seemed to peter out later in the war as the use of camouflaged helmet covers became widespread in the Corps.

In late 1942 the Marines on duty in the States and at other posts where uniforms other than combat clothing were worn started wearing rank chevrons on the left sleeves only. In the Pacific, particularly in the Solomons, chevrons were painted on the green, herringbone tweed fatigues with black stencil ink in inexpert strokes – on both sleeves.

The issue chevrons for greens and tropical khakis were made of the identical material used in the green uniform sewed on a red background for the greens and a khaki background for the khakis. The issue chevrons for dress blues had a yellow felt-like material for the chevrons and red for background. The 'store bought' chevrons of that time had shiny green and yellow embroidered centers on regulation backgrounds.

The invasion of the Solomons had been launched by the 1st Marine Division commanded by Maj. Gen. Alexander A. Vandergrift, and the targets were Guadalcanal and Tulagi. One of the division's regiment's was left in Samoa and was replaced by the 2nd Marine Division's 2nd Regiment. When the shoulder patches that the Marines were to call 'battle blazes' were authorized later, the 1st Division's red numeral '1' had the word 'Guadalcanal' written down its length. The 2nd Division, which later served as a full unit on the 'Canal' had a red snake twisted in a numeral '2' with the word 'Guadalcanal' in yellow. Although it was worn for a time, it was never officially approved, and the authorized 2nd Division patch was not similar to the 1st's.

Only one man in the U.S. Marine Corps can wear these chevrons – the Sergeant Major of the Marine Corps. The rank was created in 1957, and the man holding it serves on the personal staff of the commandant, whom he advises on all matters pertaining to enlisted Marines. Among the decorations indicated by the ribbons worn by Sgt Maj. Leland D. Crawford are the Bronze Star and Purple Heart. Among his medal ribbons are those indicating service in the Korean War and the Vietnamese War. At left below the ribbons is an Expert Rifle Qualification badge.

Many other patches were authorized for the Marine Corps during the course of the war – 42 in all, with at least a couple of unauthorized ones showing up, such as the 2nd Division's snake. However, there were only eighteen basic designs, since units within the First Marine Amphibious Corps used one basic form with the center changed for the types of units. This pattern was also followed for the Fleet Marine Force Pacific.

The Marine Aircraft Wings had an early version in a shield shape that was a fuselage marking before it was a shoulder patch, which gave rise to an erroneous designation of 'fuselage' among collectors many years after the war, as if the word was some sort of unit designation. The shield was replaced by a kite-shaped patch. In both ver-

Women were admitted to the ranks of the Marine Corps during World War II and continue to serve today. This sergeant major is wearing the light green with dark green trim summer uniform that is now obsolete. Women Marines wear their own distinctive versions of dress blues and greens.

Marines, for he is shown in some photographs wearing his 1st Marine Division patch on his right shoulder after he had moved on to higher command.

Two more Raider Battalions came along – the 3rd and 4th – but there was never a 704th Raider Battalion, although a bogus patch for the non-existent outfit has cropped up in collectors' circles. The only patch authorized for Raiders was that of the First Marine Amphibious Corps, which featured the death's head on the red diamond centered on the basic design. The Commando-like Raiders were a big hit with the Navy brass who thought this would be a good establishment for Marine units. The Marines, however, wanted to hang on to their hard-won divisions, and created the 1st and 2nd Raider Regiments out of the four battalions, which lasted until the early months of 1944. Then the Raiders were given a new designation, and the colors of a proud old regiment – they became the new 4th Marines.

The Guadalcanal campaign ended in six months with a little help from the Army. The Marines lost a total of 1207 during the campaign, but Japanese deaths numbered nearly 25,000.

To detail all Marine Corps operations of World War II would take a volume this size devoted to that subject alone. In terms of uniforms worn, there was little change until the war was over. At Tarawa atoll, where the Marines were cut down in the surf before gaining a foothold on Betio Island, the camouflaged helmet cover that virtually became the Marine trademark was used widely for the first time.

Most photographs of that period indicate that the wearing of the full camouflaged fatigue outfit was rather limited as the Marine 'island hopping' campaign continued. The Marines, sometimes supported by Army units, fought with valor, often taking heavy losses in the Marshall Islands, Saipan, Guam (where, after being retaken, the Americans found a U.S. Navy chief petty officer who had eluded the Japanese and lived off the land from 10 December 1941 to 29 July 1944), Peleliu, Iwo Jima and, finally, Okinawa. The atom bombs dropped on Japan convinced the Japanese authorities that to continue to fight would be futile.

On Sunday, 2 September 1945, the Marine detachment of the U.S.S. *Missouri*, dressed in khakis with the sea horse shoulder patch of ship's detachments on their left sleeves, snapped to attention as Japanese delegates came aboard to sign

sions, the only difference was in the Roman numeral used for the aircraft wings themselves, or in the headquarters patch that used a crown instead of a numeral in the first version and the letters 'PAC' (for Pacific Aircraft Command) in the second.

Many of the Marines in the Pacific never saw the patches until they returned 'Stateside'. The patches even caused some confusion amongst high ranking officers. The Army had authorized its soldiers to wear the shoulder patch from their old unit on their right shoulder and their new unit on their left shoulder. The Marines authorized only the current unit patch for left shoulder wear. Vandergrift apparently thought at one time that the Army practice had been extended to the

The commandant of the Marine Corps is a full (four-star) general and wears rank insignia on both epaulets and collar. This commandant, General Robert H. Barrow, wears ribbons indicating that he has been awarded the Navy Cross, the Army Distinguished Service Medal, the Silver Star, the Legion of Merit and the Bronze Star. Among his campaign ribbons are those for the Pacific Theater in World War II, the Korean War, and the Vietnamese War. The general's uniform is the service greens, now worn by Marines the year around in different weight material, depending upon the weather.

the surrender documents while the battleship lay in Tokio Bay. World War II was over. During the war, the Corps had grown to six divisions and five aircraft wings totalling 485,833 men and women.

The Marine Corps formed a women's unit – the Women's Reserve – on 1 February 1943, and before the war ended, more than 18,000 were on duty, commanded by Maj. Ruth Cheney Streeter. The women Marines had no acronym such as WACS (Army) or WAVES (Navy), but were usually called 'WRs' for Women's Reserve. There had been a handful of women in the Marines during World War I, and they had been called Marinettes, but the unit was dissolved when peace came. The 'WRs' were continued after World War II as a permanent part of the Marine Corps, and the status of Women's Reserve was eliminated.

The peaked cap they wore (and still wear) was a sort of feminine cloth shako with the crown tapering from front to back. This was worn with the forest green uniform, identical in color to the male Marines' uniform, and in a brighter green shade with the summer uniform, which was white with a small green pin stripe. The hats had knotted cords, red for forest green and white for bright green. Later, when a blue uniform was introduced, the red cord was worn on the blue cap. White caps are worn with blues only by women members of Marine bands. During World War II, the women Marines also wore a female version of the overseas (Glengarry) cap. The white with green stripe uniform was discontinued several years ago, but while in use, non-coms wearing it wore chevrons of medium green on a white background. Otherwise, all other chevrons worn by women Marines are the same colors as those worn by the men, although of smaller size.

Following World War II, the era of the China Marine returned for a few brief years, but the growing conflict between the Nationalist and Communist forces caught the Marines in the middle at times. By May of 1949, the Communist victory seemed inevitable and C Company, 7th Marines, the last members of the Corps in China, pulled out. They left from Tsingtao, where 35 years before the 3rd Sea Battalion of the German Imperial Marines had been overwhelmed by superior Japanese and British forces, ending German imperialism in Asia.

A military fashion that had begun in Europe early in World War II with the introduction of battledress spread to the U.S. Armed Forces. Before the end of the war, an adaptation of this became the standard issue for the U.S. Army. Gen. of the Army Dwight D. Eisenhower appeared in newsreels wearing the officers' version and the jacket – in the United States at least – became known as the 'Ike' jacket.

In 1946, the Marine Corps adopted the jacket to replace the single-breasted roll collar coats for greens and khakis. It had no metal buttons – the buttons it did have were concealed behind a flap – and, in general, the Marines did not like it. In a few years, it was replaced by the type of coat it had in turn replaced. Marine enlisted men, however, were not issued coats for khakis. For them, the summer uniform would be shirt sleeve order.

A month after the last Marines pulled out of China, the United States withdrew the last of its occupation forces from that half of the divided Korean peninsula that had become officially known as the Republic of Korea and called South Korea, leaving only a handful of military advisors. In the North, a Communist regime, known as the People's Democratic Republic of Korea and called North Korea, had been set up as a satellite state by Russia. The dividing line was the 38th parallel, which roughly divided the peninsula in half. On 25 June 1950, almost a year to the day that the last American occupation forces had withdrawn, eight Communist Korean divisions crossed the dividing line.

American forces, in small numbers, were quickly committed to help the reeling South Koreans. The United Nations, with a sulking Soviet Russia absent (the Soviets were boycotting the U.N. sessions because the Nationalists still held China's seat) voted to send United Nations forces to help stop the aggression. An old soldier who had virtually been dictator of Japan since late 1945 was called upon to head the U.N. forces and stop the Communists. General of the Army Douglas MacArthur, the only American ever to hold the rank of field marshal (a title he was given as head of the Philippine Commonwealth armed forces before World War II) already had a plan forming and knew what he needed. As supreme commander in the Pacific Theater during World War II, MacArthur had the six Marine Divisions under him and knew what they were capable of doing.

'If I only had the 1st Marine Division under my command again, I would land them here,' MacArthur told Lt Gen. Lemuel Shepherd, commanding general, Fleet Marine Force, Pacific, in Tokyo on 10 July 1950. He was pointing to a speck on the map of Korea labeled 'Inchon'. The name would soon appear in much larger type in headlines around the world.

Two days later, the 1st Provisional Marine Brigade sailed for Korea from San Diego. That same morning near Songjin, North Korea, five members of the U.S.S. *Juneau*'s Marine detachment rowed ashore in a whale boat and placed two explosive charges in a railroad tunnel. A short time later, a train was blown up as it passed over the charges. It was the first explosion courtesy of the U.S. Marines that the Korean Communists had heard, but it would not be the last.

The Marine Brigade landed on 2 August and,

U.S. Marine gunnery sergeant wears winter service greens with peaked cap. The chevrons and service stripes worn on the lower sleeve are green on red. Marksmanship badges are worn below ribbons.

This monument to the U.S. Marines in Washington, D.C., was patterned after the famous World War II newsphotograph that showed the Marines raising the flag on Iwo Jima. The figures were sculptured showing the fatigues and helmet covers worn by Marines in that battle.

instead of being held in reserve for the arrival of the rest of the 1st Marine Division, it became a 'fire brigade' bolstering the sagging U.N. lines and meeting with significant successes. But on 5 September, it was pulled out to await the gathering of the other elements of the division for the assault on Inchon. This was not done, however, without objections from Gen. Walton Walker, who insisted he needed the Brigade to keep the Eighth Army's front stabilized. The Marine commanders said they could not make the Inchon landing without the Brigade. Finally MacArthur settled the matter: 'Tell Walker he will have to give up the Marines.'

The 1st Marine Division sailed for Inchon as a part of X Corps, an Army formation that included the Army's 7th Division. But the Marines were to be the spearhead of the assault. MacArthur was given almost unanimous disapproval for his choice of a landing site. But he stuck to his plan and, as it turned out, it was the most brilliant stroke of the Korean War and capped the old General's career as a military genius.

Wearing helmets with camouflaged covers, green fatigues and khaki leggings, the first wave, the 3rd Battalion of the 5th Marine Regiment, hit a 1000-yard island called Wolmi-do in Inchon Harbor. They were met by surprised members of North Korea's 226th Independent Marine Regiment and in one hour and 25 minutes the battle was over. Because of the tides, the next wave did not land on the mainland until several hours later. Bolstered by heavy sea and air support, the Marines took objective after objective. By the next day, after South Korean Marines had entered the city for mopping up operations, Inchon was in U.N. hands. The next target was Seoul, the South Korean capital, just 18 miles to the south of Inchon. Marine and Army troops pressed in on the city until, on 28 September after much vicious fighting, it too fell to the U.N. troops.

MacArthur was on hand to escort the aging South Korean President, Syngman Rhee, into the National Assembly Hall. There, in pure MacArthurese, he proclaimed: 'Mr. President: By the grace of a merciful Providence, our forces fighting under the standard of that greatest hope and inspiration of mankind, the United Nations, have liberated this ancient capital city of Korea.'

It was the high tide of the Korean War for the old soldier who would soon see his victorious troops in a full and costly retreat and find himself forced into retirement because of his outspoken views on what was needed to be done to win the war.

MacArthur was authorized to destroy the North Korean Army and to cross the 38th parallel and pursue it as far as necessary, precluding any strikes into Chinese or Soviet territory. The U.N. Forces were successful – too successful for the Communist Chinese to the North, who watched the Communist Korean forces crumble and fall back. Sometime in October the Chinese, calling themselves 'People's Volunteers', began to gather in force in North Korea.

It was winter in Korea, and the Marines were wearing 'U.N. green' double-breasted overcoats with attached hoods. The troops pulled the hoods up close around their faces and put the steel helmet with camouflaged cover on top of that. Thick gloves and mittens, insulated boots and other items designed for Korea's severe winters also became items of issue before the war was over.

When the Korean War had broken out, there were just under 75,000 Marines on active duty. Less than a month passed before President Truman called up 33,000 men of the Organized Marine Reserve, the type of reservist who attended monthly drills and underwent two weeks of training at a Marine installation every summer and was paid for duty days served. By 7 August 1950, an additional 50,000 Marines from the Volunteer Reserve were recalled. They were reservists who were not participants in any kind of drills, were not paid and were essentially 'just names on lists' that would be ignored unless a national emergency was declared. Many had signed up for the Volunteer Reserve upon leaving active duty, because they could retain whatever rank they held.

Most of the men from both Reserves were World War II veterans. Some had carefully packed their old uniforms away in moth balls. For enlisted men, at least, they could leave them packed away. For greens, of course, the 'Ike' jacket had replaced the tunic. For the treasured dress blues, changes were a more bitter pill to swallow, since they were not items of general issue in World War II, and anyone who wanted the uniform had to buy it himself. Following World War II, an armed services panel called the 'Doolittle' Board heard gripes from enlisted men about treatment in the ranks and found one of the sorest points was the differences in officers' and EMs' uniforms. In the Marines, the coats of the officers blues had four pockets, while those of the enlisted men had none. Recalled reservists for the Korean War who brought their old blues along found they were obsolete. As a result of the Doolittle Board, the coats for enlisted men's dress blues now had four pockets. Even the trousers of all EM uniforms of the World War II era were obsolete. From World War I through World War II, there had been no hip pockets on the trousers of enlisted Marines, the theory being a more military smartness could be maintained if there was nothing at the back of the pants into which a man could stuff a billfold or handkerchief. By the outbreak of the Korean War, the trousers had hip pockets with flaps. But their usefulness was questionable, because sharp-eyed officers and sergeants saw to it that they remained empty.

As the U.N. Forces in Korea moved north, after fights in places with names like Wonsan and Kojo, the major elements of the 1st Marine Division found themselves concentrated in the vicinity of the Chosin Reservoir. That is where eight divisions of the 'Chinese People's Volunteers' also found them in late November 1950.

The temperature was sub-zero and there was snow on the ground when the Chinese struck. The mottled pattern of the helmet covers and shelter halves arched over the Marines' field packs stood out against the stark whiteness of the snow. For thirteen days, against overwhelming odds, the men of the 1st Marine Division fought their way through the frigid Korean terrain until they reached Hungnam and completed what some called an 'amphibious operation in reverse' as they were evacuated in landing craft. The proud Marines refused to call the entire operation a 'retreat', since, they contended, they had been surrounded and there was no rear – they simply advanced in another direction. In so doing, they had beaten off seven Chinese divisions.

The American fortunes would improve in the months and years ahead, although when the war ended in a truce on 27 July 1953, the lines were virtually where they had been when the war had erupted three years earlier – on the 38th parallel. The war was costly to all, including the Marines. They had 4262 men killed, more than the Corps had lost in World War I.

In March of 1955, the 1st Marine Division left Korea. In the years ahead, the only U.S. division to be maintained there would be one that would always have an association with the U.S. Marines: the 2nd Infantry Division, which had included the 4th Marine Brigade in World War I. The Korean conflict had been America's most unpopular war since the War of 1812. A more unpopular war was on the horizon.

Ten months before the first Marine division pulled out of Korea, the French garrison at Dien Bien Phu, in what was then French Indo-China, surrendered to rebel forces. It set the stage for native-controlled governments in the north and south of what was to be called Vietnam. In the south, the new government asked for a U.S.

Military Advisory Assistance group to help shape its new armed forces. On 2 August 1954, a member of that group, Marine Lt Col. Victor J. Croizat, arrived to take up his duties. He would eventually be followed by thousands more of his fellow Marines.

Following Korea, the Marines found themselves in a variety of roles, including a landing in strength in Lebanon in 1958 at the request of the president there who was beset by rebellion. There was no Marine blood shed there, however.

In the Dominican Republic in 1965, it was a different story. A revolt brought pleas of help from the officially elected government, and President Lyndon Johnson responded by sending troops. Although the stated purpose was to protect the lives of American and foreign nationals there, the underlying reason was to prevent the establishment of another Cuban-type Communist regime in Latin America. On 28 April, 500 Marines from the U.S.S. *Boxer* landed. Others from the 6th Marine Expeditionary Unit followed.

The Marines going into the Dominican Republic (where Marines had been stationed from 1916 to 1924) wore the now familiar olive green fatigues they called 'utilities', plus the camouflaged helmet cover. They were now wearing boots instead of the high-topped shoes and canvas khaki leggings used in World War II and in milder seasons in Korea.

On 8 March 1965, more than a month before the Marines from the *Boxer* went ashore in the Dominican Republic, the first American ground combat forces to land in Vietnam went ashore at Da Nang. They were members of the 9th Marine

Plate A Staff NCO mess dress chevrons, sergeant up: gold on red for blue mess jacket, gold on white for summer white mess jacket; authorised in late 1970s, much larger than on other uniforms.

Plate B Brassard (top): red with gold letters, gold and black embroidered emblem; for duty at Marine and Navy base and installation gates. More common brassard (right): red with yellow letters. Earlier brassard (left): white on black or navy blue; differs from Army's in letters' shape and use of periods. Badge: polished white metal with black letters; as worn by some MPs or carried by some in civilian clothes. Imperial Iranian Marine Corps' beret badge: dark brown metal with Imperial Crown, globe, light blue Persian Gulf, crossed daggers over anchor. RM patch: black with white lettering, gold sea horse, red knives.

PLATE A   UNITED STATES OF AMERICA
U.S. MARINE CORPS
NCOs MESS DRESS CHEVRONS (Current)

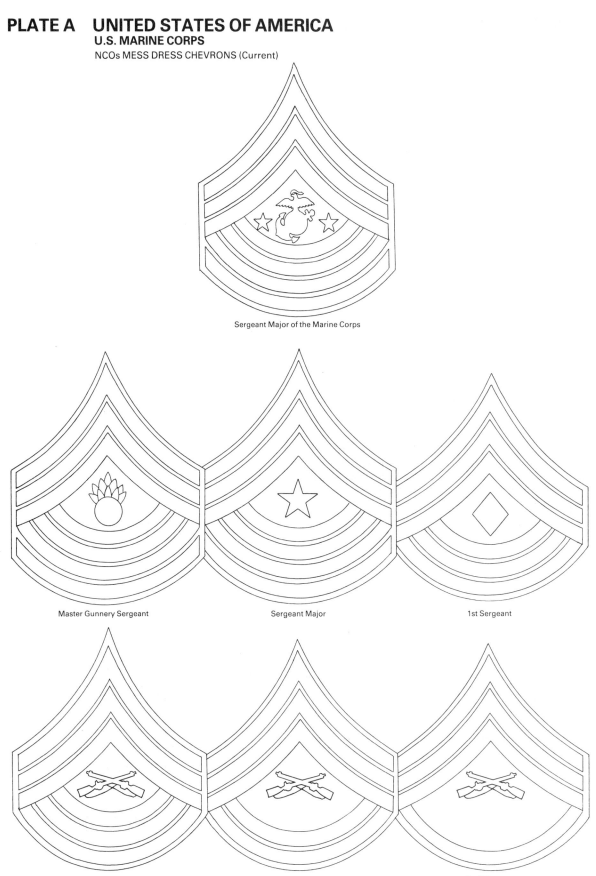

Sergeant Major of the Marine Corps

Master Gunnery Sergeant

Sergeant Major

1st Sergeant

Master Sergeant

Gunnery Sergeant

Staff Sergeant

PLATE B   UNITED STATES OF AMERICA
U.S. MARINE CORPS
MILITARY POLICE BRASSARDS AND BADGE

Brassard (Current)

Brassard (1920s to 1950s)

Brassard (Current)

4th Marine Division
Military Police Badge

UNITED KINGDOM
ROYAL MARINES

IRAN
IMPERIAL IRANIAN MARINE CORPS

Beret Badge

Commando Logistic
Regiment Jacket Patch

Expeditionary Brigade. Although Marine advisors and helicopter units had been in Vietnam for several years, this was the beginning of a commitment that would last ten years, and find 448,000 Marines seeing service there, with nearly 15,000 killed and more than 88,000 wounded. Before the Americans pulled out, there would be two Marine divisions (the 1st and 3rd), two regimental landing teams, and the 1st Marine Aircraft Group seeing service there. Nearly 130,000 more men and women were in the Marine Corps during the Vietnam War than served in it during World War II.

Yet, the Marines who fought there were just as brave, just as efficient and endured hardships just as severe, if not more so, than Marines in wars that preceded Vietnam. On the battle color of the U.S. Marines in Washington, D.C., one of the most recent streamers added is for Vietnam service: it carries three silver and two bronze stars representing seventeen campaigns.

In a book of this type, devoted primarily to uniforms, badges and insignia traced through those who wore them, when and how, it would be impossible to do justice to the battles of the Marines during the war in Vietnam, even in condensed form. Their major battles there, such as the Tet offensive and Khe Sanh, or the incursion into Laos could each fill a book themselves.

The uniforms, badges and insignia worn by the Marines there were not markedly different from those worn during the Korean War. Leaf-pattern camouflaged utilities were worn by some; otherwise, the standard green fatigues were worn. 'Bush' hats – fatigue hats with brims – became popular with some, and small unit pocket patch and beer can distinctive insignia proliferated. During this period, full khaki uniforms were phased out, although the shirt would be retained. Summer weight greens were being introduced.

On 25 June 1972, the last Marine ground forces left Vietnam, although some Marines, such as advisors and embassy guards continued to serve there. A cease-fire agreement was reached in Paris on 28 January 1973. Two months later the last U.S. combat forces in Vietnam were pulled out. In two years, the Marines would make a sudden and brief return.

In the two years after the pull out of U.S. troops, the fortunes of the South Vietnamese government ebbed and flowed. Finally, in spring 1975, its collapse and the collapse of its armed forces seemed inevitable.

Near the end, on 29 April 1975, the evacuation of Americans from the capital city of Saigon by helicopter began. Marines from the U.S.S. *Hancock*, Regimental Landing Team Four and the 3rd Marine Division assisted in this and related evacuations. In the end, nearly 1500 Americans and more than 5500 Vietnamese were evacuated at the cost of four Marine lives. Two of the dead were members of the Embassy Security Guard, the other two were members of a helicopter crew. They were the last Marines to die in Vietnam.

They would not, however, be the last Marines to die in Southeast Asia in 1975. On 12 May, a Cambodian gunboat seized an old container ship named the *Mayaguez* on its way to Thailand. The Americans sent armed forces to recapture the ship and free its crew. The ship had been taken to an island, Koh Tang, three miles from the mainland. American troops, finding the ship, also found it was empty. The ship was retaken and a search started for the crew. This search involved needless fire fights with Cambodian troops since, unknown to the Americans, the ship's crew was already being released. Eleven Marines were among the 41 Americans killed in the operation. Three others were declared missing.

It was the last mission of significance for the Marines in Southeast Asia. The focus began to shift to the Middle East. Members of the security guard in Teheran, Iran were part of the American embassy staff captured and held prisoner by Iranian revolutionaries for many months as the decade of the 1980s dawned.

A Marine unit called a Rapid Deployment Force was kept on shipboard in the Middle East, ready to move to a hot spot at a moment's notice. The Marines suffered their first casualty in that area on 6 October 1981 when Maj. Jerald R. Agenbroad, a 36-year-old observor at a military parade in Cairo, Egypt suffered a broken right leg in an attack on the reviewing stand. Little was heard about Agenbroad, since he had been among many sharing the reviewing stand with Egyptian President Anwar el-Sadat. The Egyptian leader was killed in the attack, and Marines once again were on the alert to carry their proud colors to whatever shores they might be summoned.

2

THE ROYAL MARINES

The British Marines date to 28 October 1664 when Charles II authorized the formation of the Duke of York and Albany's Maritime Regiment of Foot, which was also known as the Admiral's Regiment. During this period, the men of the regiment wore knee-length yellow coats lined red with a full length of pewter buttons down the center, two flap pockets fastened with white metal buttons at hip level and broad red cuffs decorated with pewter buttons. The breeches and stockings were red, the broad-brimmed hat black with yellow braid binding, and the shoes black with red bows. The officers' version was even more elaborate and included a gold-trimmed red sash and a white feather plume for the hat. White stocks were worn at the throat on all uniforms.

In 1685 the Duke of York became King James II, and the regiment was turned over to the King's son-in-law, Prince George, and the name was changed to the Prince of Denmark's Regiment. Although the regiment was practically dormant under this name, it cast off the yellow coats and adopted a new uniform. The coats were red with broad yellow cuffs, although one painting of the period shows them, incorrectly, as a blue-green. For officers the coat had white trimming and a white sash. Officers continued to wear the black, plumed hat, now bound in white braid.

The regiment was disbanded in 1689 because of the political climate in England, and the Marines from the unit were sent to join the Coldstream Guards. The next year, however, two regiments of Marines were ordered to be raised. They marched off, or sailed away to battle in Cork, Beachy Head and Jamaica, now in their blue uniforms with white facings. The regiments suffered heavy losses in their battles, were consolidated as one, and finally disbanded in 1699.

Within three years, a need for Marines arose again, and Queen Anne ordered six regiments of Marines to be raised. They wore red uniforms with different facings for each regiment. They fought in Spain, France and North America, but gained a lasting honor for their Corps with their capture and defense of Gibraltar.

After disbandment in 1713 there were no Marines until 1739, when Britain was again at war with Spain, and soon with France. Two Regiments of Marines were raised, followed by the raising of three further Regiments in the American Colonies. These Regiments played a prominent part in all the subsequent fighting, but with peace in 1748 were disbanded.

In 1755 the Marines were again reformed, designated 'The Marine Corps', and formed into three divisions based at Portsmouth, Chatham and Plymouth. They wore uniforms of red with white facings. Stockings were now covered by white leggings that rose to the knee and covered part of the shoes.

During this period the Marine Corps fought in battles with the French and Spanish and earned one more lasting honor. The Marines spearheaded the assault on Belle Isle off the southeast coast of Brittany, which became the first piece of French territory to fall to British arms during this conflict. The Marines were awarded the laurel wreath for their action there.

When peace with the French came with the treaty of Paris in 1763, troubles arose in the American colonies. Marines sent there were mostly attired as grenadiers (there were also Light Companies in the Battalion) with black caps, red coats with, in Light Companies, white lapels, white vests and trousers and knee-length black leggings. Officers wore tricorn black hats with gold braid binding.

Familiar old foes, France, Spain and Holland, entered the war on the American side, and the action spread back to Europe and into the West Indies. The Americans were granted independence and the war ended in 1783 with the Treaty of Versailles. By this time the black, cocked hat with a white over red plume on the left side was being worn, but little else about the uniform had changed.

The French declared war on England following the French Revolution in 1793, triggering a long series of wars between the two nations during a period that saw the rise of Napoleon Bonaparte. The tri-corn hat for enlisted men and the cocked hat for officers were the main types of headgear worn by the Marines from 1797. Officers now wore gold epaulets on red coats.

The Corps was given the designation 'Royal' on 29 April 1802 by King George III at the instigation of Admiral Lord St Vincent. Two years later, in 1804, the first companies of Marine Artillery Companies were formed.

The blue facings of a Royal regiment replaced the white facings on the Marines' uniform coats and the high-crowned, narrow-brimmed black hat sometimes termed a 'top hat' became the standard headgear for enlisted men, although some officers alternated it with the cocked hat. The red coatees now worn had standing collars of blue with white and red trim. The cuffs were also blue with white and red braid. White and red 'frogs' extended on either side of the single row of buttons in pairs on the other ranks' jackets. On officers' uniforms the white braiding was replaced by gold. White cross belts with a brass plate at the center were worn by other ranks. The breeches continued to be white and the leggings black. This uniform, with few modifications, continued to be worn throughout the Napoleonic wars during a score of battles, including the famous battle of Trafalgar where Lord Nelson was killed in the hour of victory against the combined French and Spanish fleets, on 21 October 1805. Paintings of that period indicate that Marine NCOs had begun to wear broad white chevrons point down. A year after the end of the Napoleonic wars in 1815, the Royal Marine Artillery began to wear distinctive blue uniforms of the same style as the Army's Royal Artillery,

except that the buttons and hats were the same as those of the rest of the Royal Marines.

The War of 1812 saw three battalions of Royal Marines despatched to North America, and they were amongst the British troops who sacked and burned most public buildings in Washington D.C. on 24 August 1814. The U.S. Marine Commandant's house and the U.S. Marine barracks were spared and, although many legends have arisen in Marine lore for these omissions, no satisfactory explanation has ever been given. The war officially ended with the treaty of Ghent on 24 December 1814, but isolated actions at sea continued for several months, and the last major battle – New Orleans – was fought on 8 January 1815. The slowness of communications in those days cost the British 2036 casualties in a battle fought seventeen days after peace was officially declared.

The Royal Marines continued to fight all around the world and earned so many battle honors that King George IV awarded the Corps 'the Great Globe itself' in lieu of battle honors when colors were presented by the Duke of Clarence in 1827. One engagement was selected to be inscribed on the colors as representative of all the other battles: Gibraltar.

A black, high-crowned peaked shako with a brass plate at the front became part of the Royal Marine uniform after this period and was worn by the red-coated infantrymen and the blue-coated artillerymen in the Carlist War in Spain, in the Crimea and in the China War, although the pattern changed with Army style. Dark blue trousers replaced the white trousers in the field. Non-commissioned officers' chevrons began appearing in gold on a dark blue background.

Around 1830, Royal Marine Artillery officers were wearing blue waist-length coatees with high standing, gold-braided collars, a panel of gold braid on each sleeve and a double row of brass buttons down the flap front. Gold-fringed epaulets were worn on each shoulder. A gold bullion flaming grenade edged in red was worn on each epaulet, and on the coat tails.

At the conclusion of the Crimean War, the Marines were designated a 'Light Corps', and the title of the Corps became Royal Marines (Light Infantry) while their artillery counterparts were called Royal Marine Artillery, although the official designations RMLI and RMA were not forthcoming until 1862. The shako continued to be worn, but a flat-topped peaked cap was also being worn by officers. The crown was blue with a red band below it. On the red band was a silver globe showing the eastern hemisphere. A bullion laurel wreath surrounded the globe. Above the globe was the stringed bugle of a light infantry regiment or company, but this was not worn yet on the undress cap. The Corps' famous globe and laurel was moving into prominence. It was also being worn as a collar badge.

During the 1870s the Marines put on a new headgear as they were made part of the force fighting the fierce Ashanti tribe on the West Coast of Africa. The RMLI wore their red coats with dark blue trousers, gaitered into boots, as they marched into the steamy jungle. A few wore tropical helmets, but the most common headgear for this campaign was a white 'French Foreign Legion' type képi complete with neck flap.

During the next decade the Marines operated further north, in Egypt, and wore a blue uniform with white tropical helmets as they engaged the 'fuzzy-wuzzies' and other forces of the Mahdi. The white helmets gave way to khaki ones before the fight was over. Some Marines also found a new method of transportation as they joined the Guards Camel Regiment in an attempt to rescue Gen. Gordon. This attempt failed. More than a decade passed before the Royal Marines returned to the Sudan, and when they did, in 1896, it was a small party of RMA which carried on the Corps tradition for fidelity and bravery in battle.

Although both the RMLI and RMA participated in the Boer War, they fought only one major land battle – at Graspan. The Marines who fought ashore were dressed in the tropical kit of light tan khaki, including the new wrap-around leggings, which left them virtually indistinguishable from their Army brothers-in-arms.

On 31 May 1900, 82 members of the Royal Marine Light Infantry swung through the streets of Peking on their way to the Foreign Legation enclave inside the Tartar City. They were part of the eight-nation 'winter Guard' of 340 marines and sailors called to protect the ten foreign diplomatic missions inside that section of the Chinese capital. A Chinese secret society, the 'I Ho Ch'uan', which translates as either the Righteous or Patriotic Harmony Fists, whose members, in a sort of a pun, were called 'Boxers' by Westerners, had become powerful and threatened to kill all 'foreign devils' in China.

The relatively small force sent to protect the legations was joined by another ninety men on

Drum Major John Greenfield, Plymouth Divisional Band, Royal Marines Light Infantry, 1873–1886. Bearskin caps, authorised from 1768, developed during the Seven Years' War when the grenadiers began to cover the front of their cloth caps with fur in imitation of European regiments. All bearskin caps were abolished in 1843, except those of the foot guards and Scots grays and bandsmen.

4 June. This was to be the defense line against untold thousands of Boxers who had at first tacit approval, and finally, physical help from the official Chinese government. The troops were from Austria, France, Germany, Great Britain, Italy, Japan, Russia and the United States. Although both the Dutch and Spanish governments maintained legations in Peking, they apparently contributed no troops to the defense of the Legation Quarter.

The RMLI members in the detachment were wearing the new work order uniform of white trousers, blue coat and cap. The headgear, the recently introduced 'side cap', was trimmed in red piping, and the coat had red shoulder cords. The standing collar had red embroidered stringed bugles on each side. The RMLI badge was worn on the left side of the cap. The Boxers laid siege to the three-quarter-mile square Legation Quarter. It took 55 days for an Allied relief force, which eventually numbered 14,000, to reach the besieged area. Both inside the Legation Quarter and in the relief expedition

A studio portrait of a Marine, circa 1914–18, displaying a wound stripe on his left lower sleeve, globe and laurel emblems on his collar, single patch breast pocket, and two patch side pockets. The buttons bear an anchor surmounted by a crown and encircled by 'ROYAL MARINES' and a laurel wreath.

Below right: Lieutenant G.E. Barnes, Royal Marine Artillery astride his horse Nellie, at Esquimalt, Canada, where he was commanding officer of the RMA detachment circa 1896. The cypher on the sabrétache and the bursting grenade on the collar are of interest.

Below: Captain A.B. Liardet Royal Marines Light Infantry, and his Musketry Staff, on Malta in 1885.

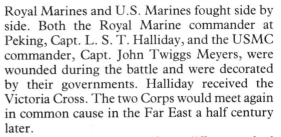

Royal Marines and U.S. Marines fought side by side. Both the Royal Marine commander at Peking, Capt. L. S. T. Halliday, and the USMC commander, Capt. John Twiggs Meyers, were wounded during the battle and were decorated by their governments. Halliday received the Victoria Cross. The two Corps would meet again in common cause in the Far East a half century later.

Although the basic uniform differences had earned the RMLI and RMA the nicknames of 'Red Marines' and 'Blue Marines', there were variations, as in the blue coats and caps worn by RMLI members during the Boxer campaign. Both also had white uniforms.

A variety of headgear was also worn in the period around the turn of the century. Both RMLI and RMA wore blue 'home service' pattern helmets which had been introduced in 1878. The former wore it with a spike, the latter with a ball top. There were several variations in helmet plates over the years. The RMLI plate was very similar to the one currently worn. It was an eight-pointed star topped by a crown, sitting on the eighth point. In the center of the star was the Corps' globe circled by a belt with the Corps' motto, *Per Mare Per Terram* – 'By Sea By Land' – used since 1775. At the bottom point of the star was the anchor and stringed bugle. In 1902, the Victorian Crowns on the plates were changed to the Imperial Crown. The RMA members wore a brass bursting grenade helmet plate. Other headgear in this period included the side cap, the 'pill box' cap, peaked caps, and the so-called 'Broderick' caps which were like peaked caps with the peaks removed.

As the new century moved into its teens, events forecast that the RMLI and RMA would soon be wearing a common helmet. The blue helmet gave way to the white tropical helmet for home service in 1905 and the Wolseley pattern helmet in 1912.

When war came, it was no surprise to the Royal Marines or any other alert member of the British Armed Forces. The government had been preparing to enter the conflict and sent mobilization telegrams to members of the forces two days before officially entering the fray on 4 August 1914.

Both the RMLI and the RMA went into what became the Great War, and, later, World War I, in blue uniforms with the blue Broderick cap. The artillerymen's badge on that cap was the brass flaming grenade, while the infantrymen wore the globe and laurel with the stringed bugle above. Officers wore a number of distinctive uniforms, among them a blue uniform that included a double-breasted, knee-length frock coat. The blue peaked cap with red band was worn with this uniform; in summer a white cap cover could be worn over the blue peaked cap. RMLI officers wore a cap badge of a gold-thread embroidered laurel wreath, a silver and gold metal globe and a metal stringed bugle. On the uniform collars the badge was similar but without the bugle. RMA officers had crossed cannon above the globe and laurel on the cap and wore horizontal flaming grenades on the collars.

Much of the service of Royal Marines during this war was afloat, but at the onset of the British entry into the conflict, a Royal Marine brigade was sent to Belgium to be part of the Royal Naval Division. One battalion of this brigade was made up of the RMA, but at the end of the month was withdrawn to become the nucleus of the Howitzer Brigade and the Anti-Aircraft Brigade.

The former was formed to man the 15-inch howitzers that gave solid backing to the British effort on the Western front throughout the war.

The new style of war on land brought new style uniforms. The Royal Marines, both infantry and artillery, were soon dressed in the same khaki uniforms as their Army counterparts. It had a single-breasted coat with stand-and-fall collar, trousers and puttees. The headgear was a soft, peaked cap with the RMLI or RMA badge in brass worn at the front. In combat the newly-adopted British shallow steel helmet was worn.

A number of special units were formed by the Royal Marines during World War I, and some of them were given a special cap badge, including the R.M. Labour Corps, which was formed in February 1917 from two companies of the Army Service Corps. The Labour Corps' badge was the globe and laurel surmounted by a sailing ship. The RME wore just a globe and laurel. Some RM officers qualified as pilots during the war and earlier, but there was no separate Marine badge for this speciality. Officers of the Royal Naval Air

The Drum and Fife Band of the RMA detachment at Esquimalt, Canada, circa 1896, identified as, left to right, rear rank, Gunners Spencer, Buxton, Hatcher, Gadsby, and Edwards, and, front rank Bugler Boyce, Gunners Davis and James, Cpl Harris, Bombardier Brennan, and Bugler Rann, with Royal. The rank stripes on Harris' and Brennan's headgear are noteworthy.

Service wore a badge above their rank stripes of an eagle in flight, and RM officers wore the eagle in flight badge on the left breast above the pocket.

The war caused heavy losses to the Royal Marines both afloat and ashore and engraved some new names on the pages of Corps history: Ostend, Gallipoli, Zeebrugge, and a score more. At the war's end the Corps' losses totaled nearly 6000 but its strength had grown to 55,000. Within a year this had dropped to 15,000. More cuts were ahead. The days of the 'Red Marines' and the 'Blue Marines' were numbered.

By 1923, Corps strength had been cut to 9500 and the decision was made to amalgamate the RMLI and RMA. By this time, the everyday uniform was primarily the blue one. The dress uniform retained by the new Royal Marines was the blue of the RMA topped by either the white Wolseley pattern helmet or the blue peaked cap with red band, which had a white cover in summer.

The amalgamation ended the use of the stringed bugle of the RMLI and the grenades and cannons of the RMA on badges. In their place, above the globe and laurel on caps, was the lion and crown (the distinguishing badge of a Royal regiment). Between the wars there was little change in the uniforms after amalgamation. There was service in China during the 1920s and in the various outposts of the Empire, and, of course, there was continued service in the fleet.

When World War II began in September 1939, Corps strength stood at 12,000. Corps members were wearing the blue uniform adopted in 1923, the World War I khaki service dress, lighter weight khaki drill for warmer climates, and a new type of uniform that had been in the works since 1937 and started being issued to selected troops in 1938. The uniform was khaki with a stand-and-fall collar on the waist length blouse. The trousers had a large, flap pocket just above the knee on the left leg. It underwent revisions during the war years, but the basic design remained the same. The uniform was the bane of the spit-and-polish British regiments, and the Royal Marines were no exception. But, being introduced as the curtain was rising on history's greatest war, the new field clothing was eventually and inevitably dubbed 'battledress'.

Early in the war the Marines wore battledress along with the khaki side cap that had two brass buttons at the front, and the Royal Marines brass cap badge on the left side. For a time, at least,

Above: RMLI buglers, aged 14 and 15, at Chatham Barracks in 1919 on the anniversary of the storming of Zeebrugge mole by HMS *Vindictive*, part of whose funnel casing mounted on a section of her upperdeck is in the foreground. This was the first use of silver bugles, while the buglers wear the last red tunics to be worn.

Right: An unusual combination indicating a Royal Naval chaplain attached to 44 Cdo, RM. The red fighting knife on a black triangle was worn by RM commandos of the Special Service Group, 1944–46.

Field Marshal Montgomery presents TSM
H.F.G. Beavan of 45 Cdo, RM, with the
Military Medal at Kiel on 1 June 1945. The
style of Beavan's shoulder flash above the
Combined Operations flash is noteworthy.
On his left sleeve, he wears a Troop
Sergeant Major's rank badge of crown
surrounded by a laurel. Montgomery wears
the 21st Army Group's formation sign.

Major-General Laycock inspects NCOs of
45 Cdo, RM (with a Royal Navy commando
in the foreground). The good conduct
stripes on the lower sleeve, the corporals'
and lance-corporals' stripes and the styles
and colours of shoulder flashes are
noteworthy.

Captain Musto, Royal Marines explains items of Special Boat Service equipment to a Royal Navy Admiral, circa 1957. Musto wears the red fighting knife on a black triangle which was worn between 1946 and 1964 by the 3rd Commando Brigade, and previously by the Special Service Group.

Below left: The colours of 41 Cdo, RM on parade for the United Nation's Medal Parade at UNICYP BRITCON (UN Forces In Cyprus, British Contingent) Base Cyprus, September 1979. In the front rank, left to right, are Lt Mark Baily, WO2 Bob Williams, and Lt Tony Airey behind whom are Colour Sgts Tony Higgins and Bill Newton.

Below: Sergeant Alan Rennles, RM, pointing out the location of the Temporary Cease-Fire Line to the Marines on escort duty, Derrick Pinnington and John Taylor, while serving as part of the UN peace keeping forces in Cyprus. The different UN cap and arm badges can be seen.

officers continued to wear the standard khaki uniform coat with lapels and four flap pockets. The globe and laurel insignia in bronze was worn on the upper lapels. A Sam Browne belt was worn. The khaki, peaked cap had the peak covered in the same material as the rest of the cap. The bronze cap insignia had the lion and crown separated from the globe and laurel, which was the standard officer style. A light green shirt and tie were worn with this uniform. This uniform soon gave way to battledress, although officers had and still have the collars open, worn with a khaki shirt and tie.

Battledress was the uniform the Royal Marines wore as they were formed into a Mobile Naval Base Defence Organization, an Amphibious Infantry Division, a Siege Regiment, and units of engineers as the war got under way.

Shoulder flashes and formation signs were beginning to appear throughout the Army, and the practice quickly spread to the Royal Marines. The Royal Marines Division wore a red, wedge-shaped shoulder patch with a yellow trident in the center. The Siege Regiment, which manned the big guns that shelled the French Coast from Dover, wore (shades of the Royal Marine Artillery) a red flaming grenade on a khaki background. The engineers wore a blue shield with a red anchor afoul with white rope and a yellow bursting grenade. While many of the Marines served aboard ship, others were waiting to perform the Royal Marine speciality – amphibious operations. The so-called 'phoney war' period in Europe between September 1939 and 10 May 1940 prevented this, but other opportunities soon presented themselves.

A group of 41 Cdo, RM and attached WRENs wearing their UN medals after the Medal Parade at the BRITCON Base Cyprus in 1979. The UN's emblem replaced the RM beret badge; another style of UN emblem was worn as an arm badge above a small cloth Union Jack on the upper left arm.

Newly-qualified RM pilot with Army wings at an Army Air Corps ceremony, with an Army major-general. The specialist badge (upper) denotes a Marksman, and the lower is a clerk third class skill badge.

Sgt Lawrence, the first RM NCO to qualify as a pilot, wears the Lovat uniform with subdued lapel badges and buttons, the latter bearing an anchor and crown encircled by 'ROYAL MARINES' and a laurel wreath.

Member of 42 Cdo, RM on street patrol in Port Stanley, in the 'mop-up' at the end of the 1982 Falklands war. His combat dress is identical to that of the Army.

A blinding snowstorm was in progress as H.M.S. *Berwick* glided as quietly as possible for a cruiser into the inner harbor of Reykjavik, Iceland. It was 4.00 am on 10 May 1940. The Marines landed without opposition in this remote northern land which had grown to strategic importance because of its position on the North Atlantic trade route. Units of the 680-man Royal Marine 2nd Battalion quickly took over the telegraph, telephone and radio broadcasting offices and then made their way to the only enemy outpost in this island nation – the German consulate.

Dressed in World War I type steel helmets and with khaki battledress buttoned tight against the late spring cold, the two platoons under Major S. G. Cutler trotted briskly through the snow with black boots sinking at times almost to the short, web anklets. The Army-style NCOs chev-

rons, blancoed white by the marines, seemed a perfect match for the snow. The consulate was secured, secret papers captured as the Nazis tried to burn them, and known Nazi agents rounded up. The net snared one German naval officer who had been put ashore from a U-boat earlier. The Marines stayed on as an occupying force until 20 May when Army troops took over the duties. These soldiers held the island against the German invasion threat until relieved in May 1941 by 147th Infantry Brigade and then by the 1st Provisional Marine Brigade. These Marines, however, were not the Royals. They wore an eagle and anchor with their globe insignia and came to Iceland to protect interests of the United States. They also freed several hundreds of British troops for service elsewhere.

Dark blue battledress was issued to Marines who were serving in ships' detachments or as landing craft crews. Although Marines were busily engaged aboard ship, little use had been made of them as ground forces, although some had been landed in Norway in rescue and rearguard operations, and other landings had been made in Holland and France. A Marine force of 2000 was sent to the Island of Crete early in 1941, but suffered heavy losses when German paratroopers attacked and captured the island.

A red patch with the Marine emblem in brass was now worn on the left side. A shoulder flash with the words 'Royal Marines' in red on dark blue cloth was also being worn on both sleeves of the battledress.

In 1942, what was to become the speciality of the Royal Marines after World War II, got under way with the formation of 'A' and 'B' Commandos within the Corps. The Army had already formed commando units which specialized in lightning raids on enemy-held territory and reportedly mounted mild protests to letting the Marines in on this speciality. But the objections were ignored, and the two Royal Marines Commandos were soon designated as 40 and 41.

The first test of a Royal Marine Commando came during operation *Jubilee*, the amphibious landings by Allied forces at Dieppe on the French Channel Coast at dawn on 19 August 1942. A German force was ready and waiting. The Royal Marines were sent in as reinforcements at about 0830 hrs. After surveying the situation Lt Col. Peter Picton Phillips, the R.M. Commando's commanding officer knew his men headed toward the beach would encounter almost certain slaughter. Only when the futility of further action was demonstrable did he don white string gloves, carried to assist him in his beach landings, and stand up, utterly exposed, in the stern of his launch, which led the assault, and wave back the landing craft astern. The gloves made him more visible to the landing craft crews. They also made him more visible to the Germans. He was shot down, but he had achieved his objective; he had saved 200 of his men. Only the two LCMs on the flanks did not see his signals and beached; all their occupants were killed or captured.

Eventually, there were nine R.M. Commandos, numbered 40 to 48. They wore red on blue shoulder flashes that varied somewhat during the war. Early flashes had the numbers written, such as 'No. 45', over a straight Royal Marines flash with a Commando flash below it. One version later had the number on top, followed by a line with the word, 'Commando' followed by another line with 'Royal Marines'. Later versions dropped the 'No.' and had the numerals standing

alone above the rest of the flash. Commandos also wore the Combined Operations patch below the flashes, but with their own little re-styling touch. The patch was originally issued with an arch-shaped black background with an anchor, an eagle and a submachine-gun all in red in the center. The Commandos trimmed the patch into a circle, after approval had been given by the Earl Mountbatten, who was Chief of Combined Operations at the time. Another patch worn by the Commandos later in the war was a red fighting knife point up, on an inverted isosceles triangle.

Royal Marine Commandos were wearing green berets when they spearheaded the invasions of Sicily and the Italian mainland in 1943. By late 1943 blue berets had become the standard head-gear worn with both the khaki and blue battle-dress. The next year Royal Marines were in the forefront of the Normandy invasion and took part in many operations throughout the balance of the war in Europe. In addition to the Commandos,

three battalions, operating under the umbrella of the 116th Brigade, fought on the Maas and at Oldenburg. They wore the old R.M. Division formation sign of a yellow trident on a red triangle. The 33rd Battalion of the 117th Brigade was sent to Germany at war's end to take part in the surrender of the German ports and harbor installations. They wore the Brigade formation sign of a six-pointed yellow star with a solid red circle in the center on which a yellow foul anchor was superimposed.

Royal Marine ground activity against the Japanese in the final years of the war was largely confined to the theater of operations where 42 and 44 Commandos wore khaki drill and field clothing most of the time. Royal Marines also served aboard ship throughout the British Pacific Fleet, Task Force 57.

Some 350 miles from the Japanese mainland on Easter Sunday, 1945, troops from the U.S. Marine Corps' 1st and 2nd Divisions joined Army comrades in what was to become the last land battle of the Pacific War. They hit the beaches at Okinawa supported by the ships of the U.S. and British fleets. As the American Marines fought on the ground below, Royal Marine pilots were among those giving close air support from above. It was among the few operations of World War II in which both Corps participated.

The strength of the Royal Marines in 1944 was 78,500 officers and men, of whom 3,999 were killed during the conflict.

Special mention should be made of the Royal Marines Band Service, which became responsible for bands in the Royal Navy in 1903. Distinctive uniforms have been and still are worn by Royal Marine bandsmen. Dating to the mid eighteenth century, when Divisional bands were formed, the bands have had their ups and downs as defense cuts reduced and wars increased the strength of the Corps. Until 1930, Divisional bands existed at Chatham, Plymouth, Portsmouth, and Deal.

Among distinctive badges worn by the bands is the Prince of Wales plumes, awarded to the Plymouth band in 1922. It is worn on the cap in white metal between the lion and crown and the globe and laurel. The Rose of York, awarded in 1902 to the Chatham band, was worn in the same position. The Portsmouth Band, now the band of CINCNAVHOME wears a special badge of bursting grenade and laurel wreath, plus the cyphers of King George V, Queen Elizabeth II, and Prince Philip. This band also wears a Royal Yacht curved shoulder flash surmounted by a crown on the right shoulder. Band members of the Royal Naval School of Music, as distinct from the Divisional Bands, from 1903–50 wore a lyre over the globe and laurel cap badge and a lyre as a collar badge. R.M.B. shoulder titles have also been worn. In addition to the standard R.M. uniforms, band members wear pre-war cere-

Left: Arriving back in Britain, the Royal Marine garrison of Port Stanley which was forced to surrender to the Argentinian invaders' overwhelming numbers and firepower. The corporal has parachutist's wing on his 'woolly-pully', the only RM item on which shoulder flashes are worn.

Right: Major General Jeremy Moore, RM, CB, OBE, MC, holds the signed Argentinian surrender document which ended the 1982 Falklands war. Just visible between his breast pockets is his rank tab, a position adopted on combat dress during the Falklands war.

monial 'blues' which had high yellow or gold-trimmed red collars with embroidered globe and laurel collar badges. A special white tunic with high collar is also worn, but has no collar badges. Recent defense cuts indicate that the Commando Forces band will be phased out. It inherited the Prince of Wales plumes from the Plymouth Divisional Band, and, so far, it is uncertain what will become of this unique insignia.

Following World War II, battledress was still the mainstay uniform for everyday dress in the Royal Marines, but as they saw service in varied places such as Palestine, Malaya, Cyprus, Suez, Aden, and Borneo, field clothing in green khaki

Right: Royal Marine Band buglers, c. 1963, wearing the pre-war blue uniform with high red collar trimmed in yellow or gold with embroidered globe and laurel.

Below: Royal Marine bandsman wearing the Prince's Badge on his left shoulder. The white Wolseley pattern helmet is a pre-war relic. The helmet plate, an eight-pointed star, is derived from nineteenth century RMLI styles, and the ball top from the RMA.

drill and other rigs more suitable for warmer weather were worn. A soft crowned, narrow-brimmed hat was also worn with some field clothing in place of the beret. Warm-weather gear was not all the Corps would be needing as the 1950s opened and new trouble spots exploded.

'They've got us surrounded. The bastards won't get away this time.' The date was 28 November 1950, the place was Koto-ri, North Korea, and the speaker was Col. Lewis B. 'Chesty' Puller, USMC. He was talking to Lt Col. Douglas B. Drysdale, commander of 41 Independent Commando, Royal Marines. Drysdale was given one of the toughest tasks of the Korean War; he was ordered to try to get a combined British-American force through the encircling Chinese Communist forces to the city of Hagaru, 11 miles away, where Lt Col. Thomas L. Ridge, USMC, was holding out with his outnumbered 3rd Battalion, 1st (U.S.) Marines.

Task Force Drysdale reached its objective two days later, but at great cost. The force consisted of 41 Independent Commando, G Company, 1st U.S. Marines, and B Company, 31st U.S. Army Infantry. Nearly half the task force, including 61 Commandos, was lost in the battle of Hell Fire Valley. Drysdale, who was wounded himself,

punched through with half the force to Hagaru to reinforce Ridge's beleaguered battalion with 300 men, 174 of whom were Royal Marines. Getting there had cost the force 321 casualties.

41 Independent Commando, Royal Marines, was specially formed in August 1950 at Plymouth to serve with the U.S. 1st Marine Division in Korea. The men of the unit, dressed in plain clothes, were flown to Japan where they were issued American equipment. American field clothing was worn by the Royal Marines in Korea, although they retained their distinctive beret. In addition to their fight to reach Hagaru during the retreat of the 1st U.S. Marine Division from the Chosin Reservoir, the Commando also participated in some coastal raids and other actions. The Commando was awarded the U.S. Presidential Unit Citation. All R.M. Commandos wear colored lanyards, the one of 41 being old gold. This Commando was disbanded in February 1952, reformed in March 1960, disbanded in 1977 but reformed and finally disbanded in 1981.

Royal Marine service since World War II has covered half the world: Palestine, Malaya, Cyprus, Suez, Kuwait, Aden, Brunei, Tanganyika, Borneo, Radfan, Hong Kong, Northern Ireland, and Belize have all echoed to the marching boots of Her Majesty's Jollies. That

---

Members of the Women's Royal Naval Service assigned to the Royal Marines during World War II, wearing WRNS uniform and rank insignia, but with the globe and laurel and lion on the seaman's cap.

Above: MARENS photographed in 1979 on the Thames. The officer (foreground) has an WRNS cap emblem, but the Petty Officers on the flanks do not, although all wear WRNS rank insignia.

Lt Col. P. G. Ferguson, RM, presenting Leading Wren Susan Smithson with a bronze medal for the winning team in the Wrens inter-unit shooting competition, 1975. The manner of wearing the cap insignia on a red patch is shown.

The King's Badge, instituted by King George V in March 1918. In July 1952 Queen Elizabeth II approved that the style and custom remained unchanged.

The Prince's Badge, awarded annually since 1978 to the best Boy Musician or Bugler in Senior, or Commandant General's Squads training at Deal.

The Prince's Badge. (The Commandant General, RM approved the title 'Commandant General's Squad' in January 1950.)

The first Royal Marine Forces Volunteer Reserve shoulder badge issued in 1948 and worn until 1952. The title has since become Royal Marine Reserve.

Marine officer's gorget, the last relic of medieval armour, worn on a ribbon around the neck. They were established in 1830.

Original style of RM gorget, 4.2in deep, and 3.75in wide. They were worn to indicate the officer was on duty.

A Royal Marine officer's shoulder belt badge, 1784–85.

Royal Marine waist belt plate bearing Queen Victoria's Royal Cypher surmounted by a Queen's Crown. The plate is 1.7in by 2.25in.

Royal Marine officer's waist belt plate, 1830–55. The King's Crown is surmounted by a lion, distinguishing of a Royal regiment, which the Marines became in 1802.

The gold on blue parachutist's wings worn two inches below the shoulder seam of the right arm of an NCO's blue uniform tunic.

Colour sergeants gold on red herring-bone pattern stripes and gold on blue Crown, worn on the right upper sleeve only, but now not worn on blues.

RM Gun Layer 3rd class badge (upper) which replaced the single gun emblem c. 1950; Marksman's badge; Good Conduct badges.

Royal Marine Artillery officer's shoulder belt plate from the reign of Queen Victoria, having a Queen's Crown and RMA bursting grenade.

Royal Marine officer's shoulder belt plate, 1830–55, with the battle honour 'Gibraltar', awarded in 1827 to represent all the many and King's Crown.

Royal Marine officer's shoulder belt plate, 1826–30, bearing the lion of a Royal Regiment upon a King's Crown, surrounded by an oak wreath.

Royal Marines Artillery Company officer's waist belt locker, 1857–59. The first official mention of the title RMA dates to 1862.

Full Dress waist belt locker, warrant officer RM Bands, 1923–39. It measures 3.78in by 1.96in.

Other Ranks valise badge, RMA and RMLI, 1877–1901.

Badge of the 21st Bombay Native Infantry, a Sepoy Marine Battalion dating from January 1777, but unconnected with the Royal Marines.

Pouch badge, 1902–70. Note that the King's Crown was not changed until 1970 due to the large stocks remaining. It is 3.15in in height.

RMLI horse martingale badge, 1893–1902. This badge is 3in high.

Royal Marine Artillery horse martingale badge, 1893–1902. It is 3.17in high.

An unidentified prototype, therefore unofficial, globe and laurel wreath badge. The laurel wreath was awarded for the Marine's assault on Belle Isle.

An unidentified prototype, therefore unofficial, Royal Marine Light Infantry cap badge, with the stringed bugle which distinguished the RMLI.

Unauthenticated belt buckle plate, 2.85in high and 2.15in wide.

A Royal Marine Artillery hat plate, 1816–21: it leaves no doubt as to the wearer's occupation! It is 4.9in high and 3.55in wide.

The badge of the Royal Marines Labour Corp, a globe and laurel surmounted by a sailing ship, from World War I.

term, incidentally, originated in the late seventeenth century and had its base in London street slang of that era. Citizen soldiers were known as 'Tame Jollies' and the Marines were called 'Royal Jollies.' The term was immortalized by Rudyard Kipling in the poem 'Soldier and Sailor, Too'.

In 1964 the Royal Marines said farewell to battledress and adopted a distinctive new dress for everyday wear. Called 'Lovat dress' it is a shade of green slightly lighter than the forestry green of the U.S. Marines. This is worn with the green Commando beret and with the blue beret with red patch and brass globe and laurel for ranks under training. Band ranks wear the white peaked cap with red band with Lovat dress. Light khaki shirts and neckties are worn with this uniform which has a tunic with turned-back lapels. Bronze collar insignia buttons and initials are worn with this uniform. Chevrons worn with Lovat dress are gold on dark green and are of a slightly smaller pattern than those worn on the blue uniform.

Chevrons are worn on the right sleeve only. Color sergeants wear a crown above their stripes on all uniforms, except the blues, when they wear the traditional color sergeants' badge consisting of a globe on crossed union flags having a crown above and a foul anchor below, surrounded by a laurel wreath. Rank chevrons are worn point down, except for drum and bugle majors and provost sergeants who wear them point up. Good conduct stripes are worn bottom point up, but on the lower left sleeve only. When greatcoats are worn, chevrons are at the cuff level, otherwise they are always worn about $10\frac{1}{2}$ inches below the shoulder seam.

In addition to Lovat and blue dress, light khaki drill uniforms are worn in tropical climates for everyday wear. They have turned-back lapels for officers. Collar badges are worn only by officers on this uniform. Either the peaked cap or the dress helmet are worn with this uniform. A variety of combat and field clothing is worn. A popular item of everyday wear is a knit sweater or pullover known as a 'woolly-pully', which is often worn instead of the tunic in Lovat dress. The sweater is an olive drab shade. It is the only Royal Marines uniform item on which the Royal Marine Commando shoulder flash and Royal Marines Band Services title are worn.

As Britain's sole Commando units, the Royal Marines and R.M. Reserve receive highly specialized training. Most of this is done at Lympstone. Because of cuts announced in 1981, the Royal Marines presence in some traditional bases is uncertain, but Portsmouth, Deal, Plymouth, Arbroath, and Poole still serve.

Some work at Marine bases is performed by members of the Women's Royal Naval Service (WRNS). Wrens assigned to the Royal Marines are often called 'Marens'. They wear the regular WRNS dark blue uniform, but instead of a cap tally wear the Royal Marine badge on a red patch.

On 2 April 1982 Argentine forces landed at Port Stanley, the Falkland's capital, and next day at Grytviken, South Georgia, overwhelming the token Marine garrisons. Britain rapidly mounted an amphibious operation to retake the islands. The initial landings being carried out by 40 and 45 Cdo and 2 and 3 Para. 42 Cdo remained afloat as reserve, landing later. The main Argentine force, concentrated around Stanley, had to be defeated, but direct sea assault was not viable. The British landed 65 miles away at San Carlos Bay. Early in May, SAS and RM Special Boat Squadron section were deployed on reconnaissance tasks critical to the selection of the landing site. The enemy believed a march from San Carlos was impossible in winter, but the Marines have a saying: 'The difficult we will do at once, the impossible will take a bit longer'. On the night of 26 May 3 Cdo Bde began its march across moors, hills and mountains in rain, sleet and freezing winds, with little helicopter lift. As decisive as a major action, it demoralized the enemy. It also promoted a new word: yomping. 5th Infantry Bde which landed later also closed in. Maj. Gen. Moore, RM who had been appointed Land Forces Commander launched the final offensive on the night of 11/12 June, and ofter determined attacks on the remaining Argentinian positions by all units, the enemy's will finally broke and surrender became in evitable on 14 June. This was unmechanized infantry war radically different to Ulster anti-terrorism and Rhine army technology, but the Marines have had considerable experience of such warfare since 1945. Marine aviators were in the forefront of supply and casevac helicopter operations throughout the campaign, the first occasion they had operated with and got awards from all three services. In the Falklands Marines wore rank on chest tabs, as in Norway where it is also worn on headgear as per NATO. The only distinctive features were the globe and laurel on green berets.

3

THE ROYAL NETHERLANDS MARINES

There was no mistaking they were Marines, but the cut and color of their uniforms seemed strangely alien on this United States Marine Corps base at Camp Lejeune, North Carolina. It was 1943 and the camp was teeming with Marines in various stages of training, preparing to go to the Pacific theater of war to battle the Japanese.

This new group of officers and men was almost swallowed up in the throngs of U.S. Marines, but they were there for the same purpose as their American counterparts. They were the detachment of Korps Mariniers – the Royal Netherlands Marines – from the Netherlands Antilles, the last of their Corps to serve on free Dutch-ruled soil in these years of World War II. They had trained a local Army to protect the islands and had come to North Carolina to form the nucleus of the largest single unit of their Corps in history – a Marine Brigade. Their gray-green uniforms with stand-and-fall collars set them off from the Americans in forestry green service uniforms and tropical fatigues. The distinction would not last long. These Dutchmen were to be American equipped as an expedient matter and would wear USMC uniforms from dress blues to jungle fatigues. They would, however, retain the insignia of their Corps on all uniforms. It was a proud Corps with a long history.

Admiral Michiel De Ruyter, who wanted a regiment of sea soldiers, and Secretary of State Jan de Witt, who won approval from the government for the unit in 1665, are considered the founders of the Korps Mariniers. De Ruyter had become dissatisfied with eleventh-hour selections of land-based troops to fight aboard ships and felt a specially-trained body of sea soldiers

was necessary. So on 10 December 1665, the unit came into being. It was called the 'Regiment de Marine', and it was the second such special formation to be created by a major European power within fourteen months. On 28 October 1664, the English had raised a similar unit and called it the 'Lord High Admiral's Regiment'. The Netherlands and England were at war during this period.

The Marines the Dutch sent into action at this time were an oddly-clothed lot by today's standards. Officers wore what appeared to be fashionable street clothing of the period. A typical uniform might be brown with a plumed, broad-brimmed hat, a knee-length frock coat with long rows of brass buttons, and knee-length trousers that met light-colored stockings. Buckled shoes and ruffled lace at the collar and cuffs completed the outfit. Within ten years the Mariniers' uniform consisted of a long, medium-blue coat with gold facings and cuffs, blue knee-length trousers, light colored stockings – probably buff – buckled black shoes, and a black, medium-brimmed hat, the forerunner of the tricorn.

By the early 1700s the Mariniers' organization had been given a new name, 'The Regiment de St. Amant'. Its members wore long gray coats with white metal buttons and wide blue cuffs. The stockings matched the cuffs and the black hat now had white edging around the brim. It was this unit that joined with its former rivals, the British Royal Marines, during the Spanish War of Succession, to storm the fortifications at Gibraltar.

In the latter part of the century, Dutch Marines were engaged in colonial uprisings and another war with England. During this time the uniforms

A Dutch Marine captain wearing ceremonial uniform topped by a cork helmet, similar in pattern to the old British Home Service helmet. These helmets, however, are not an item of issue, but are gifts to the Korps from the City of Rotterdam, where the Mariniers' headquarters is located. The stripes on the officers' ceremonial dress trousers are gold.

began to take on a more professional military look. The Zeeland Mariniers Regiment outfitted its members in navy blue coats with buff-yellow facing and double rows of brass buttons. The coat flared just above the waist in front and tapered back to a tail just above the knees. Trousers and leggings were white, and the black tricorn hat had a white edging. Grenadiers of the 21st Mariniers Regiment wore a similar blue coat with old-gold facings and white vest and trousers. Dark blue leggings were worn, and the headgear was the typical tall, black fur cap of grenadiers. When the Dutch joined once more with the English in 1816 to sail against the pirates of the Barbary Coast, the Dutch Marines were wearing a high-collared, single-breasted dark blue coat with old-gold collar and facings and red fringed epaulets. Trousers were white and were ankle length. Belts and other leather accessories were black. A black, bell-crowned peaked shako with a red and white plume and brass front plate was worn.

From 1817 to 1830 the Mariniers wore the 'top hat' headgear then popular in European military forces. It had been adopted by the Royal Marines several years before the Dutch. The hat was black with a flowing red plume on the left side. The uniform was navy blue with red facings. 'Wings' of blue with red semi-circular designs were worn on the shoulders. There was a narrow red stripe on the outside seam of the trouser legs.

The Dutch Marines were kept busy throughout the balance of the nineteenth century putting down rebellions in the Netherlands East Indies. Most of the action was centered in the Province of Atjeh and the Island of Bali. The Mariniers there probably shed the coat of the uniform being worn in Europe during that period. It was beginning to resemble the ceremonial uniform in use today, being blue with red trim and a high collar of red with double bars of gold. Solid red 'wings' were also featured. Rank chevrons were coming into use, being gold with red piping. They were worn point up on the lower cuffs. The bell-crowned shako returned, this time with a more elaborate brass front plate with the main feature being crossed anchors under the royal crown. Trousers were white.

By the turn of the century, the Korps Mariniers had added Peking, China to the outposts where they were stationed. Like brother Marines from other lands, the Dutchmen served as the legation guard. They stayed in China for 23 years.

The Mariniers of 1900 wore uniforms that set the pattern for their dress and ceremonial uniforms today. For those stationed in Europe, a cork helmet covered with navy blue cloth became the standard headgear. It was fitted with a brass helmet plate, bearing the insignia that had become the emblem of the Corps – an eight-pointed heraldic star resting on crossed anchors with the royal Netherlands crown above. A spike could be worn on the helmet on ceremonial occasions and a brass knob at other times.

The uniform was dark blue with a standing collar. Rank chevrons were red on blue, red on white, and gilt. A képi with a crowned anchor insignia was also worn during this period. A white uniform with a wide stand-and-fall collar was issued and worn with a black string bow tie. In the tropics the uniforms were similar but of lighter material. The helmet was blue but of the British 'Gunga Din' sun helmet pattern. It had no brass fittings. Officers wore dress white uniforms in East and West Indies, other ranks a dress blue coat with white trousers. The field uniform was blue with knee-length white leggings.

The Netherlands remained neutral during World War I, but its Marine detachment in Peking was reinforced to take on the additional duties of guarding the property of the German and Austrian legations. While the dress uniform changed little in the years immediately following World War I, a field service uniform was introduced similar to one adopted by the Army. It was gray-green with stand-and-fall collar. A tropical version was also issued. A broad-brimmed hat, also of gray-green, was frequently worn with the tropical uniform. Rank insignia for non-commissioned officers was worn on small collar patches with dark green background.

In 1935, the Netherlands was called upon by the League of Nations to provide part of the international military force on guard in the Saar District during the plebiscite. Holland sent the Mariniers.

A steel helmet had been adopted by Dutch forces in 1928, and the one worn by the Mariniers bore the crowned, foul anchor insignia stenciled on the front. The Dutchmen would be needing those helmets within five years. When the Nazis struck in May 1940, the Dutch fought valiantly, but were soon overwhelmed. In bomb-scarred Rotterdam, a handful of Korps Marinier recruits in gray-green uniforms with breeches

Right: The musician with the fife is called a 'piper' in the Dutch Marines. He is part of the musical unit called the 'pipes and drums' of the Korps Mariniers. Silver snare drums are used in this oldest of Dutch Marine musical units.

Far right: A drum major wearing a sash that bears the Korps Mariniers' battle honors below the lion's head badge and between ceremonial drumsticks. This man is a sergeant major, shown by the four chevrons topped by a crown on each sleeve.

Bottom right: The Korps Mariniers band wearing ceremonial uniforms prepares to step out during a parade in Rotterdam. Officially called the Marine Band of the Royal Netherlands Navy, it dates its founding to 1 August 1945, when eighteen former members of the Korps' old regimental band who had reported for duty upon the liberation of the Netherlands became the nucleus of the new band. In addition to its official duties, it appears in concerts and has recorded some 300 compositions that have topped the three million mark in world-wide record sales.

Left: Two major generals of the Korps Mariniers review an honor guard in 1958 as the command of the Corps changed hands. The outgoing commandant, Maj. Gen. H.O. Romswinckel, and the incoming commandant, Maj. Gen. H. Lieftinck, wear identical rank distinction lace on their cuffs. Dutch Marine officers wear Navy rank insignia but use Army titles. The Marine holding the Corps colors is a warrant officer. The general officers wear double red trouser stripes but a single stripe is worn by other Marines. The man to right of the color bearer is a sergeant major who wears four chevrons topped by a crown. To the sergeant's right is a captain who wears two stripes topped by a curl on his cuffs. The everyday service dress shown here has since been modified by having the stand collar replaced by turn-down lapels.

and wrap-around leggings held the Maas bridges for several days against a superior German force before the fight ended. Some Dutch servicemen eluded capture and made it to England. Some of them were Mariniers.

The problem of supplying the Dutchmen with their own type of uniforms was at the bottom of the British list of priorities in 1940. The British Isles had become an embattled haven of refugee armies from a half-dozen or more nations on the European mainland and most had escaped with the clothes on their backs and little else. Food and shelter came first – then clothing. The Dutch and all the rest were issued British battledress. The dark khaki outfits were soon modified by all of the receivers with insignias from their homelands and special emblems designed to let citizens of the host nation know where they were from. The Dutch were no exception and wore their own rank insignia when they could and British when they could not. They formed the Royal Netherlands Brigade and named it after their Prinses Irene. A battle group in that Brigade was formed by the Korps Mariniers who wore their Corps insignia and shoulder flashes to let the world know who they were. It was nearly five years before they marched on Dutch soil, but when they did, they brought along something from the British Isles besides battledress – they marched to bagpipes.

When the Japanese launched the Pacific phase of World War II in 1941, there was a Korps Marinier battalion on Java and Mariniers serving aboard ships in the fleet of Rear Admiral Karel Doorman in the Java Sea. Neither group fared well. The Mariniers aboard the Dutch light cruiser that was the flagship of the Allied fleet during the battle of the Java Sea were lost when it went down with all hands. It was the *De Ruyter*, named for the Admiral who was instrumental in founding the Dutch Marines. On 8 March 1942, the Allied commander on Java concluded that further resistance was futile. He surrendered a disorganized and scattered force that included the remnants of the Korps Mariniers battalion. A radio station on the island sent out a final message: 'We are shutting down. Goodbye till better times. Long live the Queen.' The Dutch, in time,

would return but better times were all in the past.

In Europe the Prinses Irene Brigade had landed at Normandy and fought in France, Belgium and Holland before the German surrender. The unit had adopted a badge, a Royal Netherlands crown over a scroll bearing the name 'Prinses Irene'. Although the Korps Mariniers comprised the 3rd Battle Group within the brigade, it does not appear that they wore the Prinses Irene insignia, although there may have been individual exceptions.

Following the war the Brigade became the Prinses Irene Gardefusiliers. It was an Army unit, but it traced its links in its dress uniform. The coat is red, marking its founding in England. The headgear is the spiked, blue helmet in remembrance of its association with the Mariniers.

As the war in Europe drew to a close, thousands of Dutchmen from the south of the Netherlands flocked to the United States to join the Royal Netherlands Marine Brigade training to enter the Pacific War. The Allied plan was to have this unit take part in what was to be the final thrust – the attack on mainland Japan. U.S.

uniformed and equipped, the Korps Mariniers Brigade could, at first glance, have been mistaken for a formation of U.S. Marines. With U.S. M-1941 steel helmets, USMC fatigues and tan canvas leggings, they looked as if they might step off singing 'From the Halls of Montezuma' at any moment. But one mark on the fatigues was still distinctively Dutch – the badge of their Corps stenciled on the left fatigue jacket pocket with the words 'Korps' above it, and the word 'Mariniers' below. They never got to wear this uniform into action against the Japanese. The atom bombs brought an abrupt halt to the Pacific half of World War II. The Dutch found themselves with a 9000 man Marine Brigade embarked on ships in the Pacific Ocean and no war to fight. They would soon find one.

In the homeland, the Korps kept the British-style battle dress for everyday wear while the Brigade, which had been sent to the East Indies, kept the American Marine-style uniforms which seemed more practical in the tropics. This included the light tan color uniforms designated as 'khaki' by the Americans and worn as a summer

Far left: Dutch Marine lieutenant colonel wearing 'woolly-pully' and beret discusses merits of the Land Rover with a U.S. Marine warrant officer during a NATO exercise in Norway in 1976. The Dutch officer's rank insignia of three full stripes with a curl is shown on the shoulders of his sweater. The devices are in the 'subdued' coloring of black on khaki. The shoulder title has black lettering on light khaki twill with the words, 'Korps Mariniers'. On the side of the beret away from the camera is a crowned gold anchor on a red patch.

A Dutch Marine officer in tropical whites is probably in the Netherlands Antilles. His rank is shown on shoulder boards, and he appears to have two full stripes of a captain.

Wearing the current service dress, this Dutch Marine second lieutenant has parachutists' wings above the right pocket and a commando fighting knife badge on the left pocket below his medals. The Korps' crown and star insignia is worn on each lapel, and the Korps' yellow metal crown and anchor badge is worn on each epaulet. A Dutch Marine officers' embroidered cap device is the same as that worn by Dutch naval officers.

Two gold on red chevrons worn point down mark this Dutch Marine as a corporal. Parachustists' qualification wings are worn above the right pocket of the battle jacket. Barely discernable on his left pocket is the round commando badge worn by all branches of service in the Netherlands.

A Dutch Marine captain wearing ceremonial dress worn primarily for the opening of parliament or by color guards. Officers' shoulder cord is gold, but is red for enlisted men.

service dress uniform. With this, the Mariniers often wore the American-style 'overseas' cap which the British usually call a 'side cap'. But the chevrons now worn by the NCOs showed both British and American influence. They were point down, British-style, but were of a smaller size, about the same as American chevrons.

Between 1945 and 1949 the Mariniers and other Dutch forces in the East Indies fought against the rebelling Indonesians. In 1950, independence was granted to the people of the archipelago. The Dutch had one more fight in West New Guinea in the early 1960s. After that the Netherlands withdrew as a Pacific colonial power.

Today, the Korps has men serving afloat, serving in a special joint NATO force with the British Royal Marines and garrisoning the Netherlands Antilles.

The ceremonial dress blues have been only slightly modified since World War II. The old-style large chevrons of prewar days have been retained for this uniform. They are still gold on red, worn point up. A white uniform with a peaked cap is also worn. The blues and whites are sometimes mixed, as in the Mariniers' traditional Fife and Drums Corps, where the white cap and trousers are sometimes worn with the blue coat. Gray-green, American-style field clothing is worn with a black beret. In the tropics lighter-weight khaki is worn.

The headquarters of the Korps Mariniers is located in Rotterdam. The commandant holds the rank of major general. Netherlands Marine recruits are trained at the Van Ghent barracks in Rotterdam and the Van Braam Houckgeest barracks in Doorn. There is an amphibious training center on the island of Texel opposite the Dan Helder naval base where the Dutch Naval Academy is also located. Future Korps Marinier officers receive their education there.

4

ITALIAN AMPHIBIOUS UNITS

In September 1943, the only unit of Axis ground forces in the Far East, besides the Japanese, was about to have its status changed. The officers and men of a special unit of the Italian San Marco Regiment, which had been stationed in China since 1924 as a garrison of the Shanhaikwan Fort at the end of the Great Wall and as guards at the naval station in Hankow, were facing capture and internment by their former allies.

In Italy the government had signed an armistice with the Allied Command and was extending its cooperation to them. Mussolini had rallied his fascist forces and had formed a puppet government, the Italian Socialist Republic, in northern Italy, which was protected by German Army Units.

The Japanese, never fully at ease with Western comrades-at-arms whose battles were largely half-a-world away, quickly went to the San Marco officers and asked a blunt question: 'Are you with Mussolini or the monarchy?' When the San Marcos refused to pledge allegiance to Il Duce, they, in effect, bought tickets to a Japanese prisoner-of-war camp, and the price was high. Internment was harsh and not all survived.

As naval infantry, the San Marco had its roots in the Brigata Marina (Naval Brigade) of World War I, which carried on a tradition of Italian naval units engaging in ground action dating back to 1713 in the Kingdom of Savoy. The brigade consisted of one regiment of naval infantry and one regiment of artillery. Both naval infantry and artillery units had been employed in support of the Italian Army almost from the onset of Italy's entering the war on the side of the Allies in May 1915.

The first naval artillery units to serve on land were surviving gunners of two sunken cruisers,

Garibaldi and *Amalfi*. Men from the latter unit also engaged in commando-type operations along the Piave front against the Austrians.

A naval infantry battalion, given the name 'Monfalcone', began operations against the Austrians in the Cortellazzo area in early November 1917. On 20 November the battalion was incorporated into the newly formed Naval Brigade and was joined by two other naval infantry battalions. 'Grado' and 'Caorle'. Two other such units, the 'Golametto' and the 'Navi' were attached to the regiment by June 1918. The previous April the 'Malfalcone' battalion had changed its name to 'Bafile' in honor of Lt Andrea Bafile, a hero of the Brigata Marina who had sacrificed his life to minimize the losses of his men.

While serving on land, the enlisted men primarily wore naval uniforms of a gray-green color. They were of traditional naval cut and consisted of a jumper with flap collar, British-type duck caps and trousers that were tucked into wrap-around leggings. Naval rate insignia was worn. The men also wore stocking caps and turtle-neck sweaters during colder weather and were issued the French Adrian-style steel helmets during the latter part of the war. Officers also wore naval uniforms for a time, but later switched to Army-style field uniforms with a mixture of Navy and Army insignia.

In the final year of the war, the effort of the naval infantrymen in defense of Venice was considered so valiant that at the war's end the grateful city offered the name of its patron saint, St Mark, to the Marina Regiment. The change of name became official on 17 March 1919. Less than four months later the regiment was demobilized with only one battalion remaining in service. But the unit had gained a name and, along with it, a badge – the winged lion of St Mark taken from the Venetian coat of arms. Under the lion's right paw is a pair of tablets bearing the Latin legend, *Pax tibi Marce evangelista meus* – Peace to you Mark, my evangelist. The San Marcos would find little peace in the days ahead.

Dressed in the traditional green sailor's uniform adopted during World War I, men of the special unit of the San Marco Battalion sent to China in 1924 joined with troops of other foreign powers maintaining concessions there over the years in civil wars of the warlords and later during the Japanese offensive.

Their comrades left behind marched to war again in the 1935–36 Italian campaign in Ethiopia. For this they were issued tropical dress, which again retained the traditional sailor uniform lines. The jumper was khaki with a blue flap collar with double white lines at the outside border and white stars in each corner. Instead of a sailor's cap in khaki, however, the men were issued tropical helmets in khaki with cap tallies in black with gold lettering, 'Battaglione S. Marco'. The San Marco lion in yellow or gold on a red background was worn on cuffs by enlisted men and lapels by officers. The unit was employed as regular infantry and never got to use any of its specialized amphibious training.

In 1939, on the eve of World War II, two companies of the San Marcos participated in the Italian landings in Albania. When the gathering clouds broke into the storm of war and Italy formed the Axis with Nazi Germany, the San Marco consisted of two battalions, the Bafile and the Grado. A nautical parachute battalion and a battalion of frogmen were added. Gradually, the strength was increased to seven battalions. By 1942 there were 6000 officers and men in the San Marco Regiment.

Despite the specialized amphibious role envisioned for them, the San Marcos never got to perform their speciality at any time during the war although, late in 1941, such an action seemed imminent. Two battalions, reinforced by two companies of coast artillery, were trained to act as point-of-landing troops in a proposed invasion of the island of Malta. The plan, however, was shelved by the Axis High Command in favor of reducing the island by aerial bombardment, a strategy that failed.

By November 1942, all of the San Marco units were concentrated in North Africa where they were employed generally as infantry and suffered

Left: Three Marines talk things over during a NATO exercise in Turkey in 1978. The man at the left holding a cigarette is a Royal Marine. The officer in the center is a lieutenant of Italy's San Marco Regiment. His rank device is worn above the left pocket. The officer on right is a U.S. Marine major who wears gold rank oak leaves on the lapels of his coat, and metal parachustists wings above the cloth recon wings over his left jacket pocket.

Below: A member of the Italian San Marco unit checks over his rifle during a training exercise. The insignia on his beret is of white metal, and consists of the so-called Republican crown over an anchor and crossed rifles within a circle of rope. This badge was adopted sometime after the San Marcos were revived in 1965 after a twenty-year hiatus. Members of the unit, however, still wear the traditional badge of the winged lion of St Mark on cuffs, lapels, and breasts of service and dress uniforms. The unit has its roots in the Naval Infantry battalions of the World War I. The lion badge is the symbol of the City of Venice, which awarded it and the title 'San Marco' to the naval infantrymen who defended the city from 1914 to 1918.

65

heavy losses. The Bafile battalion, because of its actions during the defense of Tobruk in September 1942, was awarded the name 'Tobruk' battalion. Another unit of the San Marco soon took the Bafile name. During this period the San Marcos in North Africa continued to wear what was virtually the same version of khaki uniform as used during the Ethiopian campaign, except that a khaki beret had been introduced. On 7 May 1943, the Axis troops in North Africa surrendered. The shattered remnants of the San Marcos were among the last to lay down their arms.

That September an armistice between Italy and the Allies was signed and, within a month, Italy declared war on Germany. The reconstituted Bafile battalion, now in British battledress with blue berets but still proudly wearing the winged lion of St Mark, teamed up with the Allied forces at the Rapido River on the Cassino front.

The regimental flag of the San Marcos – the one presented to them by the people and City of Venice – had to be left behind in German-occupied territory, but it was safely hidden. The Bafile battalion, however, borrowed the flag of the submarine *Enrico Totti* and marched under it when it went to join the British Eighth Army on the Adriatic front.

The San Marco was gradually rebuilt as the reconstituted Grado and Caorle battalions were added. They were attached to an all-Italian parachute unit, the Folgore Combat Group. Another unit, consisting of paratroopers and frogmen, was given the honor of being the first to land in the newly-liberated city of Venice. The San Marcos had returned home.

When Mussolini formed his puppet government in the north of Italy, San Marco-type units were raised there and wore the San Marco insignia, although on gray-green paratroop uniforms. Despite the intent, most experts who analyzed the units after the war – including United States Marine Corps authorities – came to the conclusion that they were Army rather than Marine or Naval Infantry Units, despite the insignia worn. The special badges they wore, however, are illustrated and explained later in this book.

When the war ended, the government could foresee no usefulness in a naval infantry force, so the proud San Marcos, carrying battle honors from both Axis and Allied sides, were demobilized.

Venice, however, was not to be long without a force wearing its symbol as an insignia. In 1951 the Italian army raised an amphibious unit to be stationed near the lagoons of the Northern Adriatic and to operate in the river estuaries and coastal waters around Venice. The unit was designated the 'Lagunari' and wear lapel, cuff and breast badges that utilize the winged lion of St Mark. They wear black berets with gold or bullion badges of a gold crown over a foul anchor over crossed rifles. Rank and specialist badges are worn as in the rest of the Army. They wear the red scarf of the Serenissima regiment to which it is attached.

In the early 1960s Italian military and naval authorities began to realize they needed a specialized naval landing force to keep up with the realities of modern strategy. So on 1 January 1965, the San Marco Battalion was raised Phoenix-like from the ashes as a truly élite group. Officers and non-commissioned officers are drawn from volunteers from both the Army and Navy (although it is a naval unit), while the lower ranks are specially selected from Navy draftees. They receive regular infantry training and special SEAL training. The old San Marco insignia are used with the addition of a beret badge that is similar to that of the Lagunari. The beret – like that of the Lagunari – is black. Special camouflaged field clothing has been added to their uniform list. Unlike its predecessors, the new San Marcos are not just land-based naval infantrymen, but are based afloat in transport vessels specially designed for amphibious operations. The new San Marco Battalion works in close cooperation with similar units of the NATO Southern Command and has participated in exercises with United States Marine units from the U.S. Sixth Fleet.

5

SPANISH MARINE CORPS

The men from the 2nd Battalion, 2nd Regiment, Spanish Royal Infantry Marine Corps had their work cut out for them. In front of them were 1800 rebels, and at the back of them was the railway line the rebels wanted to blow up. There on a line between Gibara and Holquin in Cuba in 1890, the Marines crouched with their rifles waiting for the attack to begin. Their defense plan was simple – shoot as many rebels as possible before they reached the rail line. Privates Rama and Cancela could not work up a more sophisticated plan because they were outnumbered 900 to one, and with those odds it is best to stick to basics.

Today, as Fidel Castro's green fatigue-clad troops pass that way, there is nothing left to mark where Rama and Cancela fell, after thinning the rebel ranks somewhat. There had been once, however. The Spanish built a fort there named after the two Marines, and on the fort gate was a plaque with the inscription: 'Christian Traveller, stop and remove your hat! The ground you tread on is sacred; in the name of the Royal Infantry Marine Corps.'

The Spanish Marine Corps was already old when that plaque was nailed to the fort gate. It dates its founding to 1537 under the reign of King Carlos I. In its early years, members of the unit wore the familiar Spanish sixteenth century armor with high-domed, crested helmet and front and back plates, along with pantaloons of a basic red color with yellow or white stripes. A long-sleeved jacket in a medium-brown color was worn beneath the armor. Long red stockings and black shoes completed the uniform. One painting of the period shows a white cloth collar folded down at the neck of the body armor. At each corner of the collar is a medium-blue foul anchor.

Officially, the Corps divides its history among five 'epochs' or periods, during which the Corps had a variety of names and fought in battles around the world.

The first period runs from 1537 to 1717, when it was known primarily as the Infantry of the Armada, and participated in such battles and expeditions as Lepanto, Tunis, the Azores, England, San Salvador, and Brazil. At late as 1625 Spanish Marines were still wearing body armor. They also wore broad-brimmed, plumed hats, shirts with balloon sleeves and ruffled collars, red pantaloons, long white stockings and brown shoes with red bows.

The second epoch runs from 1717 to 1827, when the primary name was Corps of Battalions of the Navy, with the battalions named, Armada, Bajeles, Marina, Oceano, Mediterraneo, and Barlovento, and were nicknamed 'Jewels of the Boats'. They fought in Napoli, Sicily, Pensacola, Florida (U.S.A.), Havana, Toulon, Ferrol and Buenos Aires. During this period the Corps adopted red and blue as its official colors. Marine grenadiers, at this time, wore tall fur shakos, high-collared double-breasted jackets with fringed epaulets and white cross belts. Because of bravery at the battle of Havana, corporals of the Corps were given the privilege of wearing gold stripes, and sergeants, gold braid on their hats.

The third epoch, 1827 to 1931, included the period of the twilight of the far-flung Spanish empire. It took in battles and expeditions in Indochina, Mexico and Santa Domingo, and in the Philippine Islands and Cuba during the Spanish-American War when Spanish Marines encountered their American counterparts in both places. Known at this time as the Royal

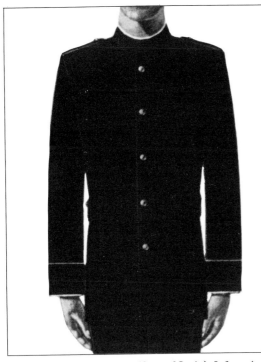

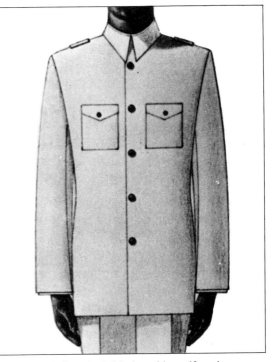

Left: The dark blue dress uniform of Spain's Infanteria de Marina has a double red stripe down outside of each trouser leg. Special shoulder boards with the Corps badge of a crown over an anchor and crossed rifles are worn with this uniform. The illustration is from a Spanish Marine Manual.

Right: The Infanteria de Marina white uniform is cut along the same lines as dress blues. Shoulder boards are also worn with this uniform.

Corps of Marine Infantry, the unit went on to more battles and expeditions in Africa.

Spain sat out World War I as a neutral, but its military leaders thought they had learned something from it. Largely because of the British debacle at Gallipoli, the Spaniards concluded that amphibious warfare had little potential. As a result, the proud Spanish Marine Corps was disbanded in 1931.

With the outbreak of the Spanish Civil War in 1936, the Marine Corps was revived, largely to provide guards for naval bases and ammunition dumps. The Corps was reformed and soon adopted the insignia in use today, crossed rifles over an upright anchor which is topped by a coronet. This is considered the fourth epoch of the Corps' history.

The other ranks dress uniform at that time was similar to the one worn today – a dark blue single-breasted coat with stand-and-fall collar, flap breast pockets and brass buttons. On each cuff are the 'sardinetas', which are small gold insignia that resemble vice jaws and were awarded to the Corps in 1817 as a distinction of troops of the Royal Household. The trousers have double red stripes down each outside leg. A black leather belt with brass buckle is worn with this uniform. The white peaked cap has a black band below the crown. The Corps insignia is worn on a black patch on the crown. Officers wear naval uniforms.

The fifth epoch which takes in the present day Cuerpo de Infanteria de Marina started in 1957 with the building of the Corps into a modern amphibious force. Today's Spanish Marine wears a dress white as well as a dress blue uniform. In the field he wears olive green fatigues with a camouflage cover over his American-style steel helmet. Some distinctive insignia are worn as shoulder patches. Dark blue berets with the Corps insignia in brass on the left side are also worn. Black high-laced boots are the standard footwear in the field.

The Corps maintains units in Madrid, the Canary Islands, El Ferrol, Cartagena, and Cadiz.

6

FRENCH MARINES

The old enemies eyed each other across the deck of the H.M.S. *Bellerophon* as the guard of British Royal Marines snapped to inspection arms. 'Much might be done by a hundred thousand soldiers such as this,' commented Napoleon Bonaparte, as he inspected the guard. It was a courtesy extended to a vanquished foe by the victorious British. It was July 1815, and the former French emperor was on his way back into exile, this time to St Helena, and the red coated British Marines would be the only ones he would see. There would be no French Marines of the Guard accompanying him, as there had been before when he was exiled to Elba. There had been thirty of them then, and they had returned with him during 'the hundred days', and many of them fell at Waterloo.

There would still be French Marines, of course, or more accurately, French Naval Infantry. There had been French Marines before Napoleon, and long after his death, they would fight in places with names like Dixmüde, Dieppe and Indo-China. The idea of a Marine-type of service occurred to another Frenchman, Cardinal Armand Jean du Plessis Richelieu, as early as 1622, some forty-two years before the British raised a similar type of unit. 'Similar' may be stretching a point, since the British and French always took a different approach to this matter. Richelieu envisioned the unit as sailors who would be trained to go ashore as infantrymen, when necessary. The British approached the matter with the theory of training soldiers to serve aboard ship. This difference has essentially prevailed down through the centuries. Richelieu called his unit Company of the Sea – 'Compagnie de la Mer'.

The name of the unit was changed to le Regiment de Marine in the late seventeenth century, as the British and Dutch influence on sea-soldiers began to be felt. Although the unit's members dressed essentially as sailors during the formative years, by the mid-eighteenth century, some ship's companies were wearing white coats and breeches and black tricorn hats.

With the arrival of Napoleon, all French uniforms became grander and the Marines were no exception. The Marines of the Guard (Garde du Marin) were seamen who had been assigned to the Consular Guard and were formed into a battalion of the Imperial Guard. They served as both crew and escort for Napoleon's barge and served in campaigns throughout Europe. They wore tall, short-visored shakos with tall plumes at the front. The shako plate was an Imperial eagle with crossed anchors behind it. The dress uniform coats had high collars, open at the front, braided shoulder knots and rows of braid across the front. After Napoleon's downfall, the uniforms of the Naval Infantry drifted back to more of a naval style. By the turn of the century, the distinctive French sailor cap with the red pom-pom had come into use and was worn by the naval infantrymen who, by now, had become known as the Fusiliers Marins (Marine Riflemen).

With the outbreak of World War I in 1914, the French raised a Naval Brigade, and the Fusiliers Marins marched off to battle in naval uniforms. In addition to the distinctive cap – which bore the words, 'Fusiliers Marins' in gold on the cap tally, seamen wore the standard dark blue jumper with blue jean flap collar and dark blue trousers tucked into black leather boots. Rank insignia was red on blue. In addition to the pom-pom (which brought the Marins the good-humored nickname of 'the girls with the red pom-pom'), the cap also had a small gold wire foul anchor worn at the center of the front crown. Standard black leather infantry equipment was also worn. Officers wore blue naval uniforms with a peaked cap that also had a gold wire foul anchor badge at the front. Gold rank stripes were worn on a band below the crown. The single-breasted coat had a stand-and-fall collar and five brass buttons down the front. Rank stripes were worn on the cuffs and on small epaulets at the shoulder seam. The dark blue breeches were tucked into black leather boots that rose almost to the knee.

As the war ground on, the naval infantrymen were issued army-style, double-breasted, horizon-blue overcoats. This color had proven too visible in the field, and by the end of the war in 1918 dark khaki uniforms were being issued. When the Marins got these uniforms, their black boots went, since wrap-around leggings were part of the new issue. The 'Adrian' steel helmet had become a standard item with the French troops and was issued to the Marins with a foul anchor plate on the front.

Between the wars, the uniforms of the Fusiliers Marins – which were still standard French Navy issue – changed little. Their speciality badge was the flaming grenade which came plain or circled and in red, silver and gold, depending upon rank and assignment. For wear on land, the Marins were issued a dark blue overcoat, a dark blue Adrian-pattern steel helmet with foul anchor plate at the front and canvas leggings.

After the fall of France in 1940 Free French Fusiliers Marins, who formed new units in Britain, were issued standard British battledress but clung to their 'matelot' caps with red pompoms. The 10th (Inter-Allied) Commando was formed, and the French Fusiliers Marins were part of it. The Frenchmen wore standard navy rank insignia with the British battledress. The

Members of the 6th French Marine Infantry Parachute Regiment march past reviewing officials during a Bastille Day parade. French Army units designated 'marine' are former Troupes Coloniales that once provided garrisons throughout the French Empire. Although considered amphibious forces, the Army's Marines do not have the same functions as the French naval infantry, the Groupement de Fusiliers Marins.

officers wore their stripes on slides that fit over the shoulder straps. A shoulder flash with the word 'France' in yellow capital letters on a curved black background was worn above the commando flash by this unit. While the Frenchmen usually wore steel helmets when participating in raids, there were other times when the traditional sailor cap seemed inappropriate. The commandos had adopted a green beret in 1943, and the Fusilier Marins commandos did likewise. A year later a new cap badge, a bronze shield incorporating the Cross of Lorraine symbol of the Free French, the commando fighting knife and a full-masted sailing ship was worn on the beret. The badge (illustrated and described in full in the plates section) is still used today with very slight modification.

The Fusiliers Marins Commandos, still in British battledress, went into the Battle of Normandy under the command of the British 6th Airborne Division. The French Marine Commandos, however, had brothers in arms who were not British uniformed and equipped.

A number of Fusilier Marins units had been formed in Africa and the Middle East and were being equipped by the Americans. Once again, however, the French sailor cap was the typical headgear, despite the U.S. Army-style field clothing worn otherwise. In a display of versatility, the Marins were formed into an Armored Reconnaissance Regiment and fought first in Italy and later helped liberate their homeland. It was not uncommon to see a head with the red pom-pomed cap peering out the top of the tank turret. These Frenchmen wore a shoulder flash with 'Fusiliers Marins' in red letters on a curved black background. The M-1941 steel helmet with a yellow anchor on the front largely replaced the Adrian style for these troops.

There were a few Fusiliers Marins in French Indo-China during World War II, but the colonial officials were pro-Vichy and let the Japanese

A civilian official chats with several members of the 1st French Marine Infantry Parachute Regiment. The man in the foreground wears the unit's shoulder patch. The para- chutists' qualification badge is worn on the right breast of the fatigue uniforms.

troops take up positions there. Towards the end of the war the French sentiment in what was to become Vietnam obviously shifted to the de Gaulle Free French movement, which caused the Japanese to round up French troops and civil servants and put them into internment camps. The Marins there, dressed in tropical-zone naval uniforms, which included white sun helmet and white shorts, never got to fire a shot. They would get to do that at a not-too-distant future date.

After the war ended in 1945, the French found themselves trying to keep the lid on colonies in Africa and Asia. The Fusiliers Marins were called upon again to fight for the honor of France, particularly in Indo-China. Their units there wore whites, light khaki and the camouflage that became known as 'tiger stripe'.

The Fusilier Marins of today operate as a battalion with five commando units. It is known as the 'Groupment de Fusiliers Marins Commando'. The green beret with the bronze badge adopted during World War II is worn.

Since the French colonial empire in Africa dissolved, there has been some confusion about some French Army units using the term 'Marine' in their titles. The confusion is compounded because many of these units use an anchor in their distinctive insignia and other badges. As the French word 'Marine' has several shades of meaning – the principle one being 'Navy' – it leans closer, in this case, to meaning troops trained for overseas operations.

They are all the former 'Troupes Coloniales' which guarded and fought in the outposts of the French empire for centuries. The colonial troops traditionally wore an anchor as an insignia – some sources insist this badge was adopted because the first colonial troops were Marines – and continue to do so under their redesignation as 'Troupes de Marine'. They are not like a Marine Corps in the sense of the USMC or the Royal Marines. They are part of the French Army and wear its uniforms and insignia. The largest of these units is the Ninth Marine Division. Former colonial paratroop units are now known as Marine parachute regiments. They are all very much modern army units and are not designed to duplicate the mission of France's true 'sea soldiers', the Fusilier Marins. Cardinal Richelieu's concept still prevails.

7

DANISH MARINES

Just outside the headquarters of I Battalion, Bornholm Force, on the Danish island of Bornholm in the Baltic Sea rests a venerable anchor that once rode the ocean waves on a ship of the Royal Danish Navy. At first glance, it would seem a strange adornment for an Army unit's headquarters, but this is no ordinary Army unit. For more than 290 years, under a variety of names, it has been part of the Royal Danish Army. But between 1670 and 1692, it was part of the Royal Danish Navy, a fact that is never forgotten by its members who, since 1963, have served in it under its original title – 'The Marineregiment'.

While black neckties are worn with service dress by other Danish Army units, the men of the Marineregiment (which is still battalion size despite the name) wear ties or scarves of navy

Men of Denmark's Marine Regiment parade on Bornholm Island, home base for the unit. The man in the right foreground is a sergeant major, as shown by both his chevrons and the bosun's pipe hanging from left shoulder. The regimental badge, a sailing ship, is worn on berets and lapels with a red cloth backing. Members of the regiment (actually a battalion, despite its name) also wear blue scarves to mark the nautical origination of the regiment, which was originally under naval control. The unit has been a part of the Army since the eighteenth century. Circular badges above the right coat pockets are for proficiency in various specialties.

blue to commemorate that long-ago association with the Navy. The battalion badge also reflects that association; it is a three-masted seventeenth century frigate riding above splashing waves. The badge, in brass, is worn on a red felt patch, the color indicating it is the first battalion in the Force, which, in Danish, is written I. bataljon, Bornholms Vaern, Marineregimentet.

While other units in the Danish Army wear rifle green uniforms, the Marineregiment members wear black, with the single-breasted blouse having turned-back lapels on which are worn the frigate badges with the ships facing inward. The coat has brass buttons. Members of this unit also wear black berets with the battalion badge worn on the left side. Otherwise, all insignia are the same as worn in the rest of the Danish Army.

The unit, either as a regiment or a battalion, has taken part in every important battle fought by the Danish Army since 1700 and carries on its red and white colors battle streamers for Torsebro, Gadebusch, Fredericia, Frederikstad and Dybbol. Between wars, it was usually garrisoned at some exposed frontier such as Christiano, Holstein, Schleswig, Zeeland, and Bornholm, the latter being, in a manner of speaking, 'behind the Iron Curtain' since it is north of Poland.

The Marine traditions of the unit go back to its early days when it specialized in fighting aboard ship and making amphibious landings. Even after its transfer to the Army, it kept for many years its functions as a unit to be used afloat. To this day they strike bells, report in naval style, and pipe the gangway at parades and inspections.

In its history, the unit has also been known as Line Infantry Battalion and Regiment, the Bornholm Infantry Regiment and the 7th Battalion. It was under the latter name that it found itself ordered by the government to surrender to invading German forces in early April 1940.

When the Nazi war machine rolled across the Danish frontier, the Danes were wearing a mixture of uniforms. Some wore dark blue coats with light blue trousers, while others wore light gray, and some khaki. Some Danes managed to get to England, where they served in a special Royal Air Force unit and wore British uniforms. Others got to nearby neutral Sweden, where a Danish Brigade was formed in case the Swedes were drawn into the war. Some members of the old Marineregiment served in the Swedish exile unit, wearing Swedish uniforms. Others, who stayed behind, joined special resistance units

A bearded sergeant major of the Danish Marine Regiment holding the battalion colors near a rugged hillside on the Island of Bornholm, the unit's headquarters.

Opposite: Danish Marine Regiment captain wearing summer-weight khaki uniform worn only on foreign service. The regimental badges on the black beret and lapels clearly show their red cloth backing. 'Danmark' shoulder flash and patch with Danish cross are worn by Danish troops only when serving outside of Denmark. This officer was assigned to the Command and General Staff College at Fort Leavenworth, Kansas, U.S.A. The three pips on his epaulets show his rank.

specializing in sabotage in the southern part of Zeeland and the southern islands. Following the war the battalion first served as a border guard along the southern frontier, then spent a year as an occupation force in Aurich, Germany.

Despite the name and the traditions, today's Marineregiment members do not receive amphibious training, but serve in a motorized infantry battalion with a headquarters, a headquarters company and two motorized infantry companies.

Officers wear a series of gold stars to indicate rank. Field-grade officers wear five-pointed stars and staff-grade officers wear six-pointed stars. General officers wear slightly larger six-pointed stars. Non-commissioned officers wear a series of chevrons point up. Top grade NCOs now wear chevrons. During the World War II period, sergeants and sergeants major wore beveled silver bars, one and two respectively, on shoulder straps, to indicate rank.

If members of the battalion are called upon to serve outside their country on special duty, they wear a curved red shoulder title with the word 'Danmark' in white lettering at the top of each sleeve. A red shield with a white Danish cross is worn as a shoulder patch on the left sleeve only.

In warmer climates officers wear light khaki twill uniforms with white shirts. Green felt slides with insignia of rank are worn on the shoulder straps of the shirt.

The motto of the battalion is *Nec Temere – Nec Timide* which means 'Neither rash nor timid'.

8

SOVIET NAVAL INFANTRY

'Schwarz tod!' The German soldier's words hung like a curse on the frozen Russian air. They were his last. He was not speaking of any medieval plague but of the black-clad figures emerging from the Baltic mists in the winter of 1943. They had seen him a split second before he had seen them, and a Soviet Moisin Nagant 7.62 mm rifle barked. Dressed in black fur caps and long black capes, the raiders, from out of the fog, hurried forward, quickly passing the German soldier's body. He had called them 'Black death', a term generally applied to those troops by the Germans on that front. They called themselves *morskaya pekhota* – Naval Infantry – and the black clothing they were wearing and the nickname they got from it would be remembered in years to come when they would be called 'Marines' in official translations, which is obviously what the Soviets wanted them to be, despite the fact there is no Russian word for Marine.

Russian naval infantry units have existed on an on-again, off-again basis ever since the first such regiment was raised by Czar Peter the Great in 1705. History indicates that such units were largely sailors sent to fight land battles, even as recently as World War II, when an estimated half-million of them fought alongside units of the Red Army to drive back the Nazis.

The Russian naval infantryman of that time did not march into battle in a special uniform, but in most cases, wore his sailor uniform topped by the visorless flat Navy cap that has come to be known, almost universally, as the 'Donald Duck' cap. But Donald Duck never wore his headgear so proudly, despite the best efforts of Walt Disney, as the Soviet Naval Infantryman.

Many of the units were designated as 'guards' and were entitled to wear a special double-tailed cap ribbon with orange stripes that hung down the back of the neck. The ribbons bore the name of the fleet the units represented in gold Cyrillic letters and had small gold anchors at each end.

There were times the sailors wore army uniforms, but they usually maintained something to identify themselves as *krasnoflotyets* or members of the Soviet fleet. This most often was the blue and white striped 'T' shirt which showed through the blouse, unbuttoned at the neck, or a gold anchor worn on the upper left sleeve.

Part of the standard cold weather gear issued to Soviet sailors during the World War II period was the long, black woolen capes and black fur caps that brought them their title from the Germans. Western intelligence sources indicate that the *morskaya pekhota* dwindled in size following the war and became an element of the Coastal Defense Forces before being disbanded in the mid-1950s. The first evidence that the Soviets had re-established the Naval Infantry came during the mid-1960s. The new-style unit came closer to being a traditional 'Marine' formation and, for the first time, included some uniforms distinct from other branches of the service.

One of the more distinctive parts of the new uniforms – all, incidentally, field uniforms – is the black beret. Officers and warrant officers wear the standard naval bullion or metal cap device of a gold wreath surrounding a circled gold anchor topped by a gold-bordered red star with a center circle of white on which is superimposed a gold hammer and sickle. Enlisted men wear a cloth cap badge consisting of a gold-circled black oval containing a gold-bordered red star with a gold hammer and sickle at the center. For winter, the officers and warrant officers wear the same badge on the berets, while other ranks wear the red star device only on black fur caps. All ranks wear a red pennant with a gold anchor at the broad end on the right sides of the beret. An earlier version featured only the gold anchor.

Both summer and field uniforms for all ranks are black, but the summer uniform is open at the collar to show the traditional sailor's blue and white striped 'T' shirt. The enlisted men have blue jean flap collar with three white stripes as part of this uniform. All ranks also wear a cloth patch midway down the left sleeve of the blouse, consisting of a red-bordered black circle with a gold foul anchor at center. Guards units wear distinctive metal badges of a wreathed red star surmounted by a gold-bordered red flag on the right breast of the blouse. A stenciled red star is worn on the front of steel helmets, and a white stenciled foul anchor is worn on the left side.

Rank insignia is identical to that of the Navy, except that the shoulder boards are always black with gold adornments for enlisted ranks, and black checkered shoulder boards with red trim and gold stars for officers and warrant officers. The shoulder boards of enlisted men have the Cyrillic abbreviations at center for the fleet to which the wearer is assigned. These are the Baltic, Black Sea, Northern, and Pacific Ocean fleets. There is also a symbol for those not assigned to fleets.

It is estimated that the Soviet Naval Infantry consists of about 18,000 men in five marine brigades. They are designed to spearhead amphibious landings and pave the way for regular infantrymen to follow. Their field uniform has proved popular in some so-called 'client' states, with the small naval infantry force of Cuba adopting it right down to the red pennant on the left side of the beret.

9

FINLAND

Next to Iceland, Finland is the northernmost state in the world. Although a small nation by most standards, it maintains crack defense forces, and among them is its counterpart of a Marine unit, the Coast Jaeger Battalion.

During the Finnish wars of 1939–45, coastal defense in Finland was based on fortified coast artillery and the Navy. Coast artillery units included some infantry for the close defense of artillery positions. Finnish military leaders concluded from experiences in battles in the archipelago of the eastern Gulf of Finland at that time that a specially trained infantry unit was needed for the coastal environment. This path was pursued further after the war and, in 1952, such a unit, called the Coast Infantry Battalion, was formed as a sub-unit of the 1st Coast Artillery Regiment. It became independent in 1960 and was given its present name. It is an Army unit and its headquarters is at a coastal garrison about 40 kilometers (25 miles) west of Helsinki. The unit was reorganized in 1979.

The battalion includes the commander, who holds the rank of lieutenant colonel, staff and normal logistic formations. Commando-type training is given to selected conscripts and volunteers at the Coast Jaeger School, and is considered one of the hardest in the Finnish Army. It includes normal infantry training plus anti-tank, mortar, sapper and signal training. Special training includes guerrilla and reconnaissance activities in the rocky islands of the coastal area. Landing exercises take place in the form of small unit strikes against occupied islands using open sea assault boats. This training is conducted in close cooperation with nearby units of Navy and Coast Artillery.

This private in Finland's Coastal Jaeger Battalion wears the unit's distinctive gilded eagle badge on a green beret. Although a part of the Army, this battalion undergoes amphibious and commando training and is Finland's version of a Marine unit. Blank collar patches show this man's rank. Non-commissioned officers wear small chevrons pointing inward on these patches.

Since the Coast Jaeger Battalion is part of the Army, its members wear Army uniforms, but with special insignia. As a jaeger unit, its background color for insignia is green. On the collars, green insignia backgrounds are worn with yellow piping. The battalion's members are authorized to wear the green commando beret with the special gilded eagle insignia of the unit.

An NCO of the Finnish Coastal Jaeger Battalion charges during a training exercise. The small metal pin-on rank device on his collar indicates that he is a junior sergeant.

A soldier of the Coastal Jaeger Battalion climbs up a mountain side with rope during commando training. He wears standard Finnish Army camouflage fatigues.

10

PORTUGUESE MARINES

For three weeks the battle had raged in Hong Kong, and the sounds had drifted across the water, and the sights had been reflected in the night sky. Two Portuguese Marines – Corpo de Fuzileiros – members of a tiny detachment serving as naval police, strained their ears against the sound of the lapping surf and heard both the noise of battle and the sounds of Christmas.

It was 24 December 1941, Christmas Eve, and this was Portuguese Macao, a five-square-mile island in the Canton River on the coast of China. The traditions of Portugal had overlapped those of the Orient here and on Christmas Eve, despite the nearby war, everybody, including the two Marines, went to midnight Mass, since Portugal was so Christian and so Catholic that its monarchs of the past had worn no crown – it belonged to the Blessed Virgin.

The British Crown Colony fell to the Japanese invaders the next day, but the residents of Macao awoke to another day of freedom. The Marines, attired in naval uniforms, would never have to fire a shot at invaders. Because of the nature of global politics at that time, Macao was spared invasion and occupation, and Portugal would sit out World War II as a neutral.

That had not always been the case with Portugal, nor with its Naval Infantry. In 1585, special detachments were assigned to handle the artillery and small weapons aboard ship. They were also called upon to defend the coast against pirates, serve as the king's personal guard, and fight in the war of independence after the Spanish occupation. Their headquarters was in St George's Castle, overlooking Lisbon and the River Tagus.

The Marine of that day wore a tri-corn hat, long frock coat and leggings which reached to the knee. The color was blue with buff facings.

These Portuguese units participated in several naval battles integrated in Lord Nelson's armada, and fought in Naples, Trieste and Tripoli, under the name of Royal Navy Brigade. This unit went to Brazil with the Portuguese royal family in 1808 and founded what would become the Brazilian Marine Corps after Brazil's independence.

The Portuguese Corpo de Fuzilieros have been an integral part of the Navy and have followed the naval system of rank over the years, as well as dressing in Portuguese naval uniforms.

In 1916, Portugal entered World War I on the Allied side and sent the Portuguese Expeditionary Corps to serve in France, but this, apparently, did not include Marines. The Marines, however, did serve with the Portuguese fleet during this war and were issued steel helmets which were similar to the British 'dishpan' style, but had fluted crowns. It was not until 1961 that members of this Corps would see extensive action. Guerrilla warfare broke out in the Portuguese African colonies of Guinea, Angola and Mozambique at that time and would continue for fourteen years. During that period, 125 Marine units totalling more than 13,000 men were sent to Africa.

In the field there they usually wore camouflaged fatigues and black berets. A special Marine insignia of a dagger point up within a wreath was worn in both metal and cloth, and as both beret and breast badges. When not in the field, the Portuguese Marine enlisted men wear regular Navy uniforms with speciality marks identifying them as Corpo de Fuzileiros and the black beret instead of the 'Donald Duck' cap worn by other naval ranks. Non-coms wear naval rank insignia, which is a system of chevrons worn point up. Officers wear naval uniforms with British-style rank insignia of stripes with the uppermost stripe topped with a curl. Naval rank titles are used.

Coats-of-arms are used for various units within the Corps, including the Portuguese Marine Corps Command, the Marine School, and the Marine Base. The headquarters is in Lisbon.

11

SOUTH AMERICA

ARGENTINE MARINE CORPS

As the color party of the Argentine Infanteria de Marina marched smartly at the head of the column down a broad Buenos Aires avenue, it passed just a few blocks from the Plaza Retiro where a monument to a Navy officer stands. In a way, the man for whom the monument was erected had much to do with the fact that there was an Infanteria de Marina color party marching so close to the spot where he had died in combat 173 years before. His name was Candido Lasala, and he was a lieutenant in the hastily assembled Naval Battalion that formed a part of the force meeting invading British troops during early July of 1807. Lasala died while directing artillery fire as the Argentines successfully repelled the invaders. He has long been considered the first hero of what was to become the Argentine Naval Infantry (Infanteria de Marina), sometimes called Marines.

The Corps dates its founding to the year Candido Lasala died, and traces its roots to that Naval Battalion that Lasala helped to lead. The nation was not yet independent at that time, but the seed had been planted as the 'criollos', the Argentines descended from Spanish colonists, rallied with their fellow countrymen to drive out an invading force. When Lasala fell, he was wearing a typical naval officer's uniform of that day. It was blue with gold facings and buttons and had a high, standing cutaway collar and fringed gold epaulets with anchor badges in the broad circles at the shoulder seam.

When Argentina's War of Independence began in 1810, troops of these types were assigned to ships of the fleet commanded by Admiral Guillermo Brown. During this period, Marine artillerymen serving aboard ship wore blue shell jackets with high collars. On the collars, gold-colored anchor badges, probably made of brass, faced point forward on a slant. A high crowned black 'top hat' type of headgear, popular in European military fashions of that day, was worn by Argentine Marines. It had a silver-colored plate affixed to the left side. A buff-colored plume rose from the top of the plate. White crossbelts threaded through the shoulder straps were worn with the jacket. A brass belt plate was worn at the point where the belts crossed.

Officers of Argentine Marine units, at that time, continued to wear high collared, double-breasted blue frock coats with gold-fringed epaulets. Officers of the rank of colonel wore two sunburst devices on the blue cloth centers of the epaulets. By the late 1830s, a large shako had replaced the 'top hat' worn by members of the organization that had now become known as the Brigade of Infantry of the Sea.

Although both Marine infantry and artillery units were part of the Argentine Naval establishment down through the years, the anniversary of today's Corps is based on the establishment of the Artillery Battalion of the Navy on 19 November 1879 and a Marine Corps Battalion a year later.

After the turn of the century, képis of both the French and the higher crowned Italian types were used by Argentine Marines. The crossed cannon barrel badge and the bursting grenade badge, both used extensively by artillery units throughout the world, were utilized by Argentine Marines during the early years of the twentieth century.

The tradition of artillery was so strongly linked to the Argentine Marines, that when a badge for the Infanteria de Marina was adopted later in the century, the familiar crossed cannons were the background for the vertical anchor, with the Argentine coat of arms at the center.

Following World War I, uniforms of khaki and olive drab were used extensively by the Argentine Marines. By the 1930s a dress blue uniform had been developed that was similar to those worn by the U.S. and British Marines.

Troop of Argentine Marines gives 'eyes right' as it parades down a city street. The officer in front wears a frock coat with fringed shoulder boards. His rank of second lieutenant is indicated by the single stripe with a curl on his cuffs. Enlisted men wear dress blue uniforms similar to those of the British Royal Marines.

A member of Argentina's Infanteria de Marina in combat dress waves a battalion flag from a seacoast hillside. He is flanked by two Argentine Marines wearing special ceremonial uniforms of a type used during the nineteenth century, with 'top hats', a headgear used by several Marine Corps of that period.

This Marine is a member of Argentina's Infanteria de Marina, but could be almost any Marine in any western nation since combat clothing is all remarkably similar. Note the goggles on his American-pattern helmet. Argentina has one of the largest Marine Corps in Latin America.

Both coat and trousers were of navy blue with gold trim. Enlisted men wore double-breasted coats with standing collars, and officers, single-breasted coats. The white peaked cap worn with the blues had a much wider crown than most uniform caps worn by other nations during that period. Officers wore naval rank insignia and used Navy titles. Non-commissioned officers used rank chevrons of the Army pattern in colors to go with the Marine uniforms.

In 1947, the Argentine Marine Corps was reorganized along the lines of a modern amphibious organization, drawing on the United States Marine Corps for advice and other assistance. The main stations of the Corps today are in Buenos Aires, Southern Patagonia, the Baterias Marine Base, located near the Puerto Belgrano Naval Base, and the Rio Santiago Naval Base.

In addition to dress blues, Argentine Marines also wear dress whites, and the two uniforms are sometimes mixed with white coats and blue trousers and vice-versa. Greens and khaki are also worn, as well as the usual fatigue and other field clothing. Black berets are worn by members of the Corps' amphibious commando unit. A U.S.-style steel helmet is also worn.

A special ceremonial dress blue uniform is worn by selected members of the Corps on certain occasions. The coat has red collar and cuffs and three rows of brass buttons. The blue trousers have bell bottoms. The headgear is the 'top hat' with red and white plume.

During the 1982 Falklands conflict, the Corps' 5th Battalion formed part of the garrison of Port Stanley, the capital on East Falkland. Whereas the Army had a large proportion of one-year conscripts, who made unreliable soldiers, and an obvious gap between them and the privileged regular officers and NCOs, the Naval Infantry Corps had a high percentage of regulars in the ranks. They invariably fought well and regarded themselves as a *corps d'élite*.

BRAZILIAN MARINES

The drums rattled, the bagpipes skirled, and the men in glengarry caps stepped off on the parade ground in perfect time to the music that had been born in the Highlands of Scotland. This, however, was no regiment of Highlanders, but a unit just as proud and just as elite, if younger – the Corpo de Fuzileiros Navais, the Brazilian Marine Corps.

This Corps, 10,000 strong, is one of the largest Marine organizations in Latin America. It traces its origins to the formation of the Royal Naval Brigade in Portugal in 1797, and its founding dates to 7 March 1808, when that brigade landed in Brazil. The brigade might never have gone there if it had not been for Napoleon Bonaparte. In his campaign of conquest, the French leader's troops marched into Portugal, forcing the Portuguese royal family to flee to the South American anchor of its dual kingdom, Brazil. The royal family did not return to Portugal until 1821, but when it departed, it left behind a battalion of the Royal Naval Brigade and a memory of the fight against Napoleon that has survived in one small way until this day. At the front of the left side of the Marine glengarry cap is a folded black ribbon worn under the Corps badge. It is said to commemorate the death of Lord Nelson at Trafalgar where he defeated Napoleon's fleet.

Brazilian Marine fashion has closely paralleled that of most European nations down through the years from tri-corn hats to shakos. The Corps has had a variety of names since its founding, with the uniforms always showing strong links to the Navy, of which it has always been an integral part. In 1822, the unit was known as the Battalion of Naval Artillery. By 1826, this had been changed to the Imperial Brigade of Naval Artillery, and just one year later, it was renamed Corps of Naval Artillery. Twenty years later it adopted the name used today, Corpo de Fuzileiros Navais, (Corps of Naval Riflemen). This, however, lasted only until 1852, when it was redesignated the Naval Battalion. The name changes continued over the years and included Corps of Naval Infantry and Naval Regiment.

The Corps was active through all of these years, being engaged in wars with Uruguay and Argentina and the War of the Triple Alliance, in which the Naval Battalion served aboard ship and in amphibious assaults against the Paraguayan forces.

Finally, in 1932, the Corps returned to its present name, the Corps of Naval Riflemen. At this time, the dress uniform consisted of a spiked, white cork helmet, similar to the British Wolseley helmet worn by the Royal Marines. It had a brass Corps insignia plate and a decorative brass scaled strap at the front. The uniform coat was red with blue facings. The stand-and-fall collar was blue with large red patches at the front, on which were centered brass foul anchors. The cuffs were blue. Officers wore naval rank stripes on the cuff with a foul anchor above the stripes in gilt braid.

During World War II, Brazil entered the conflict on the side of the Allies. Veteran Brazilian Marines thought they might get a chance to serve for the first time outside their own continent, but that role went instead to an Army division, which was sent to Italy. It was the Marines' destiny at that time to serve in garrisons guarding the principal bases located along the coast of the nation at strategic points.

On 24 April 1965 a revolt in the Dominican Republic caused the government there to request assistance from American Armed Forces. The request was granted and soon led to the formation of an international peace-keeping force from the Organization of American States. Troops were sent from Honduras, Nicaragua, Costa Rica, Paraguay, and Brazil. General Hugo Panasco Alvim of the Brazilian Army was appointed Commanding General of the OAS forces. This time the Corpo de Fuzileiros Navis got to go along. It was the first opportunity the Brazilian Marines had had to serve side-by-side with their American counterparts, the United States Marines, and friendships were forged during this period between the two Corps which have endured to this day.

The 3rd Battalion, 6th Marine Regiment, from the aircraft carrier U.S.S. *Boxer* was one of the first American units ashore. They landed at Red Beach and quickly moved toward Santo Domingo. Brazilian Marines also moved into Santo Domingo. Dressed for combat, they wore U.S.-style M-1941 steel helmets with camouflaged cloth covers. The light green fatigue uniform was U.S.-style, but of the Army rather than Marine pattern. At the point of each side of the collar, a patch with the Brazilian Marine emblem embroidered in dark thread was worn. In addition to fatigues, a uniform the Brazilian Marines wore frequently in the Dominican Republic was the light tan khaki service dress. When not wearing the steel helmet, the Brazilians wore a long-billed field cap which was slightly tapered from front to

A lieutenant of the Brazilian Marines wearing the full dress uniform. The coat is red with trim in dark blue and gold. The two stripes on each cuff indicate that he is a lieutenant commander. The Corps device in gold thread is worn above stripes.

A United States Marine Corps officer in dress whites pins a medal on to the tunic of a commander of the Brazilian Marines in 1966 for valor during the Dominican Republic intervention a year earlier in which men of both Corps served side-by-side. Officers of the Brazilian Marines, known as the Corpo de Fuzileiros Navais, wear naval rank devices with Corps insignia above stripes. The man holding the cushion at the left is a Brazilian Marine corporal, as indicated by the two inverted chevrons on his sleeves. He is wearing a white version of the uniform, which includes a Glengarry cap. This uniform also comes in a light khaki twill style.

back. The Brazilian Corps insignia of crossed rifles behind a foul anchor was pinned on the front of this cap. The badge was worn in its dark bronze version.

Brazilian non-commissioned officer chevrons, worn point down, were worn on the sleeves of both fatigues and khakis in the dark brown on khaki version. Officers wore miniature rank devices on collars and caps. Brown, laced 'paratrooper' style boots were worn with both the fatigues and khakis. The webbing equipment was similar to the U.S. pattern.

The Brazilian Marines of today wear a variety of uniforms for both service and full dress. Officers use both naval titles and rank insignia, although the Corps badge replaces the 'curl' at the top of the rank stripes. NCOs wear chevrons and usually use Army titles. The chevrons feature the Corps device at the top.

The Brazilians have never been bashful about adopting what they determine is a good-looking military or naval fashion for their uniforms. The dress uniform of their Army's Independence Dragoons is said to be derived from a nineteenth century Austrian dragoon uniform. The Policia Montada Paulista – the Sao Paulo Mounted Police – wear a uniform that in cut is very similar to the Royal Canadian Mounted Police. So it is not unusual that the Marines wear a Scottish-style glengarry cap and march to pipes and drums, although the Corps has no link with Scotland. They simply like the way the caps look and the pipes sound. The airbag of the pipes is covered in no recognizable tartan, but appears to be grass green with an overlay of broad scarlet stripes. The pipers wear the dress red coats with navy blue shoulder straps and cuffs. White glengarry, white trousers and white belt fill out the uniform. The drum major wears a type of high fur cap with a scarlet plume on the left side. The cap is encircled at the bottom by a tapered silver band with a centered insignia that appears on the Corps colors, a flaming grenade backed by crossed halberds. A red and white braided cord is worn around the cap above the silver band.

The dress and service uniforms of the Brazilian Marines are of the same cut throughout for whites, khakis and red with blue or white. The coats have stand-and-fall collars with the anchor and rifles badge at each collar point, brass for white and red coats and dark bronze for khaki. The dark badge is also worn on the khaki cap, while the brass insignia is used on the white

A Brazilian Marine marching band prepares to move out as the Corps colors are dipped during a march past. Band members are wearing Glengarry caps, while officers of the color party wear peaked caps and the military policemen in the foreground wear helmet liners. All are wearing red coats and dark blue trousers. The mascot held by the Marine second from the right is a wolfhound.

Pipers of Brazil's Corpo de Fuzileiros Navais perform at an indoor concert. They are wearing red coats with white caps and trousers. Note the distinctive shako of the drum major in the left background.

A Brazilian Marine military policeman on a motorcycle wearing a gold paratrooper qualification badge on the left breast of a brown leather jacket. One of the Corps' emblems, a bursting bomb with crossed battleaxes behind it, is at the center of the windshield and on the flag at the right. The figure '1808' on the flag is the year of the Corps' foundation.

A lance corporal of the Fuzileiros Navais wearing light khaki service dress. The Corps badge in bronze is worn on each tip of the stand-and-fall collar. All the buttons are dark bronze, but the buckle on the white belt is of yellow metal.

A Brazilian Marine officer wearing pilot's wings over his left pocket and parachute wings over his right pocket. The shoulder boards show that he is a major. The Corps emblem is worn above the stripes on his shoulder boards. Officers' whites have turn down lapels, but those for other ranks have stand-and-fall collars.

glengarry which is worn with both the white and red with blue uniforms. The liner from the M-1941-style helmet is painted white with a red band and frequently worn with several of the uniforms. It is also painted olive drab and worn with khakis by members of the Corps' military police.

The Corps M.P.s also wear a special insignia on their black brassards. It is a white circular cloth patch with a red border. In the center is a black eagle with spread wings on a yellow shield with a red bar above. Above the bar is a stylized coronet.

Officers wear naval uniforms with pressed-back lapel collars, with the exception of the red with blue dress uniform. The blue uniform has the rank stripes on the cuffs, while the white and khaki uniforms carry the rank stripes on naval shoulder boards. The red coat has small French-type shoulder crescents in blue, which curve from front to back at the shoulder seam. A white peaked cap is worn with all of these uniforms, except khaki, which includes a matching cover for the cap. The officers wear the naval cap device of a gold wreath with a silver foul anchor at the center and a gold stylized sunburst above. All of the uniforms have four flap pockets. The belt worn with the red coat is of silver-colored cloth and has a gold circular buckle. A narrow red stripe is worn on the seam of the blue trousers. Officers apparently wear the glengarry cap only when wearing summer service khakis with short-sleeved shirts. On this uniform they wear miniature rank devices on the collars.

Although units of Brazilian Marines have not been called upon for overseas service since the Dominican Republic conflict, Corps officers have served as United Nations observers in Kashmir, a territory which has long been disputed between India and Pakistan.

The modern Corps is commanded from Marine Headquarters in Rio de Janeiro and consists of the operating forces divided into the Fleet Marine Force and the Security Force. The former includes the nucleus of the 1st Marine Division, the Force Troops, and the Service Command. The latter is comprised of the detachments afloat and the district units. A support organization is in charge of the phases of recruiting and training.

Security forces are stationed at Rio, Santos, Brasilia, Uruguaiana, Ladario, Salvador, Recife, Natal, and Belem.

COLOMBIAN MARINE CORPS

In the early spring of 1951, the smallest contingent of Marines to serve with the United Nations Forces in Korea landed at Pusan as part of an Army battalion of their countrymen – the first to see service beyond their own continent. They were just a handful – officers and non-commissioned officers – of the Colombian Marine Corps, and they were dressed in khakis that would soon be exchanged for American field clothing.

Most of the U.N. troops in Korea, outside of the British Commonwealth forces, were so out-fitted as a practical matter. Eleven nations, besides the Americans and the British Commonwealth countries, sent expeditionary forces ranging from company to brigade size. Keeping each of these nation's units supplied with its own uniforms and equipment would have been a logistical nightmare, so the easiest course was taken. And so it was that the Colombians who relieved elements of the U.S. Army's 32nd Infantry Regiment around Artillery Hill in the Punchbowl area in October could barely be distinguished from the Americans they were replacing. There was a shoulder title, of course, but otherwise the M-1941 helmet and the olive green field clothing were unmistakably American.

The Colombians were the only Latin American nation to send forces to the Korean War. In addition to the battalion of infantry, they sent a Colombian Navy frigate. The exact number of Marines included in the battalion is unclear, but all were sergeants or above, and it has been said that they served with distinction. That is the type of service that had become expected of this small unit.

The exact date of this Corps' founding is uncertain, but it seems that some type of Colombian Marine unit existed in 1811 and lasted until 1845, when, as an economic matter, it was disbanded. It was re-established in 1907. Officers wore Navy-type uniforms. The Corps was reorganized in 1936 and consisted of two rifle companies. In 1940 it was expanded to battalion size.

Although Colombian Army uniforms for years resembled Prussian-style military attire, due largely to the influence of German instructors around the turn of the century, the trend apparently was not strongly reflected in Marine uniforms. As part of the Navy, the Marines, particularly the officers, leaned to Navy-type uniforms. Following World War II, the uniforms took on a more U.S.-type look as the American steel helmet and liner became standard issue. The khaki twill uniform has become a standard for Colombian Marines. The shirt has shoulder straps and is usually worn without necktie. Leggings are worn with this uniform. Marine military police wear white helmet liners, belts and leggings with khakis.

The strength of the Corps is around 2000. Its main base is in the city of Cartegena.

ECUADORIAN MARINES

One of the newest of the world's Marine/Naval Infantry organizations, the Cuerpo de Infanteria de Marina of Ecuador, dates its official founding as 12 November 1966, although the unit had existed unofficially as part of the Ecuadorian Navy since 25 July 1962.

Based at Guayaquil, the Ecuadorian Marines are charged with the protection of naval bases, cooperation in the security and control of the country, and spearheading any amphibious operations. They receive commando-type training, and their ranks include Marines who have been trained as parachutists and frogmen.

The dress uniform includes a dark blue coat piped in red with a standing collar and white trousers. A white uniform with short-sleeved shirt is also worn with the trousers, which are bloused over black, laced, paratrooper-style boots. The field uniform is camouflaged fatigues of the type almost all Marines wear, although the patterns vary from nation to nation.

The main headgear is a dark blue beret piped in red, with a red arch-shaped patch to which the Corps insignia is affixed. The cap badge has a foul anchor with a saber and rifle crossed behind it and a spread-winged condor standing on a wreathed motto in the center. The motto, *Vencer o Morir* means 'win or die'.

Insignia of rank worn by officers follows the naval pattern. Cloth insignia for other ranks, including NCO chevrons and shoulder titles, is usually dark orange on black.

Camouflage uniforms are worn by these Ecuadorian Marines engaged in a field operation. Naval rank devices are worn by members of this Corps, but no insignia is apparent on these field uniforms.

Below: A member of Ecuador's *Cuerpo de Infanteria de Marina* stands outside the Corps headquarters in the City of Guayaquil. He is wearing dress uniform consisting of dark blue, red-trimmed beret, dark blue coat with red trim and white belt and trousers. He is holding the Corps guidon. This Corps is one of the youngest in Latin America, dating its founding to 1962.

Below: A troop of Ecuadorian Marines parades down a boulevard in Guayaquil in tropical white uniform. Their blue berets have a red, arch-shaped patch on which the Corps shield is affixed. The shoulder titles on left sleeves are barely visible, but indicate that these men are commandos.

Above: The colors of Ecuador's *Cuerpo de Infanteria de Marina* are carried by officers who wear rank on shoulder boards. Army and Navy bands line the street, playing for the parade. The members of the Army band in the left background wear Prussian-style spiked helmets.

VENEZUELAN MARINE CORPS

Although the Venezuelan Marine Corps dates its founding from 22 July 1822, the Corps became inactive during the nineteenth century. It was revived on 1 July 1938, when a company of Marines to garrison naval vessels was created by presidential decree. A second company was authorized on 9 September 1943. The Corps was expanded to battalion size on 11 December 1945 during a reorganization, and this date is now celebrated as the anniversary of the Venezuelan Marines.

The Corps now has four battalions, each named after a local hero: Simon Bolivar, General Rafael Urdaneta, Mariscal Antonio Jose de Sucre, and General Francisco de Miranda.

The Corps follows naval rank structure, and its officers wear naval uniforms with some modifications for Marine duties. A green beret is worn by both officers and enlisted personnel. The Venezuelan Marine Corps includes women members whose dress uniforms resemble those worn by women in the U.S. Navy. Enlisted men wear chevrons that include the Corps device of a horizontal rifle crossed over the center of a vertical foul anchor for some ranks.

The Corps carries out a variety of duties and includes commando, paratroop and frogman units. The Corps headquarters is at Caracas. Other bases for the unit include Puerto Cabella and Maiquetia.

A warrant officer second class wearing the dress white uniform of the Venezuelan Marine Corps. The gold lace on the shoulder boards is broken in the middle by a medium blue vertical stripe used by all warrant officers. The Corps emblem is above the stripes. The medal below the Marine distinctive badge is unidentified.

A Venezuelan Marine enlisted man wearing summer service dress whites with a green beret. The chevrons barely discernible on his left sleeve indicate that he is a senior NCO. The wings on the right side of his shirt show that he has qualified as a paratrooper.

Right: Camouflaged fatigues are worn in the field by members of Venezuela's Infanteria de Marina. The beret can be replaced by a wide-brimmed field hat or by a U.S.-type steel helmet.

Below left: A captain of Venezuela's Infanteria de Marina wearing tropical khakis with a green beret. Officers of this Corps wear naval rank insignia but use Army titles.

Below right: This woman Marine lieutenant is distinguished from her counterparts in the Venezuelan Navy by the alligator breast badge on the right side of her jacket that shows that she is a member of the Infanteria de Marina. This badge is worn by officers and warrant officers. It is also used by enlisted personnel as a beret badge. The actual Corps emblem, however, is a rifle crossed behind a foul anchor.

12

KOREAN MARINE CORPS

The villagers of Tuy Hoa in South Vietnam were upset and were demonstrating so no one would mistake their feelings. Some carried signs with messages imploring some anonymous official-dom not to abandon them to the Viet Cong. It was August 1966, and they were not being abandoned. The troops that were leaving would be replaced. But the villagers felt secure with the unit that had been there since January. One sign summed it up: 'Don't leave us, Blue Dragons.'

The Blue Dragons was the nickname of the Second Brigade, Republic of Korea Marine Corps, a fighting unit that had landed at Cam Ranh Bay in 1965 and had become expert at the jungle combat that was the standard in this war-torn Southeast Asian nation. The troops that moved out of Tuy Hoa in trucks looked amaz-ingly crisp in their camouflaged fatigues and helmet covers despite the late summer heat. They represented a Marine Corps that was one of the world's largest, as well as one of the youngest.

Just seventeen years before that day in Tuy Hoa, there had been only 380 of them. They had gathered at Chinhae, South Korea, in April of 1949, mostly transfers from the fledgling South Korean Navy, to form the nucleus of the ROK Marines. They did not look much like Marines. The commissioned men wore standard naval officers' uniforms, patterned after the U.S. Navy's dark blue with double-breasted coat with two rows of three brass buttons each, white-peaked cap with Navy insignia and white shirt with black tie. Rank stripes were in gold thread on the cuffs. The uniforms of the chief petty officers were similar. For summer, the officers wore U.S. Navy-style khakis.

The enlisted men looked even less like Marines, unless you picture French Fusiliers Marines of some long past time. They wore the standard sailors' rig of dark blue with a lighter blue, white-striped flap collar and white 'Donald Duck' caps with black bands. They were to be equipped by the U.S., but for the moment, were making do with rifles left behind by the Japanese. The U.S. equipment finally arrived as did U.S. Marine advisors. The Korean Marines soon donned the ubiquitous green herringbone twill fatigue uniforms of the U.S. forces and the M-1941 steel helmets. They also had, by now, adopted a Corps insignia. It was similar to that of the U.S. Marines, but instead of a globe under the eagle and in front of the foul anchor, the Koreans chose a five-pointed star. Some sources say this was to symbolize the morning star in keeping with Korea's slogan, 'Land of the Morning Calm'.

The new Corps was quickly formed into two rifle companies, and by late 1949, had grown to a strength of two battalions. Its uniforms were modeled after those of the USMC with certain modifications. There were dress blues, khakis and greens, as in the USMC, but the greens worn by the enlisted men had the high 'choke-neck' collars of dress blues rather than the lapels of the U.S. Marine greens. The greens of the officers, however, had U.S.-style lapels instead of the high collar. The peaked caps of both officers and enlisted men had black bands below the crowns from which rose a naval-style black patch to which the Corps emblem was affixed.

The rank system followed that of the Army. The blue dress uniforms were similar in cut to the USMC dress blues, but the ROK Marine trousers were in the same dark blue color as the coat. A broad red stripe was worn down each trouser leg. White web belts with brass buckles were worn with the dress uniform, and the cap cover was also white.

There would be little time, however, for the ROK Marines to wear dress blues, or even the khakis and greens for that matter. Just fourteen months after the Corps was founded, Russian-equipped troops from North Korea pushed across the 38th parallel separating the divided peninsula, and the ROK Marines found themselves in the middle of a war which their side was rapidly losing in the mid-summer of 1950.

The South Korean Army had four divisions deployed along the border with North Korea. The ROK 1st Division managed to hold its ground, as did elements of the 6th Division near Chunchon, but elsewhere the defenses were crumbling. The ROK Marine Corps had no troops in the line on the morning of 25 June 1950, when the attack began, but its units were soon ordered into action. The Corps reached the front nine days after the attack and participated in holding actions at Kunsan, Yo-Su, Nam-Won, Chin-Ju, and MaSan.

The Korean Marines were still American-equipped, as was the Army, but found nothing in that equipment to stop the Russian-built T-34 tanks. Their 2.36 rocket launchers did not have enough punch to penetrate the Soviet armor. All along the front the troops fell back. A U.N. force that ultimately included brother Marines from the U.S. and Great Britain was on the way, but for now the ROK Marines, still in the green herringbone twill fatigues supplied by the U.S., were in a lonely fight. But they had been building *esprit de corps*. On the left fatigue coat pocket they had added something of their own – the Korean Marine Corps emblem was stenciled there in black along with the Korean symbols for the Corps' name.

Even after the first U.N. troops – initially all U.S. – arrived, the line sagged and reeled until a 100-mile long rectangle that was but 50-miles deep was all that remained in U.N. hands on Korea's east coast. A small swelling in the line was called the 'Naktong bulge' and was considered a threat to U.N. troops. The unit called in to handle this problem was the newly arrived 1st Provisional Marine Brigade, USMC. In hard fighting with heavy losses, the U.S. Marines fought two battles there and helped turn back the North Korean hordes. They also helped train

Korean Marines who would now serve in their Corps' new First ROK Marine Regiment. The U.S. Marines from the Pusan Perimeter area were being withdrawn and would become part of the 1st Marine Division, as would the new ROK Marine Regiment. It would become the division's fourth rifle regiment.

A Korean Marine colonel wearing a variety of specialist badges and decorations. The wings over the ribbons above the left pocket show that he is a Marine parachutist. The collar devices are crossed rifles over an anchor, which recently replaced the Corps emblem of an eagle, star, and anchor as the collar insignia. The uniform is dark green with yellow metal buttons. The shirt and necktie are light khaki.

The division had been selected for a bold assault by General of the Army Douglas MacArthur, who was commander of the United Nations forces. MacArthur had selected Inchon, the harbor nearest the South Korean capital of Seoul, now in enemy hands, for the landing. His strategy was opposed by about every flag-rank officer in the United States Armed Services, but, in the long run, America's top old soldier proved that he was right. Going in with the 1st (U.S.) Marine Division was not only the 1st ROK Marine Regiment, but the 5th Independent Korean Marine Corps Battalion. Both units were later recognized for their effectiveness and bravery in this action by the award of the United States Presidential Unit Citation. Members of these units were entitled to wear the citation ribbon, which has a blue bar at the top, a golden-yellow bar at center, and a red bar at the bottom. A small silver star is worn on the ribbon for each action for which the citation is awarded.

The ROK Marine Corps was essentially an adjunct of the U.S. 1st Marine Division throughout the balance of the Korean War. It participated in a score of operations, including the 'Punchbowl' operation and was hailed as the 'invincible marines' by the Korean President, Syngman Rhee.

Following the end of the Korean Conflict, the ROK Marine Corps was expanded, first by adding a 2nd Regiment and then, on 1 March 1954, becoming the First Korean Marine Brigade. Not quite a year later, the Corps again expanded, and the 1st Korean Marine Corps Division was formed. During and following the Korean War, there was no apparent move by members of various ROK Marine units to develop distinctive insignias at the battalion or regimental levels, perhaps out of deference to their American counterparts who had dropped divi-sional and other special unit emblems for wear on uniforms a couple of years after World War II. The idea behind this was to promote pride in the Corps as a single unit and not to polarize the organization with inside rivalries. This, perhaps, was the reason that the ROK Marines did not use any smaller unit insignia until its 2nd Brigade went to serve in Vietnam. That insignia, illustrated and described in detail in the plates section of this volume, was probably not worn as a shoulder patch, although it may have been worn as a small metal distinctive insignia. Photographs of the ROK Marines serving in Vietnam indicate Spartan neatness on the fatigues and other field clothing. Name tapes were worn in black lettering on white above the right breast pocket. Small subdued rank devices were worn on collar points and, occasionally, on pocket flaps. ROK Marine officers apparently did not follow the practice of some American officers of pinning a rank insignia on the camouflaged helmet cover.

Today, South Korean Marines still have uniforms similar in style to U.S. Marines, including the so-called 'campaign' hat (U.S. Marines call all types of headgear 'covers') which is worn by drill instructors.

The Republic of Korea Marine Corps, which started out as an arm of the Navy, surprisingly enough had been under control of the Army for many years. In 1973, it again came under naval jurisdiction, and the commandant, who holds the rank of lieutenant general, was designated second vice chief of naval operations.

The 1st ROK Marine Division headquarters is at Pohang. Chinhae is still Corps headquarters and also serves as 'boot camp' for ROK Marine recruits. Marine security units are based at several other points in South Korea, including the main line of resistance (MLR) along the no man's land dividing the north and south.

13

THE INDONESIAN MARINE CORPS

The 65-man platoon swung smartly down a dusty roadway in the former Belgian Congo, reflecting that special elan discernible among elite troops. Half-a-world away from their homeland, the men were making history. They were in the first unit from their relatively young nation to serve in an overseas assignment. They were members of the Korps Kommando (KKO) – the Indonesian Marine Corps – and they were part of the Indonesian 'Garuda' Battalion serving as part of the United Nations forces in those troubled parts from 1960 to 1963.

Just fifteen years before they arrived in the Congo, there had been no Indonesia and no KKO. There had been a colony called the Dutch East Indies and the Royal Netherlands Marines – the Korps Mariniers – who served there and from whom the KKO adopted their first name, 'Korps Marinirs', which was the way the Indonesians spelled it.

The Dutch Marine Brigade that had been trained in the United States to help the Allies deliver the knockout punch to the last unconquered Axis power by invading mainland Japan arrived too late. Japan had surrendered and the brigade was redirected to the East Indies archipelago to help pick up the colonial reins dropped when the Japanese invaded the islands three years earlier. But Indonesian nationalists had already been at work to prevent the recolonization, and in the jungles of interior Java, a force had been formed that would bring the Dutch Marines into battle with their namesakes.

The Indonesian Korps Mariniers had been formed as a part of the Indonesian Navy and operated largely as a guerrilla band at the onset of the Indonesian revolution. As the months wore

An officer of the Indonesian Korps Kommando wearing the naval-style uniform worn only by those assigned in foreign nations. The Corps device cannot be seen in this photograph, but is worn above the stripes on the cuff. The cap emblem is the same as for the Navy. In the field these Marines wear a lavender beret.

on, the organization's name was changed to the present 'Korps Kommando', so it would not be confused with the organization it often battled in the jungles and along the coasts. When peace and independence came in 1950, the former foes joined hands as the Netherlands sent an advisory team of Korps Mariniers to help build the Korps Kommando into a professional Marine organization.

The need for an amphibious force, such as a Marine Corps, becomes obvious when the fact is considered that Indonesia is the world's largest archipelago, consisting of 3000 islands, stretching for 3000 miles from east to west and 1000 miles north to south.

The KKO is one of the largest Marine Corps in the world, consisting of about 14,000 men in two brigades. It serves a population of more than 110 million, the fifth largest in the world.

Field clothing and khakis are the more frequent uniforms of the KKO, with officers sometimes wearing whites. There is no 'dress blue' uniform, such as worn by American and some European Marine units. The beret worn by KKO members is a color they call 'light purple', which is very close to lavender.

Indonesian armed forces have an integrated system of rank which employs the same symbols in Army, Air Force and Navy (including the KKO) for corresponding pay grades, although the colors vary.

This system has one dark purple bar for basic private, two for private, one point-down chevron for private first class and two for corporal. There is no 'buck' sergeant in the KKO. A staff sergeant wears a single gold inverted chevron; a sergeant first class, two; a master sergeant, three and a sergeant major, four. A warrant officer first class wears a shoulder board with a single stylized device that appears to be derived from the kris, the traditional Indonesian dagger. At the shoulder-seam side of the board is a single wavy gold line. The chief warrant officer wears the kris device and two wavy stripes. Officers have a rank system that employs diamonds and four-pointed stars.

Between the end of the rebellion against Dutch rule and the Congo peace-keeping assignment, members of the KKO gained combat experience in stamping out dozens of rebellions in the island chains. The commandant of the Korps Kommando holds the rank of lieutenant general and is called a 'Panglima', which roughly translates as 'Commander-in-Chief'.

14

CHINESE MARINE CORPS

Cheng Ho's Marines could be considered veterans. In twenty-eight years, they had accompanied the fleet from Java to Madagascar, and hardly a man was left in the ranks who had not seen his fair share of foreign ports, had his fill of exotic cuisine, and overcome the language barrier to discover the charms of alien enchantresses. If there were a Chinese word for 'salty', that is what they would have been called in some Corps. Not in this Corps, however. When they headed for home from the seventh of what became known as 'South Sea Expeditions', there was probably little Chinese slang around. The words for 'Marine Corps' had not even been coined yet. It was 1433.

It would be stretching a point, perhaps, to call these early day Chinese sea-soldiers Marines. Even the Nationalist Chinese Marine Corps ignores this and later evidence of their Marine-like units, and picks on 16 September 1947 as the birth date of their modern Corps.

Since an earlier unit that had been designated 'Marine' had been incorporated into the Army, the new Chinese Marines were still largely dressed in the uniforms of the Chinese World War II Army. Enlisted men wore medium khaki colored uniforms with stand-and-fall collars on the coats which had four flap pockets. Wraparound leggings were worn up to the trouser knee. A soft-crowned képi-type of headgear was worn that had the Chinese sunburst design in white on a blue circle worn in the center above two small buttons that fastened the cap's ear flaps. Officers' uniforms followed the same general design but were of sturdier material. Insignia was worn on collar patches and consisted of a series of triangular devices of several colors with various backings, such as horizontal stripes to indicate rank.

Almost from its founding date, the Corps was caught up in the Chinese Civil War, which found the Communist forces pushing the Nationalist troops further and further back, until in 1949, the island of Taiwan was about the only territory still held by the forces of Chiang Kai Shek.

Once on Taiwan, the development of the modern Nationalist Chinese Marine Corps started taking place. In 1951 a USMC advisory team started giving assistance, and soon the Chinese Corps began resembling its American counterpart. American-style helmets and field clothing were adopted. The Chinese Marine insignia was adopted and also showed the American influence. It consists of a foul anchor behind a globe on which the outline of mainland China is superimposed. The Chinese sunburst insignia is worn above this device. The Marines wear a green uniform with turned back lapels in a shade of green close to U.S. Marine green and tan-khaki uniforms for warmer weather. The buttons are gold colored for officers and silver colored for NCOs and privates, as are the lapel insignias.

Insignia of rank for officers includes five-pointed stars for generals, a series of one to three plum blossoms for field grade and one to three bars for junior grades. Non-commissioned officers wear inverted chevrons and bars on red-backed patches.

With a two-division strength and an estimated 70,000 trained reservists, this Corps is considered the second largest in the world. All of its combat has been against the Red Chinese, although its predecessor units fought against Japanese invaders during World War II. The

Corps was awarded the Presidential Banner of Honor by their President for its resupply of the Kinmen Islands operation in 1958. It was the first time this award was made to any branch of the Chinese Armed Forces.

There are two main posts for the Chinese Marine Corps – Tsoying, where Corps headquarters is maintained, and Fang-Shan, 1st Division Headquarters, where the recruit training center is also located.

15

THAILAND'S MARINE CORPS

The thunder of drums and the blare of brass filled the National Stadium in Bangkok on 5 July 1959, as the band of the 3rd Division, United States Marine Corps broke into a Marines' Hymn that had nothing to do with the Halls of Montezuma or the Shores of Tripoli. What the tune did have, however, was a royal author – his majesty King Bhumibol of the Kingdom of Thailand, who had penned 'The Royal Thai Marine Corps Hymn' and presented it to the delighted members of the Marine Brigade a few days before the concert.

The Royal Thai Marines had been around for awhile, tracing the unit's ancestry to the Royal Thai Navy transportation battalion founded in 1902. As a part of the Royal Thai Navy, the Marine Corps follows the naval rank structure and, for the most part, its members wear naval uniforms. In the field, however, American style field clothing is worn. The formal beginning of the Royal Thai Marines dates to 1932, when the nation was still known as Siam. The name 'Thailand' literally means 'land of the free', and was adopted in 1939, changed back to Siam in 1945 and to Thailand again in 1949.

The Thai Marine Corps was battalion-sized from 1932 to 1937, when a second battalion was formed, and became a regiment in 1940. That was the year that the Corps became engaged – along with other Thai forces – in border warfare with neighboring French Indo-China. French influence was seen in the enlisted men's uniforms of the Thai naval forces with the familiar red pom-pom being worn on the sailors' caps. In 1954, the Thai Corps began getting aid from USMC advisory teams and, within a year, was reorganized along the lines of a modern amphib-

ious Marine brigade. The Corps emblem shows USMC influence, using a globe with a foul anchor behind it. At the top of the globe, however, instead of an eagle, is a 'Garuda', a legendary Siamese figure with wings. The globe contains the outline of the map of Thailand.

A commander in the Marine Corps of Thailand wears light khaki naval-style uniform. The Thai Marines are an integral part of the Navy but have their own distinctive globe and Garuda insignia, which is not worn by this officer, although he would wear it on a beret. The badge above the name plate shows that he is qualified as a frogman. The wings above the ribbons are for parachute qualification. The badge on the right pocket is unidentified.

In the 1960s the RTMC participated in border warfare actions with Cambodia, and had some volunteers in covert actions in Laos. During the 1970s some Corps units participated in actions against terrorists along the Malaysian border.

During the 1960s and 1970s, enlisted men wore sleeve chevrons point down for the grades of apprentice through petty officer third class. Petty officers second class through chief petty officers wore chevrons on shoulder boards pointing toward a ship's wheel, just below the shoulder board button. Officers used British-style rank devices with curls on the top stripe for the ranks sub-lieutenant through captain. Commodores wore a single gold disc, and the rear admiral, who was the commandant of the Corps, wore two gold discs.

By 1980 the enlisted men's chevrons were modified to include an emblem above the one, two and three stripes of the bottom three grades, and the elimination of the wheel above the shoulder board chevrons of the top three grades. The new chevron emblem, which is worn by itself by recruits, appears to be the helmet or cap of traditional Siamese temple dancers above a foul anchor. Officers' insignia apparently was unchanged. Members of the Corps who are parachutists or aviators wear Army and Air Force badges for those qualifications respectively. The Royal Thai Marine Brigade, which specializes in counter-insurgency, amphibious operations and security duty at naval bases, has units at the main Marine base at Sattahip and at Chantaburi and Bangkok.

16

THE PHILIPPINE MARINES

There was trouble on Corregidor again, so a company of Marines was called in to provide security. These Marines had been there before and knew what they were doing. Corregidor, 'The Rock', carries an air of history about it, and because of that history, the Marines had returned. It was not, however, the 4th Marine Regiment, USMC, whose commander, Col. Samuel L. Howard, had stood at the mouth of Malinta Tunnel in 1942 and wept when he realized he would be the first Marine officer to surrender a regiment.

A sergeant major of the Philippine Marines wear Corps badge on both lapels of his khaki twill shirt and white cap. The shoulder flash on his left sleeve bears the legend 'Philippine Marines'. The Corps badge can be clearly seen in the center of the sign. The Philippine Marines are an integral part of that nation's Navy, although they wear distinctive uniforms which show the influence of U.S. Marine Corps.

An officer and sergeant major of the Philippine Marines wearing light khaki bush jackets and side caps. The officer's cap is of a slightly darker shade and has black and gold piping. The officer is a lieutenant and wears Army-style rank devices on his shoulder strap slides. The sergeant major wears no rank devices, but has a title printed in block letters over right pocket. A U.S. Presidential Unit Citation can be seen just above the title.

These Marines were members of the 3rd Company, Philippine Marine Battalion. It was 1963, and the conquering Japanese of 1942 had long ago left this island fortress which now is a tourist attraction. The Third Company had served there in 1961 and had returned for the same purpose as before; the Rock was a treasury of war relics, and looters and pilferers had been carting away arm loads of the historical bits and pieces. The Marines had stopped this practice before and would do so again.

But they were more than security guards, these Philippine Marines. They were fighters and had earned their membership in the world-wide fraternity of Marines in a score of battles with insurgents, pirates, bandits and rebels throughout the archipelago.

In olive green fatigues, bearing subdued pocket patches with the shield and foul anchor insignia of their Corps in black thread, members of this unit have gained battle honors without ever leaving home. Started late in 1950 with six officers and 230 enlisted men, the Philippine Marines had grown to six-battalion strength by 1980 and seemed securely established as an integral part of the Navy and a permanent branch of the armed forces.

Their uniforms are similar to those of the United States Marine Corps, including dress blues. The Philippine blues, however, do have some unique features. The dark blue coat has a standing collar that is solid scarlet. The Corps insignia, in white and yellow metal, is worn on both sides of the collar, and a larger version is worn on the white-peaked cap.

Since all Corps officers are from the Navy, they wear the Naval officers' white peaked cap with a black band with the dress blue uniform, which, American-style, has trousers of a lighter shade of blue than the coat. The Philippine Marines also wear light khaki twill uniforms. Officers wear a coat with turned back lapels with the buttons and Corps collar insignia in dark bronze with this uniform. Navy-type rank insignia is worn on slides to fit over the shoulder straps on the khaki coats. When no coat is worn, officers wear Army-type miniature rank devices on shirt collars.

A master sergeant of the Philippine Marines wears the Corps emblem on the side of his cap and on his epaulet slides. The shoulder title, worn only on the left sleeve, is red with a yellow border and lettering.

Both officers and enlisted men wear a curved khaki shoulder title with the words 'Philippine Marines' embroidered in light-colored thread. NCOs wear chevrons with points up and straight bars at the bottom. Those who qualify as parachutists wear American jump wings.

The Corps, which was founded at Cavite City, has moved its headquarters several times since its founding. Units are stationed at several locations throughout the Philippines, but the main headquarters is in Manila.

18

CONFEDERATE STATES MARINE CORPS

On 10 May 1865, a month after Gen. Robert E. Lee had surrendered the Confederate Army of Northern Virginia at Appomattox Courthouse, Virginia, a ragtag group of Confederates gathered briefly as a unit for the last time at an obscure place with the tongue-twisting name of Nanna Hubba Bluff, Alabama, and followed Lee's lead by surrendering to the Union forces. From their worn uniforms and insignia, they were virtually indistinguishable from any other Confederate unit engaged in piecemeal surrenders throughout the American South as the Civil War ground to a halt. But, despite appearances, they were different, these men in threadbare gray, creased butternut and odds and ends of civilian clothing. They were all that was left of the Confederate States Marine Corps. Three officers, two sergeants, three corporals, one musician and eighteen privates, constituting 'D' Company, CSMC, they stood in formation for the last time as the senior Marine officer, Lt David G. Raney, Jr, surrendered and accepted parole for the entire unit.

No reporter was present that day to record the final moments of the unit. What the men were wearing is merely a guess based on general descriptions of surrendering Confederates. What the enlisted men of the Confederate States Marine Corps wore is largely a matter of speculation, based on scraps of letters, faded clothing requisitions, and an 1862 sketch of a Confederate Marine Camp published in the *Illustrated London News*. No known photograph of a Confederate Marine enlisted man in uniform has even been discovered by researchers.

With the officers, however, it is a somewhat different story. Of the fifty-three men known to have served on active duty as commissioned Confederate Marine officers, nine are pictured in their uniforms in photographs that have survived for more than a century. In addition, one uniform, that of First Lt Henry L. Graves, has been preserved and is on display at the museum of the Atlanta, Georgia, Historical Society. It consists of a gray coat with a high collar and two rows of buttons, a pair of sky-blue trousers with a narrow black stripe down the outside center seam of each leg and a scarlet sash. Gold and black shoulder knots, believed to have been copied from an item of USMC officers' uniforms of that period, are on each shoulder.

The buttons, curiously enough, are of the USMC pattern. When the CSMC was formed on 16 March 1861, quite a few members of the USMC resigned or deserted to come South to join the Confederate Marines. Among them were nineteen former USMC officers. Letters from some of these men during that period show that many removed the buttons from their 'old Corps' uniforms and transferred them to their new Confederate gray. The custom apparently spread to newly commissioned CSMC officers, as Graves had no prior service in the Federal Corps, and yet, wore its buttons on his uniform.

From the old photographs, plus Graves' uniform, it is clear that the Marine officers followed the Army style, with some modifications. Some of the USMC style was retained in such items as the shoulder knots which, incidentally, are not shown on Graves' uniform in an 1860s era photograph, although his uniform in Atlanta has them. Only one of the old photographs – that of Second Lt James Campbell Murdoch – shows these items being worn. From the photographs, it can reasonably be assumed that CSMC officers favored the képi, rather than the brimmed hat that was widely worn by Confederate Army officers.

No distinctive insignia for the Confederate States Marine Corps has ever been discovered. However, it should be remembered that even the USMC of that period had not yet adopted its famous eagle, globe and anchor badge, wearing instead the infantry symbol of that era, a hunter's horn, to which had been added the capital initial 'M' set inside the circle of the handle.

One of the more meticulous researchers and historical writers of this century, Ralph W. Donnelly, retired reference historian of the United States Marine Corps, spent twenty-five years going through the relatively few CSMC records to survive the Civil War, newspaper accounts of that period and letters kept by descendants of former CSMC officers, and concluded that the Southern Corps never had a distinctive insignia.

A button bearing the capital letter 'M' unearthed near Fort Fisher, South Carolina, the only site of a Civil War battle where both Union and Confederate Marines participated – although never as face-to-face opponents – is believed to have been a CSMC button. Other Confederate buttons followed this pattern, such as 'I' for infantry and 'A' for artillery.

The sparseness of such items is understandable since the CSMC never had more than 600 members serving at any one time in the four years of its existence. Considering deaths, desertions, discharges and captured Marines, it is still doubtful if more than 800 or so men ever served as Confederate Marines. The authorized strength of the Corps eventually was 46 officers and 1024 men, but like most Confederate units, full strength was never realized. Because of their rarity, CSMC artifacts are highly prized by collectors.

Until Donnelly began his quarter-century task, which he calls a 'labor of love', to push back the veil that had fallen over the Confederate Marines, few seemed to be interested in the subject. Donnelly's efforts resulted in the book, *The History of the Confederate States Marine Corps*, which he had privately published.

Donnelly found a tantalizing reference to 'eagles and rings' on a June 1864 clothing receipt for Marines at Wilmington, North Carolina, but it was never explained, and no other reference to such items has ever been discovered. If it was some type of Confederate Marine insignia, none apparently survived.

The Confederate State Marine Corps uniform of First Lieutenant Henry Lea Graves is owned by the Atlanta Historical Society, Atlanta, Ga., and is the only known surviving uniform of that small and short-lived Corps. The coat is Confederate gray and the trousers light blue with a narrow black stripe down each leg. The sash is red and the shoulder knots are gold on a black base. The coat buttons are the same as those used by the U.S. Marines. This custom among CSMC officers apparently stemmed from the fact that so many were former officers in the USMC. Graves, however, was not. He served briefly in the Confederate Army before getting a commission in the Corps. He died in Mt Pleasant, Ga., in 1892 at the age of 51.

The chance to ask someone who had personal knowledge about Confederate Marine insignia and uniforms lasted well into this century. Fourteen Confederate Marine officers are known to have been living after the turn of the century.

One of them – perhaps the only 'famous' Confederate Marine – is a tiny footnote in American history. Israel C. Greene was an officer in the U.S. Marines when he was in command of the detachment sent to Harper's Ferry, Virginia on 18 October 1859, where the abolitionist John Brown had barricaded himself and his armed followers in a firehouse. Greene led the charge and personally captured Brown. Although a Northerner by birth (Plattsburg, New York), he found his sympathies were with the South at the outbreak of the war, and he resigned his USMC commission to join the CSMC, where he was given the rank of major and named adjutant. He died in 1909 in the state of South Dakota.

The final chance to ask a former Confederate Marine about the uniforms and insignia of the Corps ended on 28 September 1928, when former Lt Henry M. Doak died in Nashville, Tennessee, at the age of 87.

In 1970 belt buckles bearing the Confederate Marine Corps name started appearing in antique shops and at meetings of militaria collectors. Supposedly, they were discovered in places ranging from a London 'flea market' to a warehouse in London. They are assumed to have been manufactured in England, as were a great many Confederate items during the American Civil War. However, no photograph of a CSMC officer has ever shown a belt plate being worn. Moreover, although the brass buckles seem to show some 'age', their style is not of the Civil War period. Donnelly could find no basis for their authenticity.

19

GERMAN IMPERIAL MARINES

In early November 1914, at a tiny dot of land on Kiaochao Bay in the Yellow Sea, Imperial Germany was about to lose one third of its Marine force with the stroke of a pen. Navy Capt. S. Meyer-Waldeck, Governor of Tsingtao, an Imperial German colony since 1898 in the province of Shantung, China, reluctantly signed an instrument of unconditional surrender to Allied forces. It was 10 November, the final day of a siege that had begun on 27 August, when a Japanese invasion force arrived in the bay. The Germans, led by the 3rd Sea Battalion of the Imperial Marines, had put up a spirited defense, had even mounted counterattacks; but isolated, low on supplies and with casualties mounting, they found the inevitable could not be postponed.

Dressed in khaki drill uniforms with stand-and-fall collars, the Marines had little in the way of unique insignia, except white epaulets bearing golden-yellow embroidered Imperial crowns, crossed anchors and the Roman numeral III. Affixed to their tropical helmets were white metal Imperial crowned eagles superimposed on vertical anchors. The tropical uniform was unique to the 3rd Sea Battalion. The two home-based sea battalions – the 1st at Kiel, the 2nd at Wilhelmshaven – largely wore the dark blue uniform that had changed little, save for ornamentation, since the first two companies of the 'Marinirkorps' was raised in the Prussian Navy in 1850.

The name 'Seebataillon' was adopted in 1854 and survived the transition from Confederation to Imperial troops in 1871. The numbering of the units began in 1883 with the 1st, continued with the 2nd in 1889 and the 3rd in 1898.

The Imperial German Marines saw some service in the German African colonies, but, by and large, the 3rd Battalion was the only one to see any extensive overseas action, having been called in as part of the Allied Relief Expedition during the Boxer Rebellion of 1900. On 29 August 1914, the 1st and 2nd Sea Battalions were assigned to a special Naval Division, which also included units of the Marine artillery and some other naval formations. The Marine artillery was not an artillery counterpart of the sea battalions, but rather a naval coast artillery unit assigned to the defense of seacoasts and harbors. It was not similar to the British Royal Marine Artillery of the time, but rather an integral part of the navy. Such a unit did, however, exist for an eleven-year period starting in 1856. It wore the uniform of the sea battalions, but with special badges and piping. It was called the 'Seeartillerieabteilung'. After its disbanding in 1867, the German Imperial Marines were strictly an infantry unit.

It was as infantrymen that the men of the 1st and 2nd Sea Battalions marched into battle in 1914 on the Western front. They wore their standard blue uniforms with white piping, and their distinctive shakos bearing bronze frontplates of the crowned Imperial eagle superimposed on an anchor. This headgear, however, was protected by a gray cloth cover with a stenciled battalion number on the front when in the field. The officers also wore a blue, white piped peaked cap with the standard cockade, and the enlisted men wore an unpeaked version called a *kratzchen*.

In 1915 the German Marines began wearing a field gray uniform coat, but continued to wear the blue trousers and caps. The new coats were of the same cut as the blue ones, but did away with the white epaulets with yellow-gold embroidered badges. The new shoulder straps were of the same field gray color as the coats, and the badges were probably supposed to be of the yellow-gold color, but some, in fact, were closer to orange. The final conversion of the uniforms came in 1916 when caps and trousers were also changed to field gray. The introduction of the distinctive 'coal scuttle' steel helmet the same year also spelled the end for the shako.

By 1917 the men of the sea battalions were virtually indistinguishable from their army comrades, except for their shoulder straps. This was ironic, since their counterparts in the Allied forces across No Man's Land – the United States Marines – had also been ordered into Army uniforms, the theory being that their forestry green outfits were too close in color to the field gray of the enemy.

With the Armistice on 11 November 1918, the Imperial Marines were no more. When the German armed forces were reorganized in 1919, there was no provision made for Marine Infantry.

During World War II, there was no separate Marine organization in the German armed forces, although sailors were pressed into service for land battles and wore the uniforms of land-based German naval forces, primarily the Coast Artillery, which were similar to the Army's, although naval badges were worn. One of the more readily distinguishable distinctions between the Army and land-based Navy forces was the color of the Nazi cap and breast eagles. The Army wore white metal and thread eagles, while the Navy used yellow metal and thread. But in truth, authentic German Marine formations ceased to exist when the sea battalions of World War I stacked arms and marched into the pages of history.

PLATE 1 UNITED STATES OF AMERICA
U.S. MARINE CORPS
CAP AND OTHER METAL INSIGNIA

Enlisted Shako Plate, 1812

Enlisted Cap, 1834-40

Officer's Full Dress Cap, 1859-76

Officer's Fatigue Cap,
1868-76

Officer's Full Dress,
1876-92

Enlisted Helmet Plate,
1892-1904

Enlisted Cap, 1900-19

Officer's Cap, 1914-19

Enlisted Collar Discs, 1918-19

Enlisted Cap and Collar Insignia, 1930-37

Enlisted Dress Cap and Collar (Current)

Officer Cap and Collar Dress (Current)

Officer's Cap Insignia and Lapel (Green Uniform)

Enlisted Cap and Lapel (Green Uniform)

Officer's Fourragère (Top of Visor Cap)

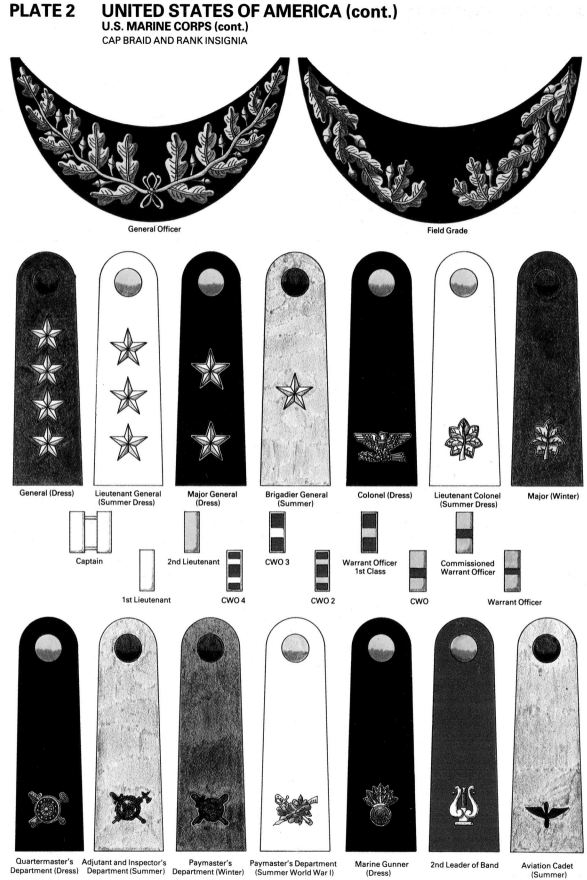

General Officer

Field Grade

General (Dress)

Lieutenant General
(Summer Dress)

Major General
(Dress)

Brigadier General
(Summer)

Colonel (Dress)

Lieutenant Colonel
(Summer Dress)

Major (Winter)

Captain

2nd Lieutenant

CWO 3

Warrant Officer
1st Class

Commissioned
Warrant Officer

1st Lieutenant

CWO 4

CWO 2

CWO

Warrant Officer

Quartermaster's
Department (Dress)

Adjutant and Inspector's
Department (Summer)

Paymaster's
Department (Winter)

Paymaster's Department
(Summer World War I)

Marine Gunner
(Dress)

2nd Leader of Band

Aviation Cadet
(Summer)

Lance Corporal

Corporal

Sergeant

1st Sergeant

Gunnery Sergeant

Quarter Master Sergeant

Service Stripes (16 years)

Sergeant Major

Sergeant Major

2nd Leader of Band

Quartermaster Sergeant

Quartermaster Sergeant, Pay Department

Drum Major

1st Sergeant

Gunnery Sergeant

Sergeant

Corporal

Lance Corporal

Sergeant Major

Master Gunnery Sergeant

Quartermaster Sergeant

Master Technical Sergeant

Master Technical Sergeant (Mess)

Paymaster Sergeant

1st Sergeant

Gunnery Sergeant

Supply Sergeant

Drum Major

PLATE 5   UNITED STATES OF AMERICA (cont.)

U.S. MARINE CORPS (cont.)
CHEVRONS (cont.), WORLD WAR I AND 1930s

Technical Sergeant

Technical Sergeant (Mess)

Staff Sergeant

Staff Sergeant (Mess)

Platoon Sergeant

Sergeant

Drum Sergeant

Trumpet Sergeant

Mess Sergeant or Chief Cook

Corporal

Drum Corporal

Trumpet Corporal

Mess Corporal or Field Cook

Private 1st Class

Drummer 1st Class

Trumpeter 1st Class

Assistant Cook

Drummer

Trumpeter

Musician

Sergeant Major of the Marine Corps

Sergeant Major

Master Gunnery Sergeant

1st Sergeant

Master Sergeant

Gunnery Sergeant

Staff Sergeant

Sergeant

Corporal

Lance Corporal

Private 1st Class

Four-Year Service Stripe

Private First Class Woman Marine

Collar Chevrons Field Uniform

PLATE 7 UNITED STATES OF AMERICA (cont.)

U.S. MARINE CORPS (cont.)

UNIT INSIGNIA, WORLD WAR I

4th MARINE BRIGADE

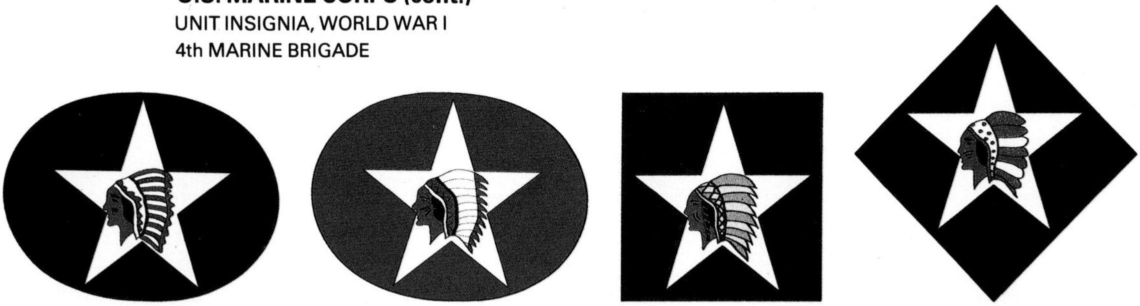

Headquarters Company 4th Marine Brigade (US 2nd Army Division)

5th Machine-Gun Battalion

Regimental Headquarters Platoon, 5th Marine Regiment

Regimental Headquarters Platoon, 6th Marine Regiment

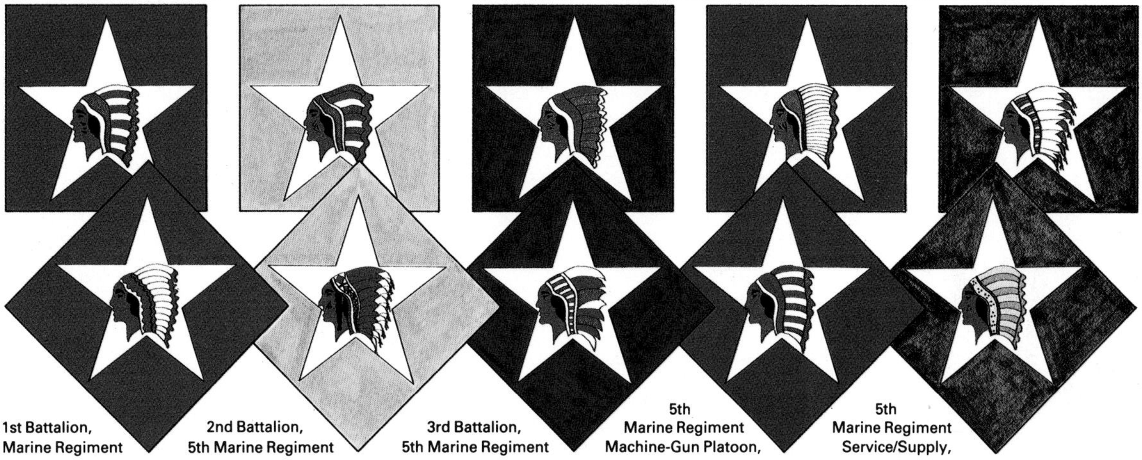

1st Battalion, 5th Marine Regiment
1st Battalion, 6th Marine Regiment

2nd Battalion, 5th Marine Regiment
2nd Battalion, 6th Marine Regiment

3rd Battalion, 5th Marine Regiment
3rd Battalion, 6th Marine Regiment

5th Marine Regiment Machine-Gun Platoon,
6th Marine Regiment Machine-Gun Platoon,

5th Marine Regiment Service/Supply,
6th Marine Regiment Service/Supply,

5th MARINE BRIGADE

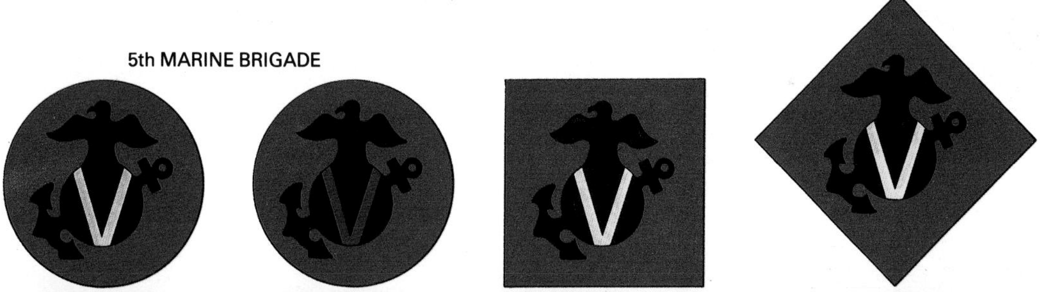

Headquarters Company, 5th Marine Brigade

Machine-Gun Battalion

Regimental Headquarters Platoon, 11th Marine Regiment

Regimental Headquarters Platoon, 13th Marine Regiment

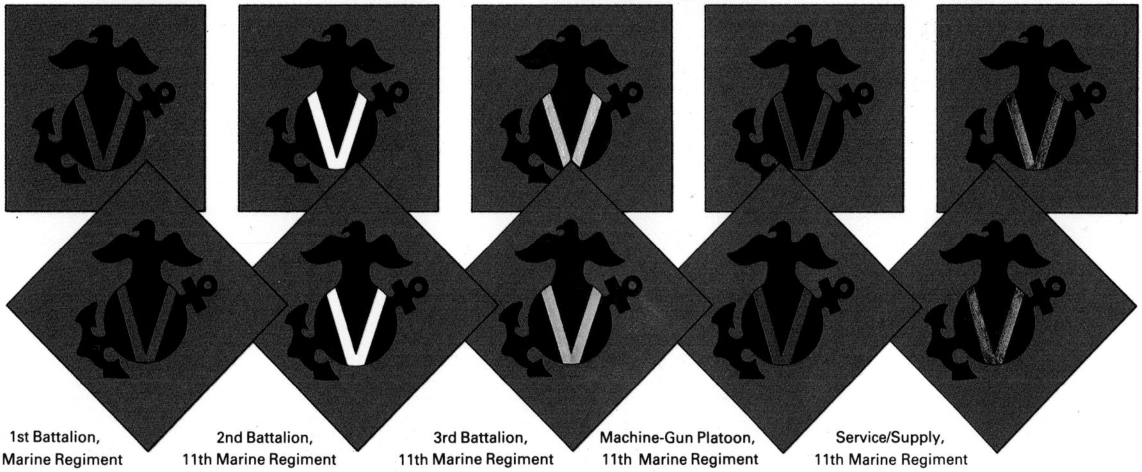

1st Battalion, 11th Marine Regiment
1st Battalion, 13th Marine Regiment

2nd Battalion, 11th Marine Regiment
2nd Battalion, 13th Marine Regiment

3rd Battalion, 11th Marine Regiment
3rd Battalion, 13th Marine Regiment

Machine-Gun Platoon, 11th Marine Regiment
Machine-Gun Platoon, 13th Marine Regiment

Service/Supply, 11th Marine Regiment
Service/Supply, 13th Marine Regiment

1st Marine Brigade
(Provisional)

1st Marine Division

2nd Marine Division
(Unofficial – 1st Pattern)

2nd Marine Division

2nd Marine Division
(Variation)

3rd Marine Division

4th Marine Division

5th Marine Division

6th Marine Division

Headquarters – Marine Airwings
(1st Pattern – 'Fuselage')

1st Marine Airwing
(1st Pattern)

2nd Marine Airwing
(1st Pattern)

3rd Marine Airwing
(1st Pattern)

4th Marine Airwing
(1st Pattern)

Headquarters – Marine Airwing,
Pacific

1st Marine Airwing

2nd Marine Airwing

3rd Marine Airwing

4th Marine Airwing

III Amphibious Corps

V Amphibious Corps

Ship's Detachments

Marine Detachment,
Londonderry, Northern Ireland

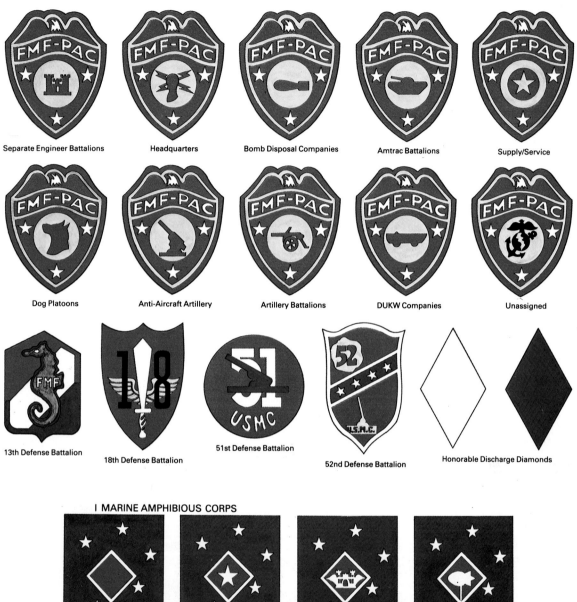

Separate Engineer Battalions

Headquarters

Bomb Disposal Companies

Amtrac Battalions

Supply/Service

Dog Platoons

Anti-Aircraft Artillery

Artillery Battalions

DUKW Companies

Unassigned

13th Defense Battalion

18th Defense Battalion

51st Defense Battalion

52nd Defense Battalion

Honorable Discharge Diamonds

I MARINE AMPHIBIOUS CORPS

Headquarters

Supply Service

Aviation Engineers

Barrage Balloon Battalion

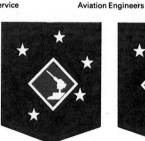

Raider Battalion

Parachute Battalion

Anti-Aircraft Battalion

Artillery Battalion

Anti-Tank Battalion

USMC Good Conduct Medal

Brevet Medal

Obverse

Reverse

Organized Reserve Medal

Expeditionary Medal

Distinguished Marksman
(Competition)

Distinguished Pistol Shot
(Competition)

Lauchheimer
Trophy Medal

Marine Corps Rifle
Competition

Marine Corps Pistol
Competition

Rifle

Pistol

Division Competitions

Expert Rifle Qualification
(Obsolete)

Sharpshooter Qualification
(Obsolete)

Marksman Qualification (Obsolete)

Basic Qualification
with Bar (Obsolete)

Expert Rifle Qualification
(Current)

Sharpshooter Qualification
(Current)

Radarman

Aviation Metalsmith

Astronaut Aviation Wings

Aviator (Unofficial)

Aviator

Naval Flight Officer

Aviation Observer

Aircrew

Combat Aircrew

Aviation Ordnance Man

Bugler

Aviation Machinist

Parachutist
(Five Jumps with Unit)

Basic Parachutist

Petty Officer 2nd Class
Companies (World War II)

Hospital Mate 1st Class
(Current)

Gun Painter

VMB-413

VMA-121

VMF-314

VMF-223

SEMPER FIDELIS

Marine Corps Aviation Insignia,
World War I

VMF-323

HMX-1

VMF-333

VMB-524

VMF-211

HMM-264

MACS-5

VMF-251

VMF-214

VMF-213

VMF-512

VMF-124

VMF-232

VMF-231

MAG-33

VMFT-20

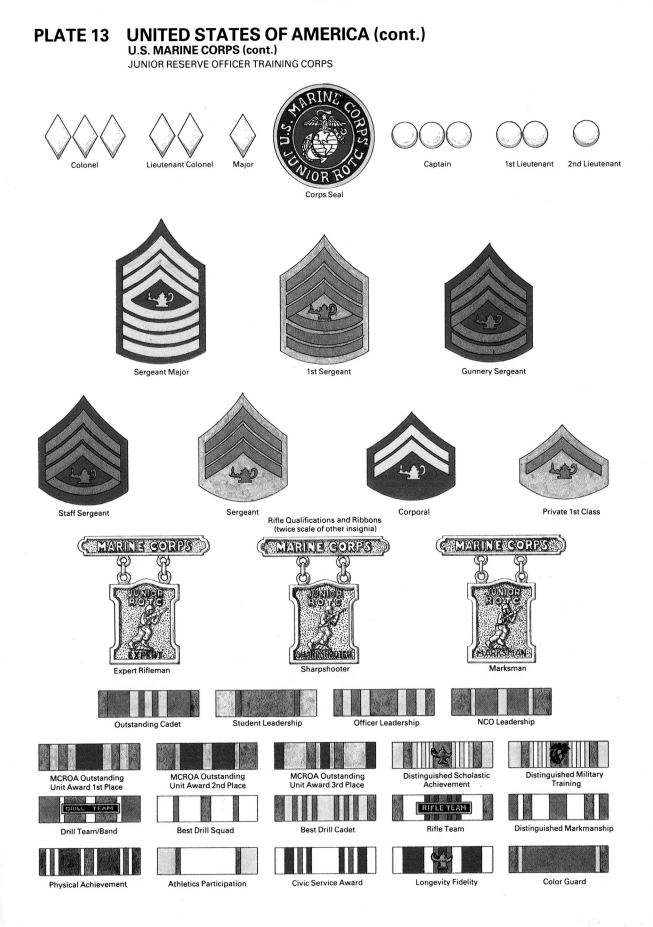

Colonel

Lieutenant Colonel

Major

Corps Seal

Captain

1st Lieutenant

2nd Lieutenant

Sergeant Major

1st Sergeant

Gunnery Sergeant

Staff Sergeant

Sergeant

Corporal

Private 1st Class

Rifle Qualifications and Ribbons
(twice scale of other insignia)

Expert Rifleman

Sharpshooter

Marksman

Outstanding Cadet

Student Leadership

Officer Leadership

NCO Leadership

MCROA Outstanding
Unit Award 1st Place

MCROA Outstanding
Unit Award 2nd Place

MCROA Outstanding
Unit Award 3rd Place

Distinguished Scholastic
Achievement

Distinguished Military
Training

Drill Team/Band

Best Drill Squad

Best Drill Cadet

Rifle Team

Distinguished Markmanship

Physical Achievement

Athletics Participation

Civic Service Award

Longevity Fidelity

Color Guard

4TH MARINE DIVISION RESERVE

Participation in NATO Exercise

4th Marine Division (Reinforced)

Mountain Warfare School, Bridgeport, Co.

Participation in Caribbean Operations

Mobilization Readiness Deployment Test

2nd Force Reconnaissance Company

3rd Reconnaissance Battalion

4th Force Reconnaissance Company

1st Reconnaissance Battalion

1st Marine Division (Korea)

MP Detachment MCAS Iwakuni, Japan

Tree Program

1st Battalion Anti-Aircraft Artillery

1st Guerrillas Company (Vietnam)

3rd Marine Division Association Patch

9th Marine Expeditionary Brigade

Military Assistance Advisory Group

Special Service Troop Marine Division

PLATE 16　UNITED KINGDOM
ROYAL MARINES
CAP, LAPEL, AND OFFICERS INSIGNIA

Officer Beret and Cap Insignia

Other Ranks Beret and Cap Insignia

Lapel

Lovat Lapel

Other Ranks Helmet Plate

Lapel

Lovat Dress Lapel

General

Lieutenant General

Major General

Brigadier

Colonel

Lieutenant Colonel

Major

Captain

Lieutenant

2nd Lieutenant

King's Badge (Dress)

Belt Buckle

Prince's Badge (Dress)

PLATE 17   UNITED KINGDOM (cont.)

Colour Sergeant (Lovat Greens)

Sergeant (Lovat Greens)

Colour Sergeant (Blues)

Lance Corporal

Corporal (Blues)

Royal Marine Division, 1941-43

104 Training Group (Reformed in 1943 as Royal Marines Training Brigade)

117th Brigade, 1945

Royal Marines Siege Regiment, 1940-45

34th Amphibious Support Regiment, 1945-46

Shoulder Tabs, Royal Marine Commandos, 1939-45

Royal Marine Engineers

Shoulder Tabs, Royal Marine Commandos, 1939-45

Combined Operations Patch

Special Service Group, 1944-46

Combined Operations Patch (Variation)

Warrant Officer 1st Class

Warrant Officer 2nd Class

Sergeant (Blues)

Corporal (Lovat Greens)

Royal Marine Police

Royal Marine Light Infantry

Royal Marine Engineers

Gunnery Sleeve Rating

Royal Marine

Sniper

Royal Marine Artillery

Royal Marine Band

Physical Training Instructor

Headquarters 3 Commando

Pilot, Fleet Air Arm
(Lovat Greens)

Pilot, Royal Marines

Commacchio Company

Parachutist

Parachutist
(Lovat Greens)

40 Commando

41 Commando

42 Commando

Officers Bell Topped Shako Plate, 1830-45

Officers Shako Plate, 1845-56

Officers Shako Plate, 1856-66

Officers Shako Plate, 1866-78

Other Ranks Shako Plate, 1866-1878

Officers Helmet Plate, 1878-1902

Other Ranks Helmet Plate, 1878-1902

Other Ranks Glengarry Badge, 1870-97

Officers Glengarry Badge, 1870-97

Officers Helmet Plate, 1902-05

Other Ranks Helmet Plate,
1905-53

Officers Helmet Plate, RMLI,
Chatham Band, 1905-50

Officers Helmet Plate
1905-53

Other Ranks Helmet Plate
RMLI Chatham Band, 1905-50

Other Ranks Cap Badge
RMLI Plymouth Band, 1920-23

Other Ranks Cap Badge
RMLI Chatham Band, 1902-23

Other Ranks Helmet Plate
RMLI Plymouth Band, 1920-53

Other Ranks Busby Badge
and Plume Holder, 1863-78

Other Ranks Helmet Plate RMA,
1878-1905 (Wide Neck)

Warrant Officers Busby Badge
and Plume Holder, 1863-78

Officers Helmet Plate RMA,
1878-1905 (Wide Neck)

Officers Busby Badge
and Plume Holder, 1863-78

Pillbox Cap Badge,
Bombardier RMA,
1874-1892

Royal Marines
Corps Cap Badge, 1916-19

Officers Helmet Plate, RMA,
1878-1905 (Narrow Neck)

Other Ranks Forage Cap, RMA

SNCOs Forage Cap, RMA

PLATE 21 NETHERLANDS
KORPS MARINIERS
OFFICERS INSIGNIA

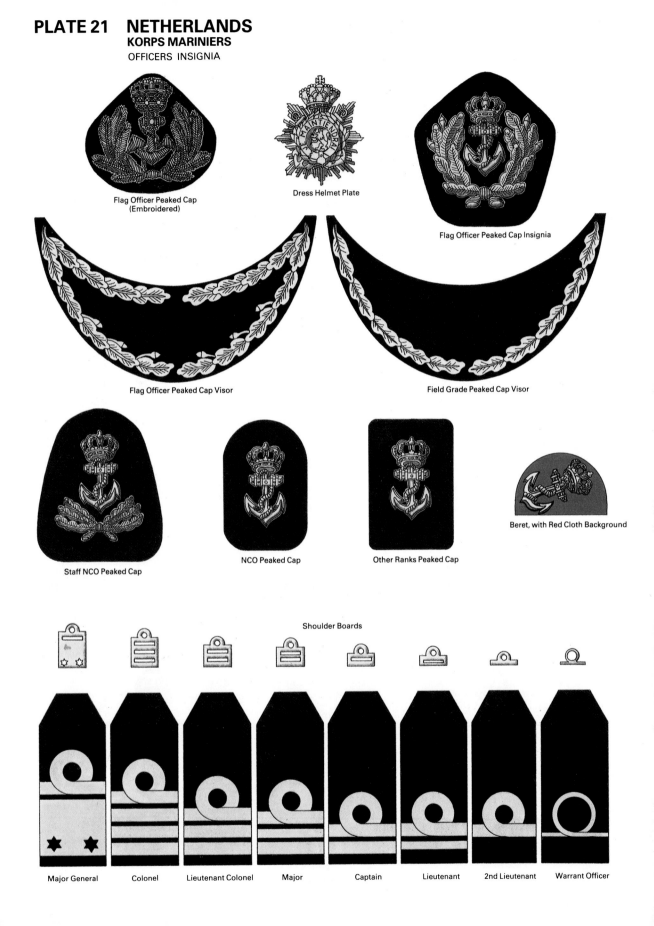

Flag Officer Peaked Cap
(Embroidered)

Dress Helmet Plate

Flag Officer Peaked Cap Insignia

Flag Officer Peaked Cap Visor

Field Grade Peaked Cap Visor

Staff NCO Peaked Cap

NCO Peaked Cap

Other Ranks Peaked Cap

Beret, with Red Cloth Background

Shoulder Boards

Major General   Colonel   Lieutenant Colonel   Major   Captain   Lieutenant   2nd Lieutenant   Warrant Officer

PLATE 22 NETHERLANDS (cont.)
KORPS MARINIERS (cont.)
OTHER RANKS EPAULET, SERVICE DRESS

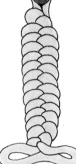

Officers Dress Shoulder Knot

Sergeant Major

Sergeant

Corporal

Marine 1st Class

Marine 2nd Class

Other Ranks Dress Shoulder Knot

Dress Blues Epaulet (World War II)

Sergeant Major

Sergeant

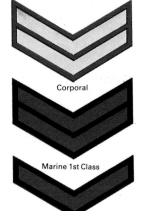

Shoulder Patch (Khaki Shirt, Current)

Corporal

Marine 1st Class

Marine 2nd Class

Service Dress (Current)

Shoulder Flash (with US Troops in World War II)

Shoulder Flash (Current)

Shoulder Flash (with British Troops in World War II)

Senior Parachutist

Field Uniform Pocket Decal

Basic Parachutist

World War II Shoulder Title

Lapel Insignia

Nationality Shoulder Title

Fields Music

Trumpeter

Communicator

Sharp Shooter

Cannoneer 2nd Class

Cannoneer 1st Class

UDT

UDT Instructor

Diver

Diver 2nd Class

Diver 1st Class

Master Diver

NCO Commando School Pupil's Sleeve Rate

FRANCE
FUSILIERS MARINS   AMPHIBIOUS TROOPS

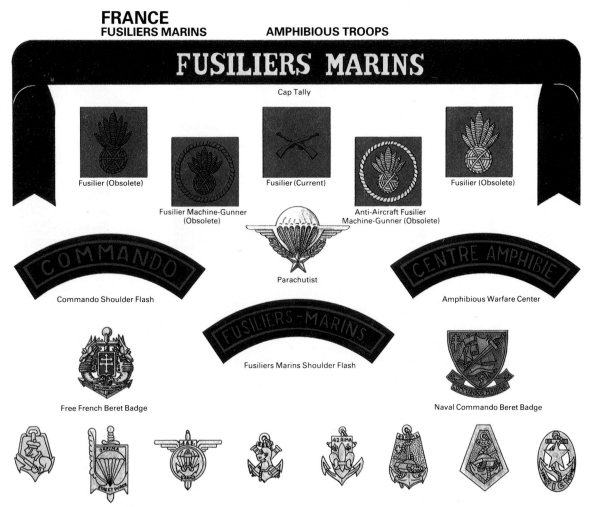

FUSILIERS MARINS
Cap Tally

Fusilier (Obsolete)

Fusilier Machine-Gunner
(Obsolete)

Fusilier (Current)

Anti-Aircraft Fusilier
Machine-Gunner (Obsolete)

Fusilier (Obsolete)

Parachutist

Commando Shoulder Flash

Amphibious Warfare Center

Fusiliers Marins Shoulder Flash

Free French Beret Badge

Naval Commando Beret Badge

Fusiliers Marins/Army 9th Marine Division Distinctive Insignia

PLATE 24   SPAIN
INFANTERIA DE MARINA
CAP BADGES AND SLEEVE RATINGS

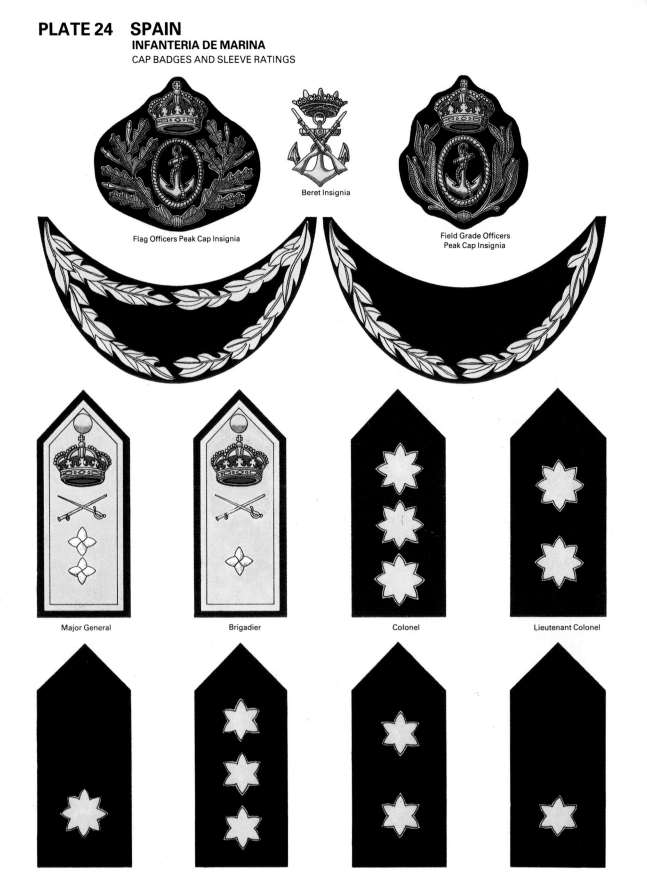

Flag Officers Peak Cap Insignia

Beret Insignia

Field Grade Officers
Peak Cap Insignia

Major General

Brigadier

Colonel

Lieutenant Colonel

Major

Captain

1st Lieutenant

2nd Lieutenant

PLATE 25 SPAIN (cont.)
INFANTERIA DE MARINA (cont.)
SLEEVE RATINGS (cont.)

Lieutenant General

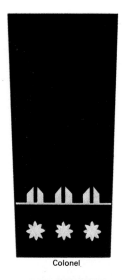

Major General

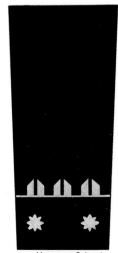

Colonel

Lieutenant Colonel

Major

Captain

1st Lieutenant

2nd Lieutenant

Warrant Officer

Master Sergeant

Sergeant

1st Corporal

PLATE 26 SPAIN (cont.)
INFANTERIA DE MARINA (cont.)
SCHOOL CRESTS

Corps Emblem,
1537-1931

Current Corps Emblem

Lance Corporal

Shoulder Board

Private 1st Class

Emblem of 3rd Armada

Coat of Arms, 1566-1664

Coat of Arms, 1682-1707

Department Emblem, Marine Infantry

PLATE 27 ITALY
SAN MARCO BATTALION

BATTAGLIONE SAN MARCO

San Marco Battalion Cap Tally

Naval Raiding Group

Right Sleeve Patch

Beret Badge

Left Sleeve Patch

Marine/Naval HQ
Co Parachute Regt

1

Company Numbers (Sleeve)

2

3

Visor Cap Badge

4

5

Company Numbers (Sleeve)

6

Collar Patch

RGT S.MARCO "BAFILE"

RGT S.MARCO "GRADO"

RGT S.MARCO "CAORLE"

Shoulder Titles

Collar Patch Variant

Sleeve Badge

Sniper's Badge

Parachutist Badge

Machine-Gunner

Artillerist

ITALIAN SOCIAL REPUBLIC SAN MARCO BATTALION

Military Police

Reconnaissance

Xth M.A.S.
Infantry

Xth M.A.S.
Infantry

San Marco

Xth M.A.S.
Naval Assault

Artillery

Xth M.A.S.
Infantry

San Marco Artillery

Reconnaissance Group

Flotilla Xth M.A.S.

Xth Division M.A.S.

Parachutists-Frogmen,
Xth Flotilla M.A.S.

Xth Flotilla M.A.S.

Swimmer's Brevet

Xth M.A.S. Helmet Insignia
(White Paint)

Lupo Battalion

Xth M.A.S. Helmet Insignia
(White Paint)

Barbarigo Battalion

LAGUNARI

Breast Badge

Lagunari Cap Badge

Cuff Badge

Collar Patch

PORTUGAL
MARINE CORPS

Breast Badge

Bullion/Cloth
Breast Badge

Marine Corps Command

Marine School

Marine Base

PLATE 29 FINLAND
COAST JAEGER BATTALION
CAP AND RANK INSIGNIA

Right Epaulet   Left Epaulet

Good Conduct

Beret Insignia

General's Collar Tab

Lieutenant General's Collar Tab

Major General's Collar Tab

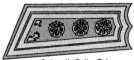

Colonel's Collar Tab

General's Sleeve Rate

Lieutenant General's Sleeve Rate

Major General's Sleeve Rate

Colonel's Sleeve Rate

Lieutenant Colonel's Collar Tab

Major's Collar Tab

Captain's Collar Tab

Senior Lieutenant's Collar Tab

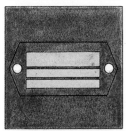

Lieutenant Colonel's Sleeve Rate

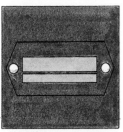

Major's Sleeve Rate

Captain's Sleeve Rate

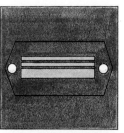

Senior Lieutenant's Sleeve Rate

Lieutenant's Collar Tab

Junior Lieutenant's Collar Tab

OCS Conscript's Collar Tab

OCS Reservist's Collar Tab

Lieutenant's Sleeve Rate

Junior Lieutenant's Sleeve Rate

OCS Conscript's Sleeve Rate

OCS Reservist's Sleeve Rate

PLATE 30 FINLAND (cont.)
COAST JAEGER BATTALION (cont.)
SLEEVE RATINGS

Cadet's Collar Tab

Chaplain's Collar Tab

Warrant Officer 1st Class Collar Tab

Warrant Officer 2nd Class Collar Tab

Cadet's Sleeve Rate

Chaplain's Sleeve Rate

Warrant Officer 1st Class Sleeve Rate

Warrant Officer 2nd Class Sleeve Rate

Sergeant Major's Collar Tab

Staff Sergeant's Collar Tab

Sergeant's Collar Tab

Corporal's Collar Tab

Sergeant Major's Sleeve Rate

Staff Sergeant's Sleeve Rate

Sergeant's Sleeve Rate

Corporal's Sleeve Rate

NCO School Pupil's Collar Tab

Lance Corporal's Collar Tab

Enlisted Man's Collar Tab

Private's Collar Tab

NCO School Pupil's Sleeve Rate

Lance Corporal's Sleeve Rate

Enlisted Man's Sleeve Rate

Private's Sleeve Rate

DENMARK
BJORNHOLM BATTALION

Beret Badge

Right   Collar Badges   Left

POLAND
COAST DEFENSE UNIT

Unit Insignia

GREECE
MARINE REGIMENT

Shoulder Flash

Shoulder Patch

PLATE 31 U.S.S.R.
MORSKAYA PEKHOTA (Naval Infantry)
EPAULETS

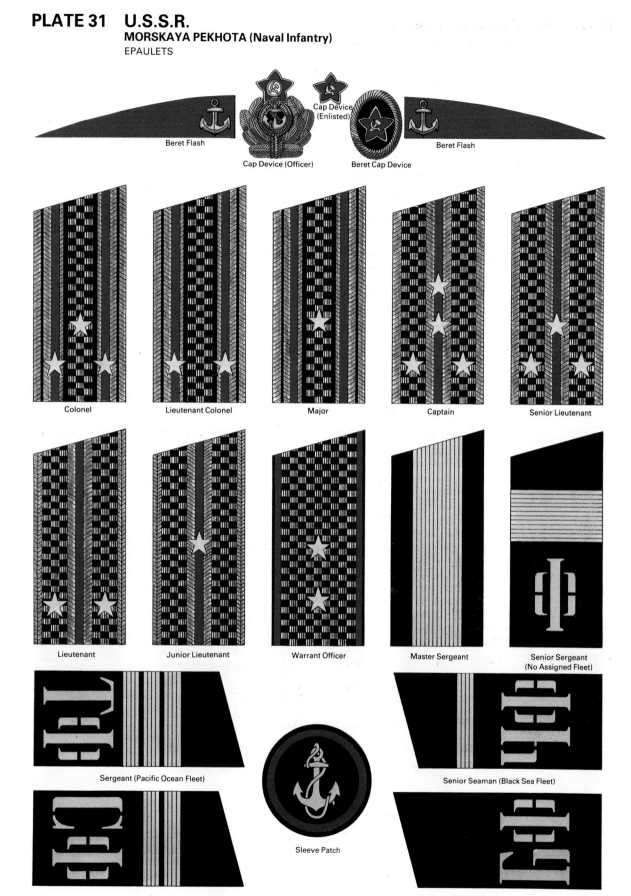

Beret Flash

Cap Device (Officer)

Cap Device (Enlisted)

Beret Cap Device

Beret Flash

Colonel

Lieutenant Colonel

Major

Captain

Senior Lieutenant

Lieutenant

Junior Lieutenant

Warrant Officer

Master Sergeant

Senior Sergeant (No Assigned Fleet)

Sergeant (Pacific Ocean Fleet)

Sleeve Patch

Senior Seaman (Black Sea Fleet)

Junior Sergeant (Northern Fleet)

Seaman (Baltic Fleet)

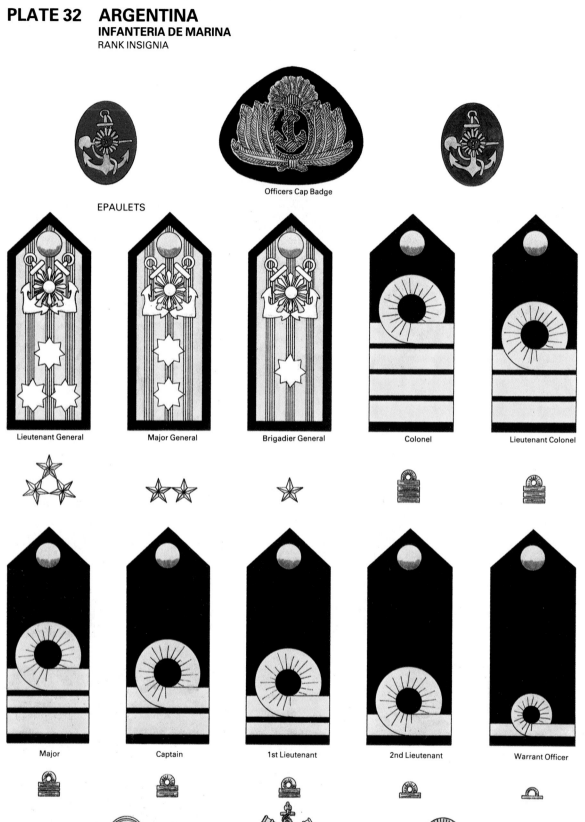

PLATE 32 ARGENTINA
INFANTERIA DE MARINA
RANK INSIGNIA

Officers Cap Badge

EPAULETS

Lieutenant General

Major General

Brigadier General

Colonel

Lieutenant Colonel

Major

Captain

1st Lieutenant

2nd Lieutenant

Warrant Officer

Arctic Badge

Breast Badge

Breast Cockade

PLATE 33   ARGENTINA (cont.)
INFANTERIA DE MARINA (cont.)
UNIT CRESTS

1st Marine Brigade

1st Marine Infantry Battalion

2nd Marine Infantry Battalion

Commando Battalion

1st Artillery Battalion

Service Battalion

NCO School

Shore Batteries

1st Force Battalion

4th Marine Infantry Battalion

5th Marine Infantry Battalion

Amphibious Vehicle Battalion

Communications Battalion

Quarters Service Unit

Amphibious Support Force

3rd Marine Infantry Battalion

Anti-Aircraft Artillery Battalion

Amphibious Commando Group

PLATE 34 ARGENTINA (cont.)
INFANTERIA DE MARINA (cont.)
SLEEVE RATINGS

Sergeant Major

Corporal 1st Class

Corporal

Private 1st Class

Officer

Enlisted

Volunteer

Variation

MEXICO
INFANTERIA DE MARINA

Parachutist

Parachutist

Sleeve Insignia

Sleeve Insignia

COLOMBIA
MARINE CORPS

Sleeve Insignia

Amphibious Commando
(Obsolete)

Amphibious Commando

PARAGUAY
CUERPO DE
DEFENSA FLUVIAL

Breast Badge

Breast Badge

CHILE
MARINE CORPS

Lapel
Insignia

Sleeve Insignia

URUGUAY
INFANTERIA
DE MARINA

Lapel Insignia

PERU
INFANTERIA DE MARINA

Sleeve Insignia (Summer)

Lapel Insignia

Sleeve Insignia (Winter)

Sleeve Rating (Summer)

Sleeve Rating (Winter)

PLATE 35 BRAZIL
CORPO DE FUZILEIROS NAVAIS

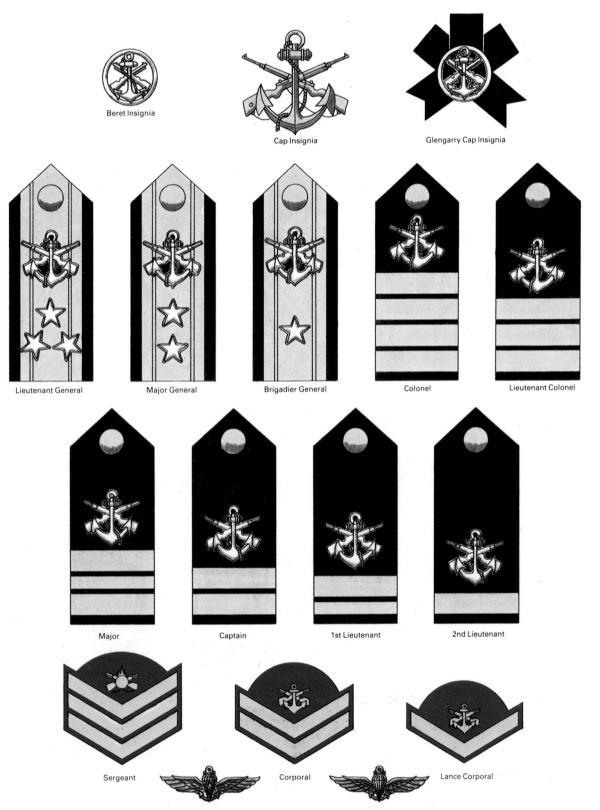

Beret Insignia

Cap Insignia

Glengarry Cap Insignia

Lieutenant General

Major General

Brigadier General

Colonel

Lieutenant Colonel

Major

Captain

1st Lieutenant

2nd Lieutenant

Sergeant

Naval Commando Instructor

Corporal

Naval Commando

Lance Corporal

PLATE 36   BRAZIL (cont.)
CORPO DE FUZILEIROS NAVAIS (cont.)

DIVISÃO ANFÍBIA

FUZILEIROS NAVAIS

1st Battalion 'Riachuelo'

Military Police

Military Police Brassard

DIVISÃO ANFÍBIA

FUZILEIROS NAVAIS

2nd Battalion 'Humaita'

ECUADOR
INFANTERIA DE MARINA

Cap Insignia

Breast Badge

Free Fall Wings

Rigger Wings

Commando Insignia

Sleeve Insignia

Sergeant Major

Master Sergeant

Sergeant

Corporal

Private 1st Class

PLATE 37 VENEZUELA
CUERPO DE INFANTERIA DE MARINA
OFFICERS INSIGNIA

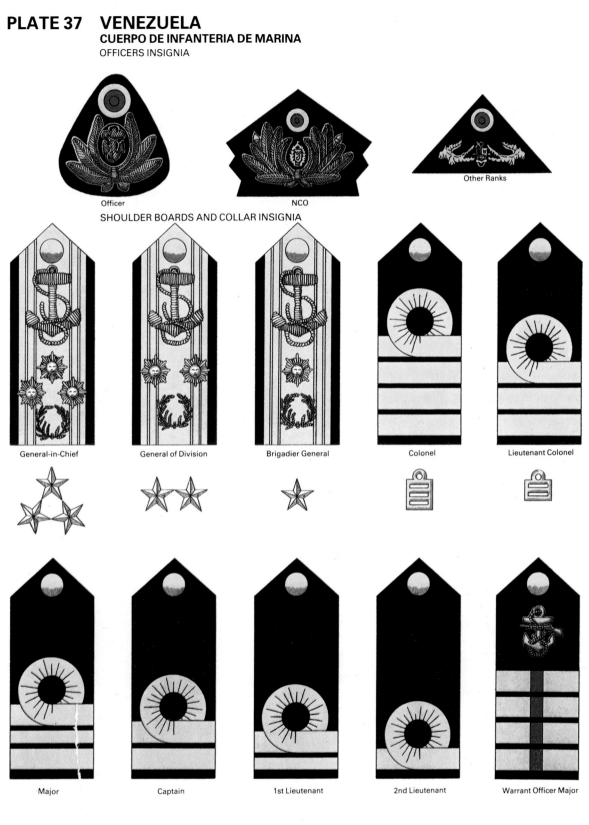

Officer

NCO

Other Ranks

SHOULDER BOARDS AND COLLAR INSIGNIA

General-in-Chief

General of Division

Brigadier General

Colonel

Lieutenant Colonel

Major

Captain

1st Lieutenant

2nd Lieutenant

Warrant Officer Major

Warrant Officer Principal

Master Warrant Officer

Warrant Officer 1st Class

Warrant Officer 2nd Class

Warrant Officer 3rd Class

ENLISTED SLEEVE CHEVRONS

Sergeant Major

1st Sergeant

Sergeant

Corporal

WEAPONS QUALIFICATION BADGES

Rifle Expert

Rifle 2nd Class

Rifle 3rd Class

Lance Corporal   Pistol 2nd Class

Pistol 3rd Class   Private 1st Class

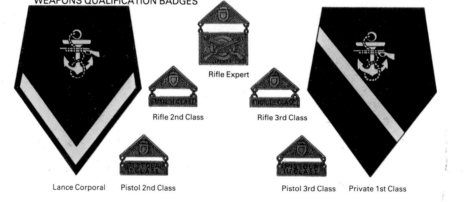

Commando Distinctive

Officer's Breast Badge

Enlisted Breast Badge

PLATE 39 CUBA
NAVAL INFANTRY

Officer Cap Insignia

Enlisted Beret Badge

Beret Pennant

Captain

Commander

Lieutenant Commander

Lieutenant

Lieutenant Junior Grade

Ensign

Aspirant

Senior Warrant Officer

Warrant Officer

Senior Chief Petty Officer

Chief Petty Officer

Sleeve Insignia Naval Infantry

Petty Officer 2nd Class

Seaman 1st Class

Seaman

PLATE 40 SOUTH KOREA
REPUBLIC OF KOREA MARINE CORPS
RANK INSIGNIA

General

Officer Cap

Officer Lapel (Old Style)

Current Officer Lapel

Lieutenant General

Major General

Enlisted Man Cap

Enlisted Man Lapel

Current Enlisted Cap

Brigadier General

Colonel

Lieutenant Colonel

Major

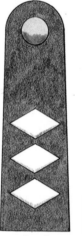

Captain

1st Lieutenant

2nd Lieutenant

Warrant Officer

Master Sergeant

Technical Sergeant

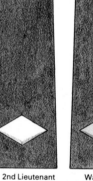

Staff Sergeant

Sergeant

Corporal

Private 1st Class

Private

Master Sergeant

Technical Sergeant

Staff Sergeant

Sergeant

Corporal

Private 1st Class

Private

PARACHUTISTS BADGES

Parachutist (Current)

Ranger/Reconnaissance Qualified

Blue Dragon D.I.

Blue Dragon Brigade Plaque

Reconnaissance Marine

Force Reconnaissance Novelty Patch

Field Uniform Stencil

Belt Buckle

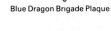

Unidentified

Seal of the Republic of Korea Marine Corps

REPUBLIC OF INDONESIA
INDONESIAN KORPS COMMANDO

Shoulder Patch

Beret Badge, 1945

Cap Badge, 1948

Beret Badge (Current)

Novelty Patch

Unidentified Shoulder Patch

Parachutist

Sky Diver's Novelty Patch

PLATE 42　NATIONALIST CHINA (Taiwan)
MARINE CORPS

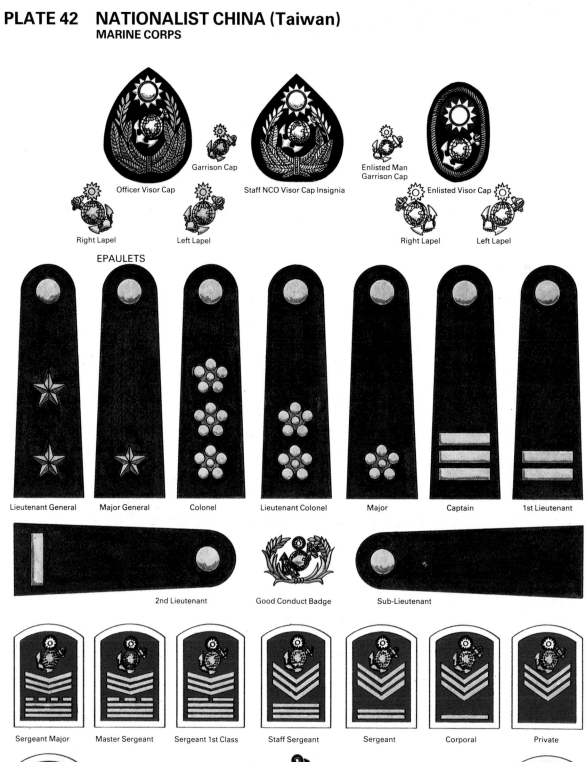

Officer Visor Cap

Garrison Cap

Staff NCO Visor Cap Insignia

Enlisted Man Garrison Cap

Enlisted Visor Cap

Right Lapel

Left Lapel

Right Lapel

Left Lapel

EPAULETS

Lieutenant General

Major General

Colonel

Lieutenant Colonel

Major

Captain

1st Lieutenant

2nd Lieutenant

Good Conduct Badge

Sub-Lieutenant

Sergeant Major

Master Sergeant

Sergeant 1st Class

Staff Sergeant

Sergeant

Corporal

Private

Private 1st Class

H.A.L.O. Scuba

Pilot Wings

Airborne Commando Frogman

H.A.L.O. Scuba

Private 2nd Class

PLATE 43 PHILIPPINES
REPUBLIC OF THE PHILIPPINES MARINE CORPS

Officer and Enlisted Cap
and Lapel Insignia (Dress)

Petty Officer 1st Class

Officer and Enlisted Cap
and Lapel Insignia (Service)

Petty Officer 2nd Class

Shoulder Insignia Field Uniform

Petty Officer 3rd Class

Seaman 1st Class

Seaman 2nd Class

Apprentice Seaman

THAILAND
ROYAL THAI MARINE CORPS

Cap Insignia (Obsolete)

Parachutist

Seal of the Royal Thai Marine Corps

Cap Insignia (Current)

Commando Qualification

JAPAN
IMPERIAL JAPANESE NAVAL INFANTRY

Parachutist Winter Service

Field Cap Insignia

Helmet Insignia (Early)

Helmet Insignia (Later)

Parachutist Summer Service

PLATE 44 CONFEDERATE STATES OF AMERICA
MARINE CORPS
SLEEVE BRAID 'CUFFS'

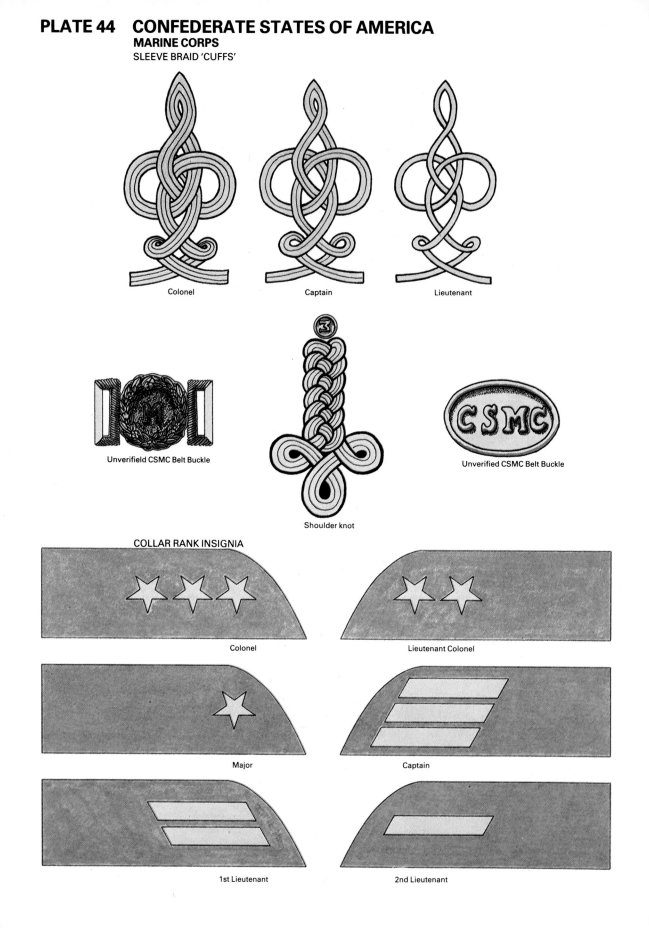

Colonel

Captain

Lieutenant

Unverifield CSMC Belt Buckle

Shoulder knot

Unverified CSMC Belt Buckle

COLLAR RANK INSIGNIA

Colonel

Lieutenant Colonel

Major

Captain

1st Lieutenant

2nd Lieutenant

Sergeant Major

Quartermaster Sergeant

First Sergeant

Sergeant

Corporal

PLATE 46 IMPERIAL GERMANY
SEE BATTALIONS

Shako Plate

Sun Helmet Plate

Garde Mariniers,
1823-51

See Battalion,
1852-74

See Artillerie,
1857-67

See Battalion,
1874-89

See Battalion Replacement,
1874-89

1st See Battalion Tunic,
1874-89

2nd See Battalion,
1874-89

3rd See Battalion Overcoat,
1874-89

1st See Battalion Overcoat,
Four-Year Volunteer, 1874-89

2nd See Battalion
Field Tunic, 1917

3rd See Battalion,
1917

1st See Battalion,
1917

2nd See Battalion,
Four-Year Volunteer

3rd See Battalion Overcoat

1st See Battalion
Field Tunic

2nd See Battalion
Field Tunic

Marine Field Battery,
3rd See Battalion

3rd See Battalion

Signalman

Gunner

Pioneer Sleeve Rating

PLATE 47   SOUTH VIETNAM
MARINE CORPS
RANK INSIGNIA

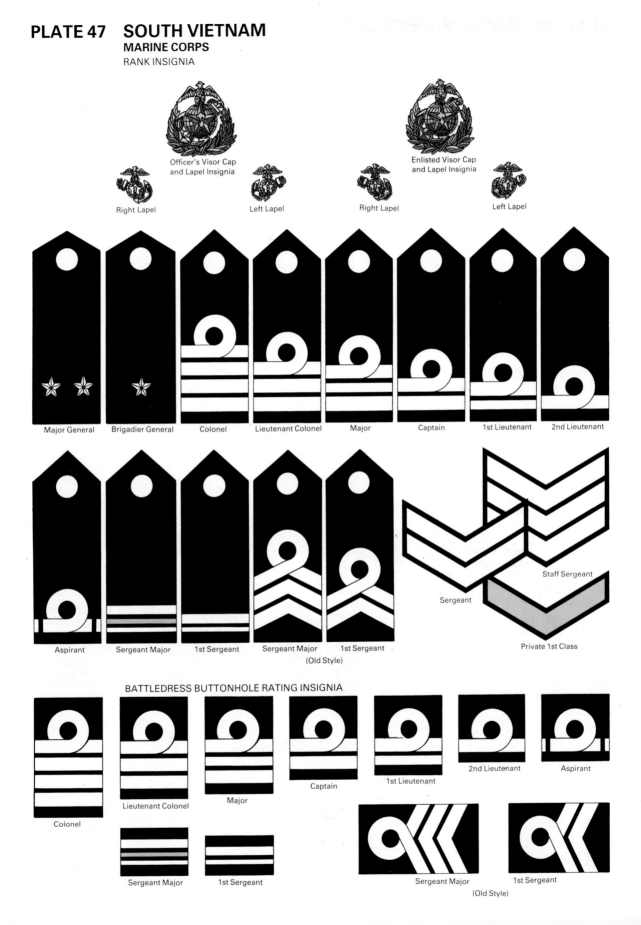

Officer's Visor Cap and Lapel Insignia

Right Lapel

Left Lapel

Enlisted Visor Cap and Lapel Insignia

Right Lapel

Left Lapel

Major General

Brigadier General

Colonel

Lieutenant Colonel

Major

Captain

1st Lieutenant

2nd Lieutenant

Aspirant

Sergeant Major

1st Sergeant

Sergeant Major (Old Style)

1st Sergeant

Sergeant

Staff Sergeant

Private 1st Class

BATTLEDRESS BUTTONHOLE RATING INSIGNIA

Colonel

Lieutenant Colonel

Major

Captain

1st Lieutenant

2nd Lieutenant

Aspirant

Sergeant Major

1st Sergeant

Sergeant Major (Old Style)

1st Sergeant

PLATE 48 SOUTH VIETNAM (cont.)
MARINE CORPS (cont.)
GENERAL CORPS PATCHES

RANGERS

INFANTRY BATTALIONS

1st Battalion

2nd Battalion

3rd Battalion

4th Battalion

5th Battalion

6th Battalion

7th Battalion

8th Battalion

9th Battalion

10th Battalion

1st Artillery

Alpha Brigade

2nd Artillery Battery

Bravo Brigade

3rd Artillery Brigade

PARACHUTISTS BADGES

Basic

Senior

Master

Basic

Senior

Master

PLATE TEXT

Plate 1 USMC   Cap and Other Metal Insignia

Although the United States Marine Corps emblem of the eagle, globe and anchor is well-known around the world, the Corps itself was 92 years old before that emblem was adopted at the behest of Brig. Gen. Jacob Zeilin, the commandant from 1864 to 1876, who was also the Corps' first active duty general officer.

Before that, the first type of distinctive badge was an elaborate (for the time) copper shako plate of the 1812-period and may have been used as early as 1807. It is known as the Octagon Plate because its corners have been clipped to produce an octagon shape. The central figure in the rather busy design is an American eagle facing to its left with the wings outspread and a fish hanging from its beak. Below and on both sides of the eagle are a variety of objects, including an anchor, a drum, cannon balls, a cannon barrel, flags and a rifle. Above the eagle's head is a streamer bearing the legend 'Fortitudine' – Fortitude, the first USMC motto.

The second badge worn by the Marines was shared with the Army in the period 1834–40 and consisted of a cut-out brass eagle with wings outspread and a bunch of arrows and an olive branch in its talons. There is a U.S. shield on its breast. The plate was worn on the high-crowned shako used by Marines during the period.

Two badges not illustrated, worn in 1840, consisted of the letters 'U.S.M.' encircled by a gold wreath which was worn by all ranks, and a foul anchor within a gold wreath.

A hunting horn in yellow metal with a white metal 'M' in the center was adopted in 1859. The type of 'M' used varied. The illustration shows the officers' full dress badge which is mounted on a U.S. shield over a laurel wreath. This badge remained in use in several variations until the official adoption of the eagle, globe and anchor in November 1868. The badge has been in continuous use ever since in variations that include showing the anchor with and without rope, and the hemisphere with and without longitude stripes. On the large helmet badge used 1892–1904, the eagle's beak was open and the wings were in a somewhat different position. Collar insignias always have had the anchors pointing inward, but have not always been worn by enlisted ranks, although Marine band members wore them in white metal from 1892 to 1900.

Because of supply problems, the U.S. Marines in France during World War I were issued Army uniforms starting in January 1918, a situation that was not always happily accepted by the Leathernecks. That August, Franklin D. Roosevelt, then Assistant Secretary of the Navy, inspected Marines of the 4th Brigade near Nancy, France and noticed that the lack of collar insignia for enlisted men made it difficult to distinguish them from their Army counterparts. Roosevelt suggested they be permitted to wear collar devices, and they were soon authorized to do so.

Brig. Gen. W. C. Neville, brigade commander, had the badges made in the bronze collar disc-style of the Army for wear on the Army uniform. In 1920, enlisted Marines started wearing the collar devices in the style of the cap ornament, except that the right device had the anchor running right to left. The E.M. version of the collar ornament, like that of the officers, had no rope.

The rope was added to the collar device for enlisted men in 1955, and for officers in 1962.

The cap and collar badges were generally in gold and silver for officers' dress, yellow metal for E.M. dress, and bronze for both officers and enlisted men for service dress. Officers' collar ornaments are slightly larger than those of enlisted men and have the rope standing free at several points, while the E.M. device has the rope stamped in with the rest of the badge. The color of the service dress ornament was changed from brown to black on 4 June 1963.

Metal buttons worn on Marine uniforms are said to bear a symbol that has been in continuous use in the U.S. armed services longer than any other. It is an eagle, head down, holding a foul anchor. A crescent of thirteen stars stretches from one wing tip to the other. There is a slight difference in the pattern worn by officers and enlisted men. The buttons are in yellow metal for dress uniforms and bronze for service dress.

Dress belt buckles have variations, but usually have the Marine Corps emblem in the center. Two versions are illustrated.

Marine officers wear a tubular braid ornamentation on the crowns of their peaked caps. It is often called a quatre foil in collecting circles, although not apparently in official regulations. Legend has it that the braid design goes back to the Revolutionary War days when men on the decks below sewed rope crosses to the tops of their caps so that they would not be mistaken for the enemy by the sharpshooters stationed in the rigging above during hand-to-hand combat. (*On plate for 'Fourragère' read 'Quatre Foil'.*)

Plate 2 USMC Cap Braid and Rank Insignia

As in the armed services of many nations, the custom of wearing gold leaf-type braid ornamentation on cap visors for higher ranking officers (thus the term 'brass hats') is practiced in the U.S. Marine Corps. General officers have heavier ornamentation than those of the ranks of major, lieutenant colonel and colonel. Officers below the rank of major do not wear it.

The Marine Corps follows the Army system of rank using stars, eagles, oak leaves and bars, although the warrant officer devices are distinctive to the Corps.

The Marines never had an active duty lieutenant general until January, 1942, when the growth of the Corps saw the commandant as the first to don the three-star insignia of this rank, then move on to the four stars of full general on 21 March 1945. As the war progressed, the number of generals and lieutenant generals increased. The strength of the Corps remained large enough thereafter that these ranks were retained.

Three departmental insignia were in use by the Marine Corps as collar and shoulder strap insignias from around the turn of the century to the middle 1940s. They served the dual purpose of being branch devices for staff officers and rank devices for non-commissioned warrant officers serving in those branches.

The badges were similar to those of counterpart departments in the Army, but a difference was the use of the Marine officers (mameluke) sword in the USMC insignia. Devices for the three departments are illustrated. They were yellow metal and enamel for dress uniforms and dull bronze for service dress. They were worn behind the Marine collar device on standing collar uniforms and on the lower lapels of service uniforms for officers. Non-commissioned warrant officers wore them on shoulder straps. During the early part of World War II, chief warrant officers wore the departmental device on shoulder straps above a special rank badge of a gold bar with a medium blue enamel stripe at the center. Warrant officer designations and rank badges were changed later in the war. Commissioned warrant officers wore a gold bar with a broad red enamel band and warrant officers a gold bar with a narrow red band. Today there are four grades of warrant officers using bars with varying patterns of red and gold.

Marine gunners use a rank device of a bursting bomb. It is in silver for dress uniforms and black for service dress. Gunners are warrant officers who serve primarily in the infantry, artillery, tank and amphibian tractor, and operational communications field. The rank was abolished shortly after World War II, but restored on 17 August 1956 for qualified Marines appointed as non-technical warrant officers. The scope of the rank was expanded to its present status in 1964.

Marine aviation cadets, during early World War II, wore a device consisting of wings with a vertical two-bladed propeller at the center as both a cap and shoulder strap badge. It was bronze for service dress and had gold wings with a silver propeller for dress.

The second leader of the U.S. Marine band wears a silver lyre device on shoulder straps.

One device not illustrated was for aides-de-camp to Marine general officers. It consisted of an American eagle standing on a U.S. shield with one to four stars in the upper portion, depending upon the rank of the general served. The device was bronze for service dress and gold with the shield in red, white and blue enamel for dress.

Plate 3 USMC Chevrons, Nineteenth Century

Chevrons to show the rank of Marine non-commissioned officers have apparently been in use since the early nineteenth century, although they may have been used in some form a little earlier since the ranks of sergeant and corporal existed in the Continental Marines during the American Revolutionary War.

Marine Corps chevrons, unlike those of the United States Army, have always been worn point up, and during the days when the coat or shirt worn was always blue, the rank stripes were always gold or yellow on scarlet backing, the color arrangement that remains to this day for the dress blue and mess dress uniforms.

The single chevron for lance corporal dates back to at least the 1830s, and the two and three stripe chevrons for corporal and sergeant respectively made their appearance even earlier. The lance corporal rating had an on-and-off existence over the years and vanished for long periods of time.

Between 1798 and 1899, there was only one sergeant major and one quartermaster sergeant in the United States Marine Corps, both stationed at Corps Headquarters in Washington, D.C. The illustrations do not show the ranks in top-to-bottom order, but the sergeant major, who wore three 'rockers' below his three chevrons, and the quartermaster sergeant, who wore three 'ties' below his stripes, were of the same pay grade, although the former was considered a 'line' rank and the latter a 'staff' rank.

The first sergeant, called an orderly sergeant until 1872, wore a diamond under his chevrons. The rank of gunnery sergeant was first authorized in 1898, and the device under his chevrons was the bursting bomb over crossed rifles. Enlisted men were entitled to wear one stripe on the lower sleeves at an angle pointing down for each enlistment. Enlistment was usually four years.

Plates 4 and 5 USMC Chevrons, World War I and 1930

By the time of the United States' entry into World War I, the Marine Corps had adopted a winter field uniform in a color known as 'forestry green', described as a grayish green. Although the large yellow and red chevrons that evolved in the nineteenth century were retained for the dress blue uniforms, the new greens and the summer field khakis called for smaller chevrons in colors to go with the uniform. As a result, the new forestry green was chosen for the stripes themselves, while the backgrounds were red for winter dress and khaki for summer uniforms.

The sergeants major wore three chevrons and three rockers. The second leader of the Marine band used the same stripes and rockers, but with a cornet in the center. The quartermaster sergeants used three chevrons and three ties below. Paymaster department quartermaster sergeants used the same pattern with a pile of coins crossed by a quill pen at center. The pattern was repeated for drum majors who wore a star in the center. First sergeants wore three stripes with an open diamond below, gunnery sergeants the same with the bursting bomb and crossed rifles below and sergeants, three plain chevrons. Corporals wore two stripes and lance corporals (also designated acting corporals), one stripe. There was apparently a crossed rifle device worn on sleeves by those designated as private first class somewhere around the turn of the century, but this does not show up in guides to World War I USMC chevrons, although some supposed examples exist in red on forestry green, which would be right for that period.

In the next decade, the number of chevrons used by the Marine Corps multiplied until, in the 1930s, at least twenty-eight were in use, many reflecting the Navy ties with the Corps by showing speciality marks in the center in the manner of naval petty officer chevrons. Of the total, only seven were unadorned with speciality devices. By this time, the large dress blue chevrons had been abolished, and all chevrons in use were of the same dimensions.

While the rockers for non-commissioned officers of the line and the ties of those of the staff were continued, some other changes had taken place.

The quartermaster sergeant had added a wagon wheel in the center of his three chevrons and ties, while his old insignia of rank was now used for master technical sergeants. Crescent moons were centered under these stripes for those assigned to the mess branch and down through one stripe over a crescent moon for assistant cook. The first sergeant had added two rockers, and the diamond at center had been filled. The gunnery sergeant also gained two rockers for that designation, and a master gunnery sergeant's rank had been created with 'three up and three down' with the bomb and rifles device at center. Drum majors had a baton at the center of their stripes, platoon sergeants a star and various grades of drummers and trumpeters respectively had crossed drumsticks and bugle devices centered under their stripes or standing alone. Musicians of the Marine band added a lyre under their chevrons. The lance corporal designation was dropped and became private first class. This system of chevrons continued until 1937, when it was modified somewhat, and again in 1941 when further modifications were made. By 1943, only the musicians' lyre remained as a distinguishing device on Marine Corps chevrons. All of the rest were unadorned, although in the top three pay grades, the same sets of chevrons were used for nine different titles. Later in the war, the diamond (also called a lozenge or mascle in some regulations) was restored in the center of the chevrons for first sergeant, now a first pay grade NCO. The ties for staff NCOs were retained until late 1946 when they were ordered phased out when the supply on hand was used up. Thereafter, only 'rockers' were used with chevrons in the upper grades.

Plate 6   USMC   Chevrons, Current

Behind the stripes worn by USMC non-commissioned officers lie bureaucratic decisions and even public relations considerations that the general public rarely hears about, or probably does not even care about.

After World War II a modernization in the records-keeping department of the Corps was encountering obstacles because of what was the apparently inefficient assignment of rank titles to job descriptions they seldom fitted. This caused problems in the new punch card system adopted for record keeping, so tradition, for the time being, was suspended in the name of modern office technology.

Eight job titles in the top NCO pay grade, for

instance, were consolidated under the one of 'master sergeant'. This meant that such time-honored titles as sergeant major and master gunnery sergeant were abolished. Quartermaster sergeants and master technical sergeants who were just getting used to wearing 'rockers' instead of 'ties' under their chevrons now found that they were classified with all of the rest who wore 'three up and three down' – master sergeants.

Twenty-three other distinctive rank titles went down the drain as the Corps condensed its next five ranks of chevron wearers into technical sergeants, with three chevrons and two rockers; staff sergeants, with three chevrons and one rocker; sergeants, with three chevrons; corporals, with two, and privates first class, with one.

At that, they may have come off lucky. One proposal was to drop the title 'sergeant' from the top three pay grades and call them chief non-commissioned officer, non-commissioned officer first-class and non-commissioned officer second-class.

The chevrons had nothing in the middle, except for the band members who continued to wear the lyre.

This system lasted less than a decade. In 1954, the title of sergeant major was resurrected as the new top NCO pay grade. First sergeants were also returned to the rank chart and got their diamonds back.

By 1959 the grade structure had been revised again. Except for PFC, there would be no more unadorned Marine chevrons. A new rank – sergeant major of the Marine Corps – was established in May 1957. Only one man could hold the title, and he would be on the staff of the commandant and would be the senior NCO of the Corps. His unique chevrons are three chevrons with four rockers below. In the center is the Marine eagle, globe and anchor flanked by two stars.

Regular sergeants major and master gunnery sergeants wear the same rank stripes, but have a star and a bursting bomb in the center, respectively. The first sergeant still wears the diamond. All other NCOs, down to the revived rank of lance corporal, wear crossed rifles under their chevrons, symbolic of the fact that all Marines are basically infantrymen despite other specialties. The service stripe, awarded for each enlistment, is now for standardized four-year terms.

Miniature pin-on NCO devices were first used on field clothing during the Korean War. They have come in both metal and plastic and were first issued to Marines in dull bronze and later in black. They are identical in pattern to the cloth stripes.

The top four grades of sergeants are now entitled to wear mess dress. Chevrons for this uniform are in the large style of the nineteenth century stripes and are gold on red for blue mess dress and gold on white for tropical mess dress.

Plate 7 USMC Unit Insignia, World War I

Shoulder sleeve insignia, commonly called shoulder patches, were first worn by members of the United States Marine Corps in the latter part of World War I. The practice was started by an Army unit, the 81st Division, and authorities soon determined that the small and colorful bits of cloth were morale boosters.

During World War I, the 4th Marine Brigade, consisting of the 5th and 6th Regiments and the 6th Machine-Gun Battalion, was detached for duty with the Army and became half of the 2nd Infantry Division. The basic insignia of this unit was the head of an American Indian in a feathered war bonnet, centered on a five-pointed white star. The star was set on backgrounds of a variety of shapes and colors to indicate specific units.

For the Marines, the 5th Regiment used a square background, the 6th, a diamond-shaped one, and brigade headquarters and the machine-gun battalion, an oval. The basic design for the 2nd Division patch supposedly originated with a truck driver in the unit who painted the design on the doors of his truck. What gave him the inspiration has never been recorded.

The patches were worn in the waning days of the war, but were not actually authorized until 14 November 1918 – three days after the Armistice. The order called for the Indian head to be embroidered or stamped in red and blue on the star, with the head facing to the left. The order was signed by Maj. Gen. John A. Lejeune, the only Marine general ever to be a commander of an Army division.

The assumption that the shoulder patches worn by U.S. troops in World War I were of uniform size, design and color is erroneous. Most worn in the field were homemade at best. They were made of blanket scraps, pieces of material begged from French tailors and dressmakers, and even chunks of material cut from tents. In the case of the 2nd Division, the Indian heads were not only embroidered or stamped, but also drawn in ink and applied with paint.

Because many of the members of the unit had never seen the order authorizing the patches and describing the various shapes and colors, there was a good deal of confusion about who was to wear what. Even Lejeune, who signed the authorization order, is shown in a photograph of that period wearing a pentagon-shaped shoulder patch, which was the shape authorized for the 9th Infantry (Army) Regiment. Later, he is shown correctly wearing the shield-shaped patch authorized for divisional headquarters. The shield-shaped patch became, in later years, the one and only patch for the 2nd Infantry Division, being worn in World War II and the Korean War and by members of the division currently stationed in Korea.

The background color of the patch became black, which in World War I had been the color for headquarters units. Other colors during that period were: red, 1st Battalion; yellow, 2nd Battalion; blue, 3rd Battalion; and purple, machine-gun unit.

Other colors and shapes did show up when the Marines returned home. There were many variations of the 'official' versions. Years after the war ended, manufacturers mass produced many of the patches for sale to veterans who wore them on their old uniforms at conventions, or on their veterans' organization uniforms. Many of the veterans had never actually worn the patches while in service but wore them proudly long after the Armistice was signed. Some of these patches were accepted by collectors as authentic World War I insignia, instead of as reproductions.

Members of the 4th Marine Brigade were not the only Marines of the World War I era to wear shoulder patches. A late arrival in France, the 5th Marine Brigade, never saw combat and never actually functioned as a unit, but shoulder patches for the brigade were recommended two months before it returned to the United States in August 1919 for demobilization. The time was probably too brief for the men of the scattered elements of the 5th Brigade to get many of the patches made. In addition, the Service of Supply recommended that the insignia be approved for wear when the brigade was concentrated as a unit, but it never was. The first elements of the brigade arrived in France in mid-September 1918. The last units of the 5th landed on

9 November, two days before the Armistice ending the war was signed.

Members of some units of the brigade were siphoned off to serve as replacements in the 4th Brigade, a factor that reportedly angered Brig. Gen. Eli K. Cole, its first commander, as well as Brig. Gen. Smedley D. Butler, the colorful two-time winner of the Congressional Medal of Honor who replaced Cole. Butler was the commander who recommended the authorization of the 5th's shoulder patch. The background color of the patch was to be crimson, and it was to have had three basic shapes: circular, square, and a square placed on end. The device in the center of the patch was a black eagle, globe and anchor on which the Roman numeral 'V' was superimposed. The color of the 'V' varied with each unit. With the three background shapes, and the combination of colors for the numeral, there were fourteen different 5th Brigade shoulder patches. Insignia experts in the U.S.A. seem to be in agreement that there probably never was a full set of the patches worn or even made while the brigade was in France.

Butler noted in his letter of recommendation that the Brigade Headquarters patch be circular and have the 'V' in gold-yellow to represent the highest rank of the units. The machine-gun battalion also wore the circle patch but with the purple 'V'. The senior regiment of the brigade, the 11th, used a square background, and the 13th Regiment, the square on end. Color schemes for the numerals in the patches for each of the battalions in the two regiments were based on the national colors of red, white and blue. The 1st Battalion wore red, the 2nd, white, and the 3rd, blue. All headquarters units wore a gold-yellow 'V', while the supply units used green.

Butler was also the commander of Camp Pontanezen in Brest, France, a sort of replacement depot with grounds that became a muddy quagmire during rains. The general ordered wooden, ladder-like walks known as 'duckboards' to be installed to combat the mud. The boards became a Butler trademark, and a patch for camp personnel featuring a white duckboard on a red circular background was authorized. There is no indication, however, that Butler ever wore either the 5th Brigade or 'duckboard' patch.

The shortage of genuine 5th Marine Brigade shoulder patches was probably a factor contributing to an error during World War II that has never been fully cleared up among collectors.

Patch collecting began to bloom as a hobby in the 1940s, causing some enterprising manufacturers in the U.S.A. to begin making reproductions of World War I patches. The same mass-production methods were used in producing these insignia as in the manufacture of the World War II patches then in use. They were fully embroidered, which genuine World War I patches seldom were.

But in the 5th Marine Brigade patch, this error was compounded by reversing the colors. The patches were first marketed about 1944 as black discs with a red U.S.M.C. insignia in the center containing a black 'V'. Over the years this became accepted in some collecting circles as the authentic combination of colors, although the fully-embroidered patches were seldom passed off as genuine World War I relics. Some reference books on U.S. military insignia even use the erroneous 5th Brigade patch as the genuine article. Manufacturers have continued to reproduce this patch, and they are sold by dealers as faithful reproductions of the World War I 5th Brigade patch. The false patches have been circulated so widely that it is doubtful if the truth will ever catch up with the unintentional lie.

One other Marine Corps unit in France used a shoulder patch. It was the 1st Marine Aviation Force which landed in France at the end of July 1918, the only Marine aviation unit to serve there during the war. The patch was a copy of the insignia painted on the sides of the unit's aircraft. It was a cockade of red, blue and white, with the circles in that order from outer to inner. The cockade was surmounted by an eagle with a streamer bearing the Marine Corps motto, *Semper Fidelis* (Always Faithful). Behind the cockade was a foul anchor running at an angle from right to left, making the insignia a replica of the official Marine Corps insignia, except that the cockade replaced the globe. Again, it was a case of arrival so near the end of the war (the last squadron of the unit did not land until October) that it is doubtful if the patches were widely used before the 1st Marine Aviation Force was shipped home.

The largest concentrated Marine force, the 4th Brigade, sailed for home about nine months after the Armistice. A notation from the Marine Corps Historical Center states: 'The 4th Marine Brigade arrived in the U.S. and was detached from service with the U.S. Army on 9 August 1919 and disbanded at Quantico, Virginia, 13 August 1919. Marines of the 4th Brigade discontinued wearing the 2nd Division shoulder patch when detached from service with the Army. Apparently, there was no written order.'

It was twenty-two years before U.S. Marines donned shoulder patches again.

Plate 8   USMC   Unit Insignia, World War II

In July of 1941, the 1st Marine Brigade (Provisional), landed in Iceland to replace the British garrison there that included the 49th (West Riding) Division. The U.S.A. was not yet at war, but through some of the political ma-neuvering of the time, it was decided that the Marines should 'protect' the somewhat reluctant Icelanders as the British troops, who were needed elsewhere, departed.

The commander of the British forces, Maj. Gen. Harry O. Curtis, as a gesture of good will, presented the Marine commander, Brig. Gen. John Marston, with 4000 of the 49th Division's polar bear patches for distribution to his troops. Marston sought official permission for his Marines to wear the patch, but it was never given. The Marines started wearing the patch anyway. It was worn, British-style, on both sleeves with the bear facing forward. This prac-tice was extended briefly to the 1st Division patch when it was adopted. Thereafter, patches were worn only on the left sleeve. It was pointed out in official circles at that time that the polar bear was not native to Iceland, and a similar patch had been used by an Army unit, the North Russia Expedition, in World War I.

Back in Britain, the 49th Division encountered dissatisfaction with its formation sign, too. Critics said that the polar bear had a bowed head, making it appear less than aggressive. The design was changed in 1943, showing the bear with raised head.

In March 1942, the last battalion of U.S. Marines – still wearing the polar bear patch – sailed for the U.S.A. Their country had been in the war for three months by then, and the Marine Corps part of that war would be largely in the Pacific theater of operations.

A year after the Marines left Iceland, Gen. Thomas Holcomb, Marine Corps commandant, issued the first letter of authorization for shoul-der patches of World War II. What the Marines initially had in mind for these insignia can only be guessed at now, since there were apparently no written records kept. But, because the patches were widely referred to as 'battle blazes' when first authorized, it seems that some thought must have been given to keying the insignia to the battles fought by the units.

The first U.S. offensive in the Pacific in World War II took place on the Solomon Islands, with the Island of Guadalcanal as the center of the thrust by the 1st Marine Division. The division, the first unit of that size in the history of the Corps, had been formed in February 1941. When its shoulder patch was approved in 1943, it was indeed a 'battle blaze'. The central point of the patch was a red Arabic numeral '1', similar to that used by the Army's 1st 'Big Red One' Infantry Division. But the Marine patch had the word 'Guadalcanal' embroidered in white letters down the length of the numeral. It was placed on a diamond-shaped, medium-blue background. The five stars of the constellation of the Southern Cross, under which the battle for the Solomons took place, are embroidered on the diamond, bordering all sides of the numeral. The patch was designed by Lt Col. Merrill B. Twining, division operations officer.

As with nearly all World War II Marine Corps patches, some variations took place, particularly at the onset of their use. Primarily, these were in the background material, which included twill, felt and fully embroidered.

The 2nd Marine Division, which also had units fighting on Guadalcanal, attempted to follow the 'battle blaze' path set by the 1st Division. The 2nd Division patch, virtually a duplicate of the 1st's, was worn for a short time before it was disapproved by Marine Corps Headquarters as being too similar to the patch worn by the 1st. It was a white-bordered, blue diamond with a red snake twisted to form a primitive numeral two, bordered by the Southern Cross. The word 'Guadalcanal' in yellow thread was embroidered down the length of the snake. The patch finally approved for the 2nd Division retained only the Southern Cross; otherwise, it was completely different. It consisted of a spearhead-shaped scarlet background with a white hand holding aloft a lighted gold torch. The scarlet numeral two is superimposed on the torch. There were variations in this patch, too, particularly in the color of the hand. One variation illustrated here shows the patch as heart shaped rather than spear shaped. It is doubtful if the heart-shaped patch was ever actually worn.

The expanding Marine Corps was eventually

to have six divisions before the end of World War II. The 1st Division's patch was to be the only divisional insignia that did not consist primarily of the official Marine Corps colors of scarlet and gold.

The battle blaze idea seemed to have been shelved after the 2nd Division's unsuccessful attempt, although some members of the 1st Division reportedly sewed tabs (flashes) with the name 'Cape Gloucester' above their patches when they returned from the battle for that town on the coast of New Britain Island. If they actually did, it was short-lived, and the tab was never approved.

The Marine Corps Historical Center puts the shape of the 3rd Marine Division patch in something close to layman's language when it is described as a 'scarlet triangular shield with a narrow gold line near the outer edge.' It had earlier been described in an official release as a 'scarlet patch in the shape of an equilateral curvilinear triangle.' The insignia, authorized in August of 1943, also contained a three-pointed device in the center which the Historical Center described as a 'gold and black caltrop, an ancient military instrument with four metal points so disposed that any three of them being on the ground, the other projects upward thereby impeding the progress of the enemy's cavalry.' The three visible points of the device also represent the division's number.

The 4th Marine Division patch consists of a scarlet patch with a gold block numeral '4' edged in white in the center. Although there seems to be no official record of it, the central design supposedly evolved because of the pattern of the Japanese airstrip on the twin islands of Roi and Namur in the Marshall chain where the newly formed 4th won a vital victory early in 1944. From the air, the landing strip appeared to be a giant numeral '4'.

The 5th Marine Division apparently was the only division in the Corps to hold a contest to select a design for its shoulder patch. The winner, out of 588 entrants, was 1st Lt Fergus F. Young. It consists of a scarlet crusader's shield bordered in gold. A blue spearhead superimposed on a gold Roman numeral 'V' is in the center of the shield. The spearhead signifies the role of Marines in spearheading amphibious operations, and the 'V' symbolizes both the number of the division and 'victory'. The design was approved in March 1944.

No contest was held for the 6th Marine Division's patch design, but it seemed to be the product of a committee. The busiest of all the divisional patches, the insignia is a cobalt-blue oval with a scarlet border. Wreathing the border are the words, 'Melanesia', 'Micronesia', and 'Orient' in gold, separated by five-pointed gold stars. In the center is a gold block numeral '6' shaded in white, superimposed on a white crusader's sword. A variant has the numeral shaded in red. Credited with contributing to the design were Maj. Gen. Lemuel C. Shepherd, Jr, commander of the 6th Division; Cpl Michael W. Pawl, 29th Marine Regiment; Col. Victor Bleasdale, and Lt George Thompson, the artist who actually drew and colored the design.

The elements of the patch were largely associated with the feats of some of the individual units that had been gathered under the umbrella of the 6th Marine Division. The word 'Melanesia' commemorates the Raider Battalions comprising the 4th Marine Regiment, which fought in the Solomon Islands. 'Micronesia' is for the fighting of the 29th Regiment in the Marshalls, 1st Battalion, 29th Regiment at Saipan and the 1st Provisional Marine Brigade at Guam. Finally, the word 'Orient' was selected to signify the long service of the old 4th Regiment in China, and the fact that the division was on the road back to the Orient, heading for Japan. The crusader's sword was symbolic of the crusade against the Axis.

The Marine Corps' philosophy of having its own close air support for its ground troops led to a burgeoning air arm during World War II. By the end of the war in the Pacific, the Marines had an HQ organization and four aircraft wings.

At the onset of World War II, before shoulder patches were authorized for Marines, the 1st and 2nd Marine Aircraft Wings had shield-shaped insignia painted on the fuselages of their aircraft. The shields were scarlet with wings, stars and Roman numerals in yellow-gold. The 1st Wing had one star above stylized wings and the numeral 'I' below. The 2nd Wing had two stars and the Roman numeral 'II'.

The design was transferred to shoulder patches after their authorization and included a patch for Headquarters, Aircraft, Fleet Marine Force, Pacific, which was the basic design with two stars above the wings and a coronet below. The 3rd and 4th Wings were added with the appropriate Roman numeral and number of stars to fit each designation. Because this design first appeared on the fuselages of aircraft, it was often called the 'fuselage' patch in collecting circles, and over the years, began to be identified on sales and trade lists, and even in books, as the Marine Aircraft Fuselage, despite the total ridiculousness of the term.

The confusion started because, early in the war, the patches for the Marine Aircraft Wings in the Pacific underwent a design change. The new design was a scarlet kite-shaped background with gold and black eagle, globe and anchor Marine emblem in the center, bordered at globe level by aviation wings. Below the emblem were the letters PAC for Pacific Air Command for the headquarters patch, and Roman numerals for the four Wings. Because of this change, some collectors, years after the war, believed the two sets of patches were from two separate Marine aviation units. Of course, they were the same unit. The later patches came from a design by Cpl Thomas J. Cooke of 3rd Aircraft Wing, which was approved in July 1943, and eventually adopted by all air wing units in the Pacific.

The first shoulder patch used by a Marine Amphibious Corps was a crimson shield with a gold alligator head centered below three five-pointed white stars, and was first known as Amphibious Corps, Pacific Fleet. The insignia later became the patch of Fifth Amphibious Corps. Third Amphibious Corps also had a crimson shield as a background, and featured a golden Chinese dragon centered below the Roman numeral 'III'. (Whereas the Army placed Roman numerals before 'Corps', pronounced as a letter, I as 'eye', the USMC placed numerals before 'Amphibious', pronounced as words.)

Despite all of the amphibious activity, the Corps still maintained ships' detachments with the fleets, and these Marines started wearing a shoulder patch in January 1944. It consisted of a scarlet diamond field with a golden sea horse superimposed on a blue anchor in the center. A variation has the anchor in black. It was designed by 1st Sgt K. F. Krollman of the U.S.S. *Massachusetts* Marine detachment.

Although most U.S. Marines served in the Pacific Theater of Operations in World War II, some did serve in Europe. The largest such unit was stationed in the Marine Barracks at Londonderry, Northern Ireland. The patch worn by these Marines consisted of a scarlet shield with a thin gold border just inside the rim, and a Marine insignia in gold and black above a green shamrock. Although the patch was widely worn,

it was disapproved by Marine Corps Headquarters. Most of the units stationed at Londonderry were disbanded by July 1945.

Plate 9 USMC Shoulder Patches, World War II

In December 1944, the Marine Corps extended authorization of the wearing of shoulder patches beyond the divisions, aircraft wings and certain smaller units that had received such authorization in March 1943.

The largest single unit to be authorized use of a shoulder patch was the Fleet Marine Force, Pacific, a sort of umbrella organization that apparently encompassed groups of specialized units not otherwise attached. The patch was a scarlet shield with a gold line forming an inside border and outlining an eagle's head and outstretched wings at the top. Under the eagle's wings are two gold lines with the letters 'FMF-PAC' in white in between. The eagle's head is also in white, as are three stars at each side and the bottom of a gold circle in the center of the patch which contained variable insignia to indicate individual units.

These units and their respective insignia are as follows:

Headquarters: two scarlet bolts of lighting clasped in a scarlet hand;
Command Service: a gold star superimposed on a small scarlet circle;
Anti-aircraft Artillery: a scarlet anti-aircraft gun and mount;
Amphibian Tractor Battalions: a scarlet amphibian tractor;
Dog Platoon: a scarlet dog's head;
Bomb Disposal Company: a scarlet bomb;
Separate Engineer Battalion: a scarlet castle;
Artillery Battalion: a scarlet cannon;
DUKW Company: a scarlet amphibian truck;
Unassigned: a black Marine Corps emblem. This particular patch was never officially authorized, although apparently it was worn by some Marines.

Although the use of shoulder patches for defense battalions was authorized in 1944, by the end of the war only four had been adopted.

The patch of the 13th Defense Battalion was a shield divided into three diagonal sections of red, white and blue, with a green sea horse outlined in cobalt blue superimposed in the center. Centered across the sea horse are the white letter 'FMF' standing for Fleet Marine Force.

The 18th Defense Battalion adopted an insignia that, at first glance, might easily be mistaken for an air unit's insignia. It consisted of a scarlet crusader's shield with gold wings in the center. A white broad sword is superimposed upon the center of the wings. The black numeral '18' overlays the wings with the '1' and '8' separated by the sword's blade.

The 51st and 52nd Defense Battalions represented what might be called social change for the Marine Corps. Recruiting regulations for the Corps dating to 1798 prohibited the enlistment of any 'Negro, Mulatto or Indian', although there were probably a few exceptions to this rule made knowingly or unknowingly over the years.

President Roosevelt sought to erase discrimination in the armed forces, and by mid-1941, steps in this direction had been taken. By August 1942, the first Negro recruits were being trained by the Marine Corps. They were, however, assigned to a segregated unit, the 51st Defense Battalion. Later, a second such segregated unit, the 52nd Defense Battalion, was activated. Both units had white officers, and it was not until November 1945 that the first Negro officer was commissioned in the Marine Corps.

The 51st Defense Battalion adopted for its insignia a red oval with a large white '51' in the center and the white letters 'USMC' below. Superimposed upon the '51' was a blue 90 mm anti-aircraft gun and mount.

The 52nd Defense Battalion adopted a red shield with a blue diagonal bar in the center upon which were superimposed four white stars. A gold 90 mm anti-aircraft gun and mount were in the lower half of the shield, and a gold shell burst with the scarlet letters 'USMC' was in the upper left-hand corner.

In 1937 the Secretary of the Navy decided that former Marines who had occasion to wear their old Marine uniforms in public needed some type of distinctive insignia to show they were no longer on active service. The insignia chosen was a diamond, $3\frac{1}{2}$ inches long, which was to be worn on the right sleeve of the uniform, $\frac{3}{4}$ of an inch below the shoulder seam. The diamond was to be white on blue, green and khaki uniforms, and blue on white uniforms, which were worn only by commissioned officers and warrant officers. The insignia was never widely used and was replaced by the so-called 'ruptured duck' which

was an emblem given to discharged members of all of the United States armed forces as World War II ended. It was a gold eagle facing right with wings spread through a ring. The background varied according to the color of the uniform, but was worn over the right breast pocket (not illustrated).

Another Marine Corps shoulder patch that was similar in function to the FMF-PAC patch, in that it was a basic patch with a multitude of uses, was that of First Marine Amphibious Corps. It consisted of a blue shield with three straight sides and a pointed bottom. The constellation of the Southern Cross in white, also used on the 1st Division patch, was used on the blue background. In the center was a scarlet diamond with a white border.

Authorized in July 1943, the patch originally was for use by six types of units which were to be designated by devices within the diamond. Headquarters was designated by a blank diamond. Others were:

Service and supply: a white star;
Aviation Engineers: a winged, white castle;
Raiders: a white skull;
Parachute Battalion: a white parachute;
Defense Battalion: a white anti-aircraft gun and mount.

Later, two other units were authorized to be included under the First MAC umbrella. They were barrage balloon units which used a white barrage balloon in the center of the diamond, and artillery units which used white crossed cannon barrels. Another type of unit which used the First MAC patch, although apparently not authorized to do so, was tank destroyer outfits which used a white tank destroyer vehicle on the diamond. Like almost all Marine Corps shoulder patches, there were variations, sometimes with slight color or shape differences. Most of these patches could be found in versions that were fully embroidered, or on twill or felt backgrounds.

Plate 10 USMC Medals, Shooting Badges, Wings, etc.

As a naval service, the Marine Corps' members have long shared the decorations and medals designed for the Navy. There are, however, some medals and one decoration that are or have been exclusively for Marines.

The oldest medal designed exclusively for Marines is the Good Conduct Medal, which was authorized on 20 July 1896 and designed by Maj. Gen. Charles Heywood, a commandant of the Corps. According to regulations, the obverse has a rope encircling a gunner and a gun (both appear to be Civil War period) with an anchor behind. The inscription reads 'United States Marine Corps'. The reverse of the medal has the name and serial number of the recipient, which enlistment the award is for and the final year of the enlistment. The medal is suspended by a ribbon with two broad stripes of medium red and a narrow center stripe of dark blue. The ribbon hangs from a rounded bar with a rope edge inscribed 'U.S. Marine Corp'. At the bottom of the ribbon is a clasp in the shape of a musket. The medal is awarded only to enlisted men and is for 'obedience, sobriety, military efficiency, neatness, bearing and intelligence'. Bars engraved with the number of enlistments are attached to the ribbon for subsequent awards. When the ribbon only is worn, a yellow metal number for each award is affixed to the blue stripe.

The Marine Corps Brevet Medal was designed and authorized long after the actions for the award had taken place and was held by only 23 men, three of whom had also been awarded the Congressional Medal of Honor, the highest decoration offered by the United States Government. In fact, the ribbon for the medal is similar to that of the Congressional Medal. The Brevet Medal has 13 white stars on a deep red ribbon, while the Congressional Medal has the same pattern with a medium blue ribbon.

The Brevet Medal was designed by Marine Quartermaster Sergeant Joseph A. Burnett. It is a bronze cross pattee with a smooth, raised edge border around the mottled arms of the cross. In the center a smooth circle surrounds the words, 'United States Marine Corps' with a single star at the bottom of the circle. An inner circle contains the stylized lettering of the word 'Brevet'. The reverse is smooth with the words 'For Distinguished Service' arching around the words 'In the presence of the enemy'. A miniature Marine Corps emblem suspends the medal from the ribbon.

Following World War I, Maj. Gen. John A Lejeune, the Marine Commandant, felt a special award should be given to officers who received Brevet Commissions in combat during the Mexican War, the Civil War, the Spanish-American War, the Philippine Insurrection and the Boxer Rebellion. The men who received the commissions had nothing other than a certificate to show for the award. So on 7 June 1921, the decoration was authorized and presented to the 23 living men eligible to receive it. It has not been awarded since. Almost any example of it that shows up in collectors circles is either a rare authentic prize, or more likely a bootleg replica, since it is illegal to duplicate or even sell (trades are all right) U.S. military decorations. Ribbons and miniatures can be sold.

Incidentally, the term 'decoration' is applied to those awards made for bravery in action, even though the word 'medal' appears in the title of some of these awards. The term 'medal' generally applies to awards for service during specific campaigns. The latter in the United States Navy usually has two reverses – one for the Navy, the other for the Marines, but otherwise are usually identical. The difference is usually only in the wording of the inscriptions on the reverse, either 'United States Navy' or 'United States Marine Corps'.

The Marine Corps has its own Expeditionary Medal awarded for landings on foreign shores in which armed opposition is encountered and for which no other specific campaign medal is awarded. The ribbon has two narrow red stripes on either side with two broad gold stripes bordering a broad red stripe in the center. The medal itself shows a Marine with full field pack charging ashore through the waves with a fixed bayonet. The word 'Expedition' arches around the figure. The reverse has an eagle perched on an anchor and a branch and the words, 'For Service – United States Marine Corps'.

The Marine Corps Reserve Medal is awarded to reservists after four year service. It was authorized on 19 February 1939. The obverse shows a Marine and civilian walking side-by-wide and the words, 'Marine Corps Reserve' and 'For service'. The reverse has the words, 'Fidelity, Zeal and Obedience'.

The Marine Corps emphasizes marksmanship and has a good supply of medals to award for this skill. The Distinguished Marksman and Distinguished Pistol Shot medals are both gold and are the highest awards for marksmanship.

The Lauchheimer Trophy Medal is awarded for annual competition in small-arms firing and is presented in three degrees – gold, silver and bronze – by the family of the late Brig. Gen. Charles H. Lauchheimer. Both the Marine Corps Rifle and Pistol Competition Medals are awarded in gold, silver and bronze. The Expert Rifleman and Sharpshooter Badges are shown in the early style without a Marine Corps emblem affixed and in the current style. The basic qualification badge can be worn with a great number of weapons bars depending on the skill of the holder. The Marksman badge can be worn with requalification bars with the years for requalification inscribed.

Marines wear the same aviation badges as their counterparts in the Navy. Few need explanation, but the pilot's wings with a Marine emblem overlaying the shield was never authorized, and those that have shown up in collecting circles appear to be homemade. The Naval Aviator's badge was authorized in 1919, and others followed one at a time. The Combat Air Crew Member was adopted during World War II. The larger Air Crew Member Wings in gold were authorized after the war for non-combat service.

The first jump wings used by Marine parachutists were the same as those used by the Army and continue to be used today as the basic badge. The Marines and Navy personnel qualified as parachutists share the gold wings which are awarded after five jumps are made with an assigned unit.

The Marines have also shared some other insignia with the Navy in the past and some areas today. The gunpointer cloth badge (*note plate annotation is wrong*) was worn on the right sleeve. Specialty marks were worn on the right sleeve and were in use for a brief period by Marines during World War II and were red on green for the winter service uniform and gold on red for the dress blues. A few are illustrated here. Aviation general utilitymen wore plain wings; aviation radiomen wore lightning bolts; aviation machinists mates wore wings with a propeller, aviation metalsmiths wore crossed hammers in the center of wings, aviation ordnancemen wore wings with a bursting bomb. Many others were also authorized.

Navy hospital corpsmen have served alongside of Marines in several wars and have often worn Marine uniforms when on duty with that service. Shown here is an illustration of a rating badge for a hospital corpsman second class, worn with Marine greens. The red cross also is used for the pharmacist mate specialty. Third class petty officers wear one chevron, first class three, and chiefs three with a rocker. The rating badge for a hospital corpsman is the pay grade E-3. Only the

greens, field clothing and khaki shirts are worn by naval personnel serving with Marines. The full khaki Marine uniform has now been discontinued in favor of a lightweight summer green that matches the winter uniform. When dress uniforms are called for the sailors don their own blues. When in Marine uniforms they wear special lapel badges of black shields bearing the medical caduceus symbol. A 'D' is worn over the caduceus by those in the dental branch.

Plates 11 and 12 USMC Aviation

Aircraft insignias were born during World War I and were used by all branches of service with aircraft, including the U.S. Marines. Although the insignia shown in the center of the page of Plate 11 was used in general on Marine aircraft during World War I, it is often thought of as the distinctive insignia of the 1st Marine Aviation Force which saw service in France in the closing months of the war. The insignia, in addition to being painted on the sides of their aircraft, was also worn as a shoulder patch by unit members.

Most Marine aviation units use the designation 'VM' to indicate Marine aircraft and one or two following letters to indicate the type of service the plane is used for. VMF means fighter, VMB, bomber, VMA, attack, and so on.

Some of the units started out as one type and were redesignated as another, particularly older units, but kept the same insignia. One example is shown at the bottom of Plate 11. This is the famed fighter squadron that fought at Wake Island in the early days of World War II. It was designated 'VMF 211' at that time, but has since become VMA 211, an attack squadron. The illustration is a variation and is more colorful than the original, which had a brown lion and brown outlined islands of the atoll on a white background.

Counting those currently in use and those that have been authorized over the years, there have probably been more than 1000 Marine aircraft insignia not including variations. Only a few examples can be illustrated here. Few need to be explained. The letters HMM mean Marine Medium Helicopter Squadron; MACS, Marine Air Control Squadron; MAG, Marine Aircraft Group, and HMX, Marine Helicopter Experimental.

Insignias of several units that won wartime fame are illustrated. One of them, on plate 12, is Marine Fighter Squadron 214, the 'Black

Sheep' of Col. Gregory R. 'Pappy' Boyington, a former Flying Tiger, who was the top Marine ace of World War II with 28 victories. The bar sinister on the insignia signifies an illegitimate son. Under 'Pappy' the squadron was known as 'Boyington's Bastards' and legend has it that those who were misfits in other outfits were shipped to 214 where they felt right at home. They flew the Corsair, a part of their insignia.

The insignias were not only painted on sides of aircraft, but worn as patches on flight jackets. Some during World War II were hand painted on leather, and some were painted directly on the jackets. Most produced today are embroidered.

During World War II, the Walt Disney Studios mobilized Mickey Mouse and Donald Duck and sent them to war in the form of unit insignias, many of which were for aircraft outfits. Marine Fighter Squadron 223 may be one of the Disney designs, because the Marine bulldog in boxing gloves seems to be in the Disney style. Relatively few Marine aircraft insignia seemed to employ Latin mottoes, but one shown here, Marine Bombing Squadron 524 shows a top hatted death's head with the motto 'Caedentes superbi' above, which roughly translates as 'arrogant slayers'. (*Plate 11: top left is patch of VMFAW-114.*)

Plates 13 and 14   USMC   Junior Reserve Officer Training Corps, 4th Marine Division Reserve

Although Junior Reserve Officers' Training Corps units have been in American high schools (secondary schools) for decades, they were always Army JROTC units until the 1960s, when, first Navy, then Marine Corps JROTC units were approved. The Marine Corps JROTC program was authorized in 1966 and was installed in high schools throughout the USA, principally in major metropolitan areas, since one of the requirements for eligibility is for the school to attain and maintain an enrollment of 100 eligible cadets 14 years of age or older. No more than 1200 schools may participate.

Unlike senior ROTC programs in US colleges and universities, the junior program does not lead to an officer's commission or any other special advantage if a cadet later joins a branch of the regular armed forces. The junior program is designed to develop informed responsible citizens, strengthen character by the teaching of disci-

pline, and develop an understanding of the responsibilities of citizenship.

The cadets wear USMC uniforms with ROTC insignia. Cadet officers wear silver disc rank devices for 2nd lieutenant through captain and silver diamonds for major through colonel. Noncoms wear USMC-style chevrons with a lamp of learning emblem below the stripes.

A universal USMC JROTC patch is worn on the left shoulder and patches designed for the individual participating high school are worn on the right shoulder. The second patch in the top row is that of the Marine Military Academy in Harlingen, Texas, a private institution that is the only military academy in the U.S.A. with MCROTC. The patch for United Naval and Marine Cadets is not fully identified, but may represent an amalgamated unit. The patch for the 'Young Marines' is worn with individual State identifications. This is not an ROTC or cadet program, but an auxiliary of the Marine Corps League, an organization of veterans.

MCJROTC members can be awarded ribbons (but not medals) for various achievements as cadets. Small metal devices, such as the lamp of learning, can be attached to ribbons for a second award. Various shooting badges are also awarded.

The 4th Marine Division (Reinforced) is currently the division made up of Marine Corps reservists who undergo, in their individual units, two weeks of active duty training annually, in addition to weekend duties throughout the year. Some of the operations the division has been engaged in over the years have been commemorated by novelty patches handed out to participants. (*Note: 'Bridgeport, Ca.' not 'Co'.*)

Plate 15   USMC   Novelty Patches

Although the Marine Corps abolished the use of shoulder patches on 23 September 1947, distinctive designs for various units within the Corps continued to be used on signs at camp sites, letterheads, shooting jacket emblems and so forth. In 1956, Headquarters Marine Corps approved the use of organizational distinguishing marks for use on about anything but official uniforms. The former shoulder patch designs are now used as organizational distinguishing marks.

Often called 'novelty patches', the emblems began to pop up during the Korean War and hit full stride during the Vietnam War. Just a few examples are shown here. Many adopted were based on World War II divisional patches.

The emblem of the 1st Recon Battalion is reminiscent of the 1st Marine Division patch in shape and coloration. 'Swift, silent, deadly' was a popular motto for Marine units during the Vietnam War. The 3rd Recon Battalion, which had elements of the 3rd Marine Division insignia in its emblem, also used the motto. The 2nd Recon Company, with the Fleet Marine Force, Atlantic, used a Pathfinder-type emblem.

Strictly a novelty patch, and more of a joke than an emblem, the Korean War corruption of the 1st Marine Division patch clearly showed the sentiment of the troops stationed there with a hand with extended forefinger expressing the universal sign of disgust.

Another somewhat risqué theme pops up in the novelty patch of the Military Police of the Marine Corps Air Station, Iwakuni, Japan. It features the stuttering cartoon character, Porky Pig, giving an order that might be considered vulgar. Marine MPs today wear brassards with the gold initials MP on a red arm band. During World War II, the brassard was navy blue with white letters which, unlike the Army's, were separated by periods.

Another Vietnam era patch is the 1st Guerrillas Company. The Marine Corps Tree Planting Program was a Corps sponsored venture in 1975. The patch was given to participants in the program. They were not necessarily Marines.

The patch two below the tree planting patch is supposedly for the 1st Coastal Shore Guard and was used in Korea. It apparently is an unofficial patch. The First 90 mm Anti-Aircraft Artillery patch is also of the Vietnam era.

The 9th Marine Amphibious Brigade operated from Okinawa and in Vietnam during the 1960s and 1970s. The trident shows its sea-related nature, the map its area of operations. The patch of the Military Assistance Advisory Group (MAAG) Taiwan is probably unofficial since it is the same as the Army's, except that it has a Marine emblem overlaid. The Special Service Troop of the 1st Marine Division served in Vietnam.

Plate 16 Royal Marines Cap, Lapel and Officers Insignia

The cap badge worn by the Royal Marines since the amalgamation of the RMLI and RMA in 1923 is the lion and the crown (the distinguishing badge of a Royal regiment) over the globe which is surrounded by a laurel wreath. Officers and warrant officers wear a divided badge with the lion and crown separate from and above the globe and laurel. For dress, the badge is gilt with a silver globe for officers and anodized in gold color for other ranks. Lapel badges and collar badges have the globe and laurel only. For officers, the badge is a silver globe in an anodized laurel wreath or the same badge in bronze. Other ranks wear the badge in yellow metal, anodized or bronze.

In place of the Corps cap badge, all officers above lieutenant colonel wear Army pattern badges – colonels and brigadiers, the lion and crown, and general officers, a crossed sword and baton in a wreath surmounted by a crown. Colonels and above wear the Corps Crest on the lapels of mess dress uniforms. Since 1953, the Corps badge has been topped by what is generally known by collectors as the 'Queen's crown'. Prior to that, and dating back to the end of the Victorian era, the crown was the 'King's crown'. Many of the latter became available to collectors after the Coronation of Her Majesty Queen Elizabeth II, when the crown was changed.

The helmet plate shown here is what is termed the 'other ranks' plate, although it is worn generally by officers, too. The so-called officers' pattern, which has a silver globe and a blue enamel circle with the gold lettering of the Corps motto, is out of production, although a few are kept on hand and issued on a temporary loan basis for special ceremonial occasions at some RM bases. The plate is worn on the white Wolseley pattern helmet. RM regulations describe it as an eight-pointed star with dead and bright rays and a crown above. On the star is a laurel wreath on the inside of which is a garter with the Corps motto. 'Per Mare Per Terram' (By Sea By Land) surmounting the globe, and above the garter a scroll with the word 'Gibraltar' and below it an anchor.

Officers rank badges follow the Army pattern. Although until recently the rank of general was held by the Commandant General of the Royal Marines, the top rank today is lieutenant general. Although not illustrated on the shoulder straps on Plate 16, officers below the rank of colonel wear the letters 'R.M.' in $\frac{1}{2}$-inch block letters below the badges of rank. In the field today the rank badges are black cloth and may be worn on removable slip-on sleeves. Until fairly recent times, the stars (often called 'pips' by collectors) crowns and crossed batons and swords, which make up the rank badges, were usually in metal, although some embroidered versions existed. During World War II worsted badges were worn on battledress and after the war these were worn on a worsted background. Today most of the badges worn are anodized or bronze.

The belt buckle worn by other ranks features the lion and crown with GIBRALTAR and the Corps motto encircling it.

In 1918, King George V directed that the senior recruit squad at the Royal Marine Depot in Deal be designated the 'King's Squad' and the best recruit in the squad be awarded the gold wire embroidered King's badge that bore his cypher within a wreath. The practice of awarding this badge continues to this day. In 1978, Prince Philip, the Duke of Edinburgh, instituted the Prince's Badge, which bears his cypher within a lyre topped by a coronet. This badge is silver wire embroidered and is awarded to the best musician or bugler on completion of training under conditions similar to the award of the King's badge but whilst the latter is awarded to every squad, the Prince's badge is only given annually.

Plates 17 and 18   Royal Marines   Other Ranks Rating, Cloth Shoulder Insignia, etc.

The use of chevrons to indicate rank of non-commissioned officers in the Royal Marines appears to have become established in 1807. Over the years the stripes have had various thicknesses and colors, but today they are principally of two types, the gold on green worn on the Lovat uniform and the gold on red worn on the blue uniform. White on khaki (not illustrated) is worn on khaki shirts and sometimes in reduced versions worn on armlets. The current chevrons are shown on Plate 17, and the types used in World War II on Plate 18. During that war and while battledress was being worn, the herringbone chevrons were often made white by Royal Marines using a whitening substance made for belts, helmets, etc. Red on blue chevrons were issued for blue uniforms, and the gold on red ceased to be issued.

Senior non-commissioned officers – Regimental Sergeants Major and Quartermaster Sergeants – wore, respectively, the Royal Arms and a crown in a laurel wreath. The insignia of the Royal Arms is now worn by Warrant Officers

1st Class, and the crown in a wreath by Warrant Officers 2nd Class. The title of Regimental Sergeant Major is now an appointment instead of a rank and is held by a Warrant Officer 1st Class.

Shoulder sleeve insignia, were apparently used officially by the Royal Marines during World War II. Some of the patches started out to represent one unit, then had the designation changed. The gold trident on red segment was the Royal Marine Division sign between 1941 and 1943, then became the badge of the 116th Brigade which was composed of the 27th, 28th and 30th Royal Marine Battalions. The golden sea horse partly in a blue circle on a red triangle was the sign for the 104th Training Brigade.

The 117th Brigade was formed in 1945 and consisted of the 31st, 32nd and 33rd Battalions. Its sign was an eight-pointed gold star with an inner circle of red on which a gold foul anchor was centered. The patch had a khaki background. The R.M. Siege Regiment was an artillery outfit between 1940 and 1945. It dipped back into the old Royal Marine Artillery for its bursting grenade badge, which was red on a khaki background.

The 34th Amphibian Support Regiment came along late in the war and existed from 1945 to 1946. Its insignia was a blue shield overlaid by a red triangle on which a gold foul anchor was centered. Royal Marine Engineers used a blue shield with a red anchor, white rope and gold bursting grenade. Royal Marines wore two types of combined operations patches, but the rounded one, which was usually trimmed from the arch-shaped one, was the type most often seen. The patch consisted of an eagle, anchor and submachine gun in red on a blue background. These color combinations were also used for most R.M. shoulder titles, although a lighter blue background was seen on some of those used early in the war. Some of the titles used the words 'Royal Marines' only, and others combined these with the word 'Commando', and still others used the number of the Commando. Royal Marine Commandos also wore a triangular-shaped black patch with a red fighting knife in the Special Service Group from 1944–46 and in the 3rd Commando Brigade from 1946 until 1964. The only shoulder flash still in use (other than by the R.M. band service) is the Royal Marines Commando title, which is worn on the so-called 'woolly-pully' khaki sweater. There is also a scarlet diamond worn on the left arm by recruits under training appointed section leaders.

A number of insignia known officially as branch, specialist qualification, skill and special badges are worn by qualified Royal Marines. Senior NCOs above colour sergeant do not wear branch or specialist qualification badges. Colour sergeants wear branch badges on the right arm a quarter inch above the point of slash. NCOs below that rank wear it on the right arm above the chevrons, fitted into the 'V' of the chevrons as close as possible. Others wear the badges on the right arm, six inches below the shoulder seam. Radio technicians (Light) wear a circle with three lightning flashes on each side. Other tradesmen wear a hammer and pincers crossed. Band members wear a metal lyre with oak leaves below and crown above, while buglers wear an embroidered drum.

Specialist qualification badges, often called 'tombstones' because of their shape are worn above chevrons on the right arm for 1st Class except by colour sergeants and on the left lower sleeve by most other NCOs and Marines for 2nd Class. Not more than one of these badges can be worn. There are 13 basic badges. Most contain the letters of the specialist qualification inside a wreath. They range from Assault Engineer (AE) to Swimmer Canoeist (SC). Those that use devices rather than letters are Drill and Platoon Weapons Instructors, crossed rifles; Driver, steering wheel; Physical Training Instructors, crossed clubs, and Signaller, crossed flags.

There are different grades of specialist qualification badges indicated as follows: Instructors (except DL and PW), crown above badge and two stars below; first class, crown above badge; second class, star above and below badge, and third class, star above badge. Royal Marines on provost duty wear the same M.P. armband as provided for the Royal Military Police. It is worn immediately above the right elbow. When chevrons are worn, the armband should cover the lower point of the bottom chevron with the 'M' and 'P' on either side of the apex of the chevron.

Skill badges are worn on the left arm a quarter-inch above the point of slash, or a quarter-inch above a specialist qualification badge if one is worn. A Marksman wears crossed rifles and a sniper crossed rifles with the letter 'S' above. Observers wear a single gold wing attached to a silver 'O' surmounted by a crown.

Special badges include Naval Pilots' and Observers' badges worn by qualified RM officers.

The Naval Pilot badge consists of gold wings with a centered wreath enclosing a silver anchor surmounted by a crown. The Observers' badge had upward-thrust gold wings with an 'O'-shaped circle of rope containing a silver anchor. A crown tops the rope circle. These badges are worn on the left breast above ribbons or above the pocket when ribbons are not worn. Royal Marines are also entitled to wear the Army Pilots' badge. These are usually worn by pilots of light aircraft, particularly helicopters. On blue, Lovat and khaki tunics the wings are silver embroidered with gold lion and crown on a black or navy blue background and a red background for mess jackets. On combat dress the wings are light blue and the background khaki. They are worn in the same position as the Naval Pilots' badge.

Parachutists badges are worn on the sleeve of the right arm, two inches below the shoulder seam. There is some variety in this badge. On blue tunics it is worn full size in gold on blue. On Lovat tunics the badge is gold on green and is two-thirds the size of the full-sized badge. On khaki tunics the full-sized badge is worn in light blue, with white parachute on khaki drill. Officers, WOs and SNCOs wear a miniature gold on scarlet badge for mess dress. There is a badge widely accepted in collecting circles as a Royal Marine parachutist badge worn before battle-dresss was discontinued. It is red on black, which would have matched the shoulder flashes, Commando dagger, etc. of that period. However, it appears that the Royal Marines actually wore the Army pattern badge of light blue wings and white parachute on a khaki background, rather than red on black when battledress was worn.

A variety of shoulder strap initials have been worn over the years in gilt, brass, bronze, and now, anodized. They have usually been in half-inch and three quarter inch sizes. R.M.L.I. shoulder strap letters were worn by the Royal Marine Light Infantry and R.M.A. by the Royal Marine Artillery. Other combinations include R.M.P. for Royal Marine Police and R.M.B. for Royal Marine Band. Some special shoulder strap titles have been used in the past, e.g. R.M.E., R.M.L.C., R.M.S.M., respectively Enginers, Labour Corps and Submarine Mariners, the latter a World War I submarine – watching unit based along the East Coast. At one time Royal Marine Cadets also used special metal shoulder strap titles. Today, about the only variance from the letters 'R.M.' are those worn by the Royal

Marines Reserves – R.M.R. Before the Lovat uniform replaced battledress, the reserves also wore special shoulder flashes, the first having the words 'Royal Marine Forces' in red on a black arch over a straight bar with the words 'Volunteer Reserve'. Later the letters 'VR' were worn in red on black under the regular shoulder flash, and today the letter 'R' is worn.

Plates 19 and 20 Royal Marines Helmet Plates and Cap Badges

Shako and helmet plates used by the Royal Marines date back to about 1816 when the round-domed Artillery plate topped by a royal crest was first used. A foul anchor was in the center around which was a garter with the words 'Royal Marines Artillery' inscribed. The eight-pointed star first was used on the plates in 1839, but the globe in the center of the star did not appear until 1845, when an officers' plate that was topped by the Victorian crown became regulation. With relatively minor variations, except for the change of crowns, this pattern was used down through the years by the Royal Marine Light Infantry and is used by the Royal Marines today. The Royal Marine Artillery used a variety of bursting grenade with the 'Per Mare Per Terram' motto surrounding the globe in the center of the bomb and in 1905 adopted the universal helmet plate. The Royal Marines Bands had some variations in helmet plates with special added devices described in previous chapters. There often were variations in materials and colors in the plates of officers, NCOs and other ranks.

Cap badges used by the Royal Marine Light Infantry varied somewhat over the years but, in general, incorporated the stringed bugle or hunter's horn with the globe and laurel wreath. The RMA had the globe and laurel topped by the bursting grenade in 1921, although officers wore crossed cannon barrels over the globe and laurel during some periods. In the 1850s, the RMA also used special cap badges for NCOs that incorporated chevrons of rank with the flaming bomb.

A unique but short-lived Royal Marine cap badge was issued during World War I to members of the Royal Marines Labour Corps. Above the globe and laurel was a sailing ship, bow forward. It bears no resemblance to the badge of the Royal Army Service Corps, from which it was formed, it disbanded with the war's end. (*Plate annotation: insert 'Labour' before 'Corps'.*)

Plates 21 and 22 Netherlands Korps Mariniers, Officers Shirt Collar Insignia, Other Ranks Epaulet, Service Dress

The use of a crown and anchor as a headgear badge by the Corps Mariniers of the Netherlands dates back to the early 1800s when crossed anchors were used on a brass helmet plate below a crown. Double anchors were used until the end of the nineteenth century. About 1900, the badge of a crown over a foul anchor appeared on the peaked, flat topped caps of officers and has remained essentially the same to date. During and immediately after World War II, it came in both yellow metal and dark bronze versions. Today, this badge is worn in metal only on the beret where it is affixed at an angle on a red arch-shaped patch. Embroidered crowns and anchors appear on the white peaked caps and have backgrounds of varying shapes depending on rank. Junior officers wear a small wreath below the anchor, while officers from staff through flag grades wear a full wreath. Staff and flag officers wear 'scrambled eggs' gilt wreath patterns on the visors of their caps.

The helmet plate worn on the spiked, cork helmet for ceremonial occasions is an eight-pointed star surmounted by a crown with the Royal Dutch Lion in a center circle surrounded by a belt with the motto 'Je Maintiendrai' resting on a wreath over crossed anchors.

The Dutch Marines use the Naval Rank insignia with Army titles for officers and warrant officers. The rank devices also come in yellow metal miniatures for wear on shirt collars. The top Korps Mariniers rank today is Major General, which is held by the commandant.

Non-commissioned officers wear chevrons on both sleeves on dress and blue service uniforms and slip on shoulder straps with rank devices for field jackets. The shoulder knots are worn on the ceremonial dress uniforms and are gold for officers and warrant officers and red for other ranks. During World War II, the navy blue uniforms had shoulder straps trimmed with red and yellow borders for NCOs and red for other ranks.

An embroidered shoulder patch is worn today on khaki shirts and some combat jackets. The words 'Korps Mariniers' are in red above a gold crown and star emblem with the wreath in green and the interior circle blue. The Corps' motto 'Qua Patet Orbis' – 'As far as the world goes' – is on a scroll below. This symbol in black was also worn on the left breast pocket of fatigue jackets by Dutch Marines serving in the Pacific during World War II.

A curved shoulder title in khaki with the border and words 'Korps Mariniers' in black was used on khaki shirts and other field clothing during the 1950s. During World War II, a number of shoulder flashes were worn, including a straight flash in dark khaki with the words 'Korps Mariniers' in dark red. Other versions had the English words 'Netherlands Marines' in red on khaki or forestry green.

Parachute qualified members of the Corps wear their wings on the right breast of their tunics. The wings come in basic pattern and master grade which has a star below the parachute.

Plate 23 Netherlands Korps Mariners, Speciality Rating Sleeve Badges; and France

As part of the Royal Netherlands Navy, the Korps Mariniers share many of the same badges, including the speciality rating sleeve badges. The twelve specialist rating badges most used by the Dutch Marines are illustrated on Plate 23, and their titles, in general, require no further explanation. The Commando Training Badge is not, strictly speaking, a speciality rating and is worn in various forms, including metal, by all services.

France, Fusiliers Marins, Amphibious Troops

The Fusiliers Marins are the infantry of the French Navy and today are all Commando trained. During World Wars I and II, they wore cap tallies with the words 'Fusiliers Marins' in gold on a black band on the traditional French sailor cap with a red pom pom. Although they still wear the French Naval uniforms, they also wear special combat clothing that includes a green beret with a bronze Marine Commando badge that was adopted in 1944. During World War II, Fusiliers Marins wore bursting grenade speciality sleeve badges in red, gold and silver thread. Today they wear crossed rifles in the same colors as a speciality badge.

During World War II, they also wore a curved shoulder flash with the words 'Fusiliers Marins' in red on black. The same type shoulder title was also worn in Indochina in the 1950s. Distinctive metal badges for these French Naval Infantry-

men were also worn as breast insignias in both of those conflicts. Other shoulder titles include those for the Amphibious Center and Commandos. The latter is still worn and comes in red on black, blue on white and gold on navy blue. As an integral part of the Navy, the Fusiliers are eligible for most Navy speciality badges, including parachutists wings, which are worn on the right breast.

Former French colonial troops began being redesignated as Marines in the 1960s, although they are a part of the French Army and are not, strictly speaking, Marines in the sense of the U.S. or British usage of the term. Since the old Colonial Army units used the anchor as a basic insignia for decades, the new Army 'Marines' continue to do so and some of these insignia are illustrated.

Plates 24, 25 and 26 Spain Infanteria de Marina, Cap Badges, Sleeve Ratings, School Crests

The Spanish Infanteria de Marina uses both a crown and a coronet over an anchor with crossed rifles as cap badges, and the former on shoulder straps of other ranks' dress uniforms. The coronet is used above the crossed rifles on the beret badge.

Officers wear both shoulder boards and sleeve insignia as rank devices depending on the uniform. Non-commissioned officers wear diagonal sleeve stripes. Between 1537 and 1931, the insignia was a crown over crossed anchors. The Corps was temporarily disbanded in 1931, and when it was revived toward the end of the 1930s, the crown, anchor and crossed rifles was adopted.

Coats of arms for various speciality schools and other Corps functions are or have been used over the years, and a few have been selected for illustration on this plate. The motto, 'Por Tierra Y Por Mar' means 'By Land and by sea', virtually the same as that of the British Royal Marines.

Plates 27 and 28 Italy San Marco Battalion and Lagunari; Italian Social Republic San Marco Battalion; and Portugal

One of the more confusing areas for insignia collectors is found in the matter of Italian amphibious units, since during World War II rival governments – one siding with the Allies, the other with the Axis – both fielded units using the same names and virtually the same insignia.

The San Marco Battalion was the name given a naval infantry unit following World War I in honor of St Mark, patron saint of the City of Venice, which the unit defended. It adopted the city's symbolic Lion of St Mark as its insignia. Although the unit apparently had a strength of more than one battalion between wars (some San Marcos were stationed in China), the cap tallies worn on the traditional sailor caps and sun helmets used the wording 'Battaglione San Marco' or 'Battaglione S. Marco'. The insignias at the left and right of Plate 27 under the cap tally are in current use. The one on the right is a breast badge worn by a Naval Raiding Group, and the one on the left is for a Marine/Naval Headquarters Company.

During World War II, the San Marcos fought against the Allies in North Africa, but, following the Armistice, joined the Allies in fighting the Germans. Mussolini, meanwhile, formed the Italian Social Republic in the north and eventually a 'San Marco' Division was formed there to fight against the Allies.

In the top half of Plate 27 several different Lion of St Mark insignias are illustrated. In the second row flanking the beret badge currently worn by the San Marcos are the cloth cuff patches worn by enlisted men in units loyal to the monarchy during World War II. Below the beret badge is a breast badge currently in use. On either side of it are the white on black patches worn to denote the company of the wearer during the war in Ethiopia. The two collar tabs at either end of the fourth row were worn by officers. The one on the left is currently in use. The three shoulder titles were used by members of those battalions in what was now a regiment.

The anchor sleeve badge leading off the fifth row was given to enlisted men assigned to all companies of the unit. The rifle sleeve insignia was awarded to expert riflemen, the machinegun to experts with that weapon, and the crossed cannon to those assigned to artillery units. The eagle, parachute and dagger was a metal breast badge worn by members of the Nautical Parachute Battalion.

The bottom part of the page shows some of the insignia worn by the Republican San Marcos and similar units. The Lion of St Mark bore the Latin motto for 'The Lion Roars Again' and held a closed bible, which, according to regulations, was the way the insignia was to appear during wartime. The Monarchist San Marcos in the south, however, failed to observe this and continued to use the insignias with the bible open and the inscription 'Peace to you, Mark my Evangelist'. The Republicans used the star under the lion on lapel tabs for a short time, then substituted the 'gladio', a gladiator's sword on a wreath. The tabs appeared in various colors and forms. A Marine-type unit, the 10th Flotilla Anti-Submarine Motor Boat, was redesignated the 10th Division and had a distinctive insignia of a death's head with a rose in its teeth over a Roman numeral 'X'. It also had its own parachutist badge and one for para-swimmers. The Republican San Marco artillery wore a yellow metal breast badge of a foul anchor over crossed cannon barrels.

A number of distinctive insignia were worn, including the para-swimmer school badge, with a fish curved around a sword blade. The 'Lupo' or Wolf battalion of the San Marcos and the 'Barbarigo' Battalion of the 10th Division pictured a ship with that title on its bow and the words 'Front of Neptune' at the top of the wreath. Both the Roman numeral 'X' and the foul anchor were worn on steel helmets by Fascist amphibious units.

Following the war, the San Marcos were disbanded and remained so until revived in the 1960s. Between those periods an Army unit called the 'Lagunari' was formed and used San Marco-type insignia. Its cap, breast and cuff badges are illustrated. It is still in service.

Portugal, Marine Corps

The Portuguese Marine Corps is an integral part of the Navy, and its members wear naval insignia. A distinctive breast and beret badge is worn consisting of a dagger within a wreath. A number of coats-of-arms are also used by this Corps. Among them are those of the Portuguese Marine Corps Command, which features three red lions; the Marine School, with three lamps of learning, and the Marine Base.

Plates 29 and 30   Finland   Coast Jaeger Battalion, Cap and Rank Insignia, Sleeve Ratings; and Denmark, Poland and Greece

The units on these two Plates are all part of the Army of their respective nations, although each one is a Marine-type unit. The Finnish Coast Jaeger Battalion has an eagle's head as a beret badge and uses the same device superimposed on hunters' horns for shoulder straps. The device appears in the center of one other badge peculiar to this unit, a blue Maltese cross with a gold border called the Trikari Cross, which is semi-official and worn without ribbon under the right breast pocket. It is awarded to regular personnel for good conduct after a minimum of three years' service, and to conscripts for good conduct before the end of their national service period.

The badges of rank are as in the rest of the Army and are worn on both collars and sleeves. The background color of all Jaeger units is bright green and the trim, yellow. The top rank in the Coast Jaeger Battalion is colonel, but the three ranks above that are also illustrated since general officers are links in the command above it. Most of the rank devices need no explanation. One, however, may need to be explained since it is unique to the Finns; it is the fir tree twig worn on many of the collar patches and also used as a sleeve patch by regular NCO school students.

The Marine Regiment of the Royal Danish Army started out in 1672 as part of the Navy, but was transferred to the Army 20 years later and has remained there ever since. It still maintains some naval traditions, and its members wear a badge that clearly shows its roots are in the sea. The insignia is a three-masted ship with sails furled. It is made in brass for all ranks and is worn on a red cloth patch on berets and collars. The ships face inward on collar badges. The rank badges are as in the rest of the Danish Army.

Although some references show insignia identified as worn by members of Polish Marine units, said to be part of the Army before World War II, Col. Henryk Krzeszowski of the Office of the Military, Air and Naval Attaché of the Polish People's Republic Embassy in Washington, D.C., says the Polish Armed Forces do not have any Marine units, that the closest they come is the Jednostka Obrony Wybrzeza, or Polish Coast Defense Unit. It is a part of the Army, and its members wear a white anchor inside a white wreath on a light blue round patch on the left sleeve of uniform coats. All other insignias are the same as the rest of the Army.

Greek Marine units are also part of their Army but wear distinctive shoulder flashes and patches. The flash illustrated is roughly translated 'Strength of the Marines'. The inscription at the top of the 32nd Marine Regiment patch is in ancient Greek and says 'To possess courage'. Greek Marines otherwise wear badges the same as in the rest of the Army.

Plate 31   USSR   Naval Infantry, Epaulets

The Soviet Naval Infantry, or 'morskaya pekhota', has roots dating back to 1705, when Czar Peter the Great ordered two infantry regiments transferred to the Baltic Fleet, but over the years, there is little to show that special uniforms or insignias existed for these types of units until very recent times. For the most part, Russian Naval Infantrymen in both World Wars seemed to be largely sailors sent to fight on land. A few insignias, such as that of the Odessa Sea Battalion of World War I, which is illustrated on this Plate, and a plain yellow foul anchor worn on the left sleeves of uniforms in World War II (not illustrated) were about the only types of distinguishing marks such troops wore.

When the Soviet Naval Infantry was re-established in the early 1960s, after nearly two decades in limbo, distinctive black field uniforms made their appearance, although rank devices were still based on those of the Navy. The officer's cap device is the same as a Soviet Navy line officer's with a wreathed anchor in yellow metal topped by a red enameled star with a white circle containing a gold hammer and sickle. Warrant officers also wear this badge. Other ranks wear a beret badge of a red, gold-bordered star inside a black circle with gold border. The red star with hammer and sickle is worn on the front flap of the fur winter service cap. Both officers and other ranks wear an additional beret badge of a red enamel pennant with a gold anchor at the broad end. These are worn on the left side of the beret, while the other cap badges are centered. Another insignia shared by all ranks is the patch worn just above the elbow on all field service coats. It has a red outer circle with a black interior, on which a gold foul anchor is centered.

Officers' rank insignia for the field uniforms are black shoulder boards with an embossed checkerboard pattern, on which red stripes and gold stars are worn. Other ranks wear shoulder boards with the Cyrillic initials for the fleet in which they serve – Baltic, Black Sea, Northern and Pacific, or no assigned fleet, centered between rank stripes in yellow or gold cloth.

Plate 32   Argentina   Infanteria de Marina, Rank Insignia

Argentina's Infanteria de Marina is one of those Corps which does not use its official insignia as a cap badge. Enlisted men wear a cloth oval on which is embroidered a device of a foul anchor, sunburst, sword and liberty cap. This is in blue for most units (top right on plate) but is used in red by Corps musicians (top left).

Since Infanteria de Marina officers wear naval uniforms, they wear the naval cap device of a gold wreath with a foul anchor surrounded by a golden-braided loop in the center. Above the anchor is an eleven-pointed sunburst in gold thread. Rank insignia for officers is worn on shoulder boards, coat cuffs and collars, depending on the uniform worn. The Admiral of the Navy is, of course, in overall command of the naval forces, which includes the Marine infantry. His insignia is three eight-pointed stars below crossed silver anchors on gold shoulder boards. The collar insignia is three five-pointed silver stars with one at the top and two at the bottom. The commandant of the Corps is a vice-admiral whose insignia is the same, but uses only two stars. A rear admiral has one star.

From captain through midshipman, the ranks are shown in stripes that have become known as 'British' style. They consist of half-stripes and full stripes with the uppermost stripe topped by a 'curl'. The shoulder boards, which are black with gold stripes, are worn on the dress whites and the service green uniforms. The stripes are worn on the cuffs of the blue uniform.

Officers wear the emblem of the Corps as a breast badge over the right coat pocket. It consists of crossed cannon, symbolizing the Corps' origin as a naval artillery unit, behind a foul anchor, which has the coat of arms of the Argentine Republic centered on it.

In addition to paratrooper wings, certain other specialty insignias are worn as breast badges in the Argentine Infanteria de Marina. Among these is the special insignia for Arctic service. It consists of a stylized gull below an arc in the Argentine national colors. Officers wear a rosette below the Corps device on the right breast which indicates command. It is a raised, fluted gold device with a black center.

Plate 33 Argentina Infanteria de Marina, Unit Crests

The Argentine Marine Corps has a number of distinctive insignia for units within the Corps, not all of which are illustrated here. Most follow the more formal traditions of coats of arms, although some, such as the amphibious com-mandos group badge, look more modern.

In the first row on this plate are the insignias for the 1st Marine Brigade, the 1st Marine Infantry Battalion, and the 2nd Marine Infantry Battalion. The brigade's motto translates roughly as 'Our nation forever'. The scroll at the bottom gives its unit designation as the 1st Brigade, Marine Infantry, Argentine Armada (Navy). The 1st Battalion's motto means, 'For the glory of the nation'. The initials B.I.M. mean Marine Infantry Battalion. The 2nd Battalion's motto means 'Always forward'.

The second row starts with the Commando Battalion badge which has a motto of 'Strength in union'. The 1st Artillery Battalion's motto translates as 'Win or die'. The Service Battalion is one of the few without a Latin motto. The badge of Non-Commissioned Officers' School has the letters ESIM at the top. They stand for Escuela de Suboficiales, Infanteria de Marina.

The ornate badge leading off the third row is that of the Shore Batteries of the Marine Infantry, and its motto means 'The work boils.' The motto of the 1st Force Battalion means 'Liberty and justice.' The 4th Marine Infantry Battalion uses no motto, nor does the 5th Battalion.

In the fourth row the Amphibious Vehicle Battalion's motto assures us that it hopes to perform 'with glory in the arena of waves'. The Communications Battalion, which is second in the row, and the following, Quarters Service unit, do not have mottoes. The last badge in this row is of the Amphibious Support Force which also does not use a motto.

The last row shows the 3rd Battalion's insignia with its motto promising to die for the nation. The Anti-Aircraft Artillery Battalion uses the well-worn 'By this sign I will conquer'. The Amphibious Commando Group uses no motto.

Plate 34 Argentina Infanteria de Marina, Sleeve Rating; and Mexico, Peru, Chile, Paraguay, Colombia, Uruguay

The Argentine Marine Corps uses naval titles for officers and enlisted ranks as well. Chevrons for non-coms are worn in varying color combinations depending on the uniform. These include red on white for white uniforms, gold on blue for blue uniforms and black on olive drab for green uniforms and field clothing. Senior chief petty officers wear two broad and two narrow inverted chevrons. Chief petty officers wear two broad and one narrow chevron, first class petty officers one broad and one narrow chevron and second class petty officers one broad chevron.

All branches of service in Argentina use the same insignia for paratroops. The officers wear gold-colored wings, the enlisted men white and both wear black, subdued wings on field clothing. The arc above the wings is in bands of sky blue and white, the Argentine national colors.

Mexico, Infanteria de Marina

Mexico's small Infanteria de Marina uses naval rank structure and insignia with few exceptions. Naval jump wings in both gold and silver versions are authorized. The long triangle shoulder patch is worn with field clothing, with or without a number at the bottom designating the wearer's company. The units device consists of crossed rifles over an anchor. Members wear curved shoulder flashes bearing 'Infanteria de Marina'.

Peru, Infanteria de Marina

Peru's Naval Infantry basically follows the rank and uniform structure of the rest of the Navy. The Corps device, however, is worn above chevrons. The insignia is also worn separately on a circular patch with a white or blue background, depending upon the uniform worn. Officers wear the badge on the collars of khakis and field uniforms. It consists of bayoneted crossed rifles behind a foul anchor. At the center of the anchor is a shield-shaped crest divided into light blue and white squares at the top and a single red bar at the bottom. In the blue square is a gold llama, in the white a gold tree, and in the red bar, an overflowing cornucopia. The Peruvians also wear an 'Infanteria de Marina' shoulder title in blue lettering on a white, blue-bordered strip.

Chile, Marine Corps

The Marines of Chile wear a Corps emblem that incorporates several armed forces specialties. The central feature of the badge is a plain anchor. Halfway up the anchor shaft is a turreted castle, a device that has been used in infantry badges, engineers insignia and fortress artillery emblems by various nations. Above the castle is a five-pointed star. Below the castle are crossed cannon, an almost universal symbol for artillery. The emblem is mounted on a black oval bordered in red. A smaller unmounted badge is worn on collars.

Paraguay, Cuerpo de Defensa Fluvial

Although Paraguay is a landlocked nation, it has a relatively small Navy that patrols inland waters. It includes a naval infantry unit that specializes in riverine defense. Its badge, which dates back to 1865, consists of an anchor with wide flukes with crossed rifles behind it. The Corps was founded as the Regimiento de Marina 'Riachuelo'. At the point where the rifles cross is a five-pointed gold star. Naval uniforms and rank insignia are used. The commandant is a Navy captain. A commando unit is included in this Corps. They wear standard green field clothing. (*The cap not breast badge is illustrated.*)

Colombia, Marine Corps

The Colombian Marine Corps insignia is more of a coat of arms than a badge. It consists of a shield with a plumed knight's helmet at the top, sea horses at each side, and a rifle crossed over an anchor inside the shield. At the bottom is a scroll with the inscription 'voluntas omnia superat' which roughly means 'desire conquers all'. The Corps includes amphibious commandos who wear the current gold badge which was adopted in 1974. Prior to that date, the commandos wore the silver insignia. Officers wear naval uniforms, and their cap badge is Navy-style with a gold wreath and an eagle at the top, but the Corps badge of rifle and anchor is in the center.

Uruguay, Infanteria de Marina

Uruguay maintains a small naval force which includes a unit of naval infantry. Its insignia is a plain anchor with a bayoneted rifle crossing behind. On the front is an outline of the nation. It is brass. (*The cap not lapel insignia is illustrated.*) The unit wears naval uniforms and uses the naval rank structure and insignia.

Plates 35 and 36 Brazil Corpo de Fuzileiros Navais; and Ecuador

The colorful uniforms of the Brazilian Corps of Naval Riflemen (Corpo de Fuzileiros Navais) are marked with special insignia that shows its connection with the Navy. The badge of the Corps indicates graphically what the unit is, with crossed rifles behind a foul anchor. This emblem is worn by enlisted men and non-coms as a cap and collar badge. Officers, however, do not use it as a badge on peaked caps. Instead, they wear the regular naval officer's cap device of a gold laurel wreath enclosing a silver foul anchor, which is topped by a sunburst (not illustrated). They do wear the Corps emblem on cuffs and shoulder boards above rank stripes in place of the curl worn by regular Navy officers.

The only time the officers wear the emblem as a cap badge is when they are in the khaki dress with glengarry cap, which is also worn in a white version by other ranks. On this cap the badge is backed by a multi-folded black ribbon, which is said to be a traditional sign of mourning for the death of Lord Nelson. Marine Commandos wear it in a circle on berets (recent research shows *it is yellow not white metal*).

The rank insignia for non-coms are chevrons worn point down with an arc above containing the Corps emblem. The chevrons are golden yellow and scarlet for both the red and white coats and dark brown on khaki for khaki coats and shirts, as well as field clothing.

Marine Commandos belong to an amphibious reconnaissance company and wear jump wings consisting of golden wings with a parachute over an anchor at center. Instructors wear a silver star in the center of the chute. Officers who qualify as pilots wear a badge of golden wings with a shield over a foul anchor in the center (not illustrated). The jump wings are worn over the right breast pocket, the pilot wings over the left. A silver version of the jump wings appeared in the 1960s but, apparently, has been discontinued. Officers may also qualify for other Navy specialists insignia, such as the submariners badge.

Although it appears that Brazilian Marines seldom, if ever, wear shoulder or pocket patches, there are a number of unit insignias that are used otherwise. Two of the examples here are shown on pennants for the Divisao Anfibia (Amphibious Division). The background of both patches appears similar to some USMC World War II patches, in that they show the stars of the Southern Cross constellation. What the American Marines saw on Guadalcanal, the Brazilians see in their homeland since the constellation is visible only south of the equator. The 1st Battalion insignia has a red background with yellow numeral and anchor. It is known as the 'Riachuelo Battalion', and is named after a Brazilian city, as apparently are the other battalions. The 2nd follows the same pattern but with a light blue background. Both numerals are crowned, which

shows Brazil's Imperial antecedents. Each shield has at the top a type of coronet with two sailing ship masts protruding. The emblems are used on vehicles of their units and are possibly worn in some way on field uniforms.

The emblem shown between the two pennants is carried on the Corps colors and is used as a vehicle marking and is sometimes painted on white helmet liners. It consists of a yellow shield, a black bomb and flames, and battle axes in red. The date 1808 is the year the Corps was founded.

The brassard worn by military policemen has the initials for the Portuguese words for 'service police' below an emblem of a black eagle on a yellow shield below a red bar with a coronet device above it.

Ecuador, Infanteria de Marina

The cap badge of the Infanteria de Marina of Ecuador is a foul anchor with a rifle and saber crossed behind it and a condor perched over a wreathed oval bearing the words Vencer O Morir – 'Win or die'. The device is also used within a gold circle with the words, 'Infanteria De Marina – Ecuador' around the interior of the circle. This is worn as a breast badge. The emblem appears in black on an orange background as a shoulder patch worn below a curved shoulder title bearing the name of the unit. The non-com chevrons in the same color combination correspond to the ranks private first class through sergeant major. A Commando flash is also worn as is an octopus patch for frogmen.

Plates 37 and 38 Venezuela Cuerpo de Infanteria de Marina, Rank Insignia and Ratings, Weapons Qualification Badges

The Cuerpo de Infanteria de Marina of Venezuela has a distinctive Corps insignia of a rifle over a foul anchor, but it apparently is not worn as a cap badge. It appears on shoulder boards and chevrons. Since the Corps is a naval service, its officers wear the Naval officers' cap badge of a wreath surrounding the nation's coat of arms topped by a cockade with an outer circle of gold, an inner circle of light blue and a center red dot. For non-coms a foul anchor replaces the coat of arms. Commandos wear a unique insignia showing open-jawed alligators on each side of the coat of arms with the cockade at the top.

Naval-style rank insignia is worn on shoulder

boards, cuffs or collars by officers, warrant officers and senior NCOs, depending upon the uniform worn. NCOs and other ranks from sergeants major to third class corporals wear inverted chevrons with the Corps device centered above. A variety of marksmanship badges and jump wings are also worn.

Plate 39   Cuba   Naval Infantry

The Cuban Marine unit is so small that Western intelligence sources have not fully figured out what it is supposed to do and Castro is not telling. It is not certain if any of its members are part of the Cuban expeditionary units in parts of Africa.

It is obvious that its uniforms are patterned after those of the Soviet Naval Infantry. The uniform is black with the blouse open just below the neck to show a blue and white striped T-shirt. For parade dress, the Marines add a white belt with brass buckle and a white cord worn from the right shoulder. Like their Soviet counterparts, the Cuban Marines wear black berets. Also, like the Russians, they wear a red enamel pennant on the left side of the beret.

Naval-pattern rank insignia is worn on shoulder boards. A shoulder patch in the shape of a shield is worn on the left sleeve just below the shoulder seam. It is black with a yellow border, and the Cuban coat of arms and a foul anchor in yellow thread in the center. The officers wear the coat of arms as a cap badge, while other ranks wear the coat of arms above crossed anchors.

Plates 40 and 41   Republic of Korea
Marine Corps, Rank Insignia, Parachutists Badges; Republic of Indonesia

The South Korean Marine Corps shows the USMC influence in its cap badge, as do most of the Asian Marine Corps. In the ROK version, the globe is replaced by a five-pointed star. In the officers' and one enlisted man's examples shown here, the eagle's legs are shown in front of the top point of the star. A variation, also illustrated, has the eagle's legs behind the point of the star.

A new collar badge was adopted during the 1970s. It consists of crossed rifles over an anchor. These replaced smaller versions of the cap badge which, USMC-style, had the anchors facing inward from left and right. They were usually in a dark bronze shade that became known as 'subdued' during the Vietnam War. The new collar

insignia are in yellow and white metal.

Officers' rank devices follow the Army's system of diamonds, eight-pointed stars and five-pointed stars. All of these rank devices are in silver-colored metal, except the warrant officer, who wears a single gold diamond.

Staff sergeants through sergeants major wear a system of inverted chevrons, with one for the staff sergeant and so on up to three with a 'rocker' for the sergeant major. An anchor with crossed rifles is centered above the chevrons. Until the late 1950s, this device was not used on ROKMC chevrons. For the lower grades, privates first class wear a single stripe on a slant, corporals, two, and buck sergeants, three. The chevrons and stripes are usually red on forestry green. The anchors and crossed rifles, which combine the device used above chevrons in the Army with the one used by the Navy, are also red on green. The rank devices for the enlisted grades are the same on the miniature pin-on insignia in either metal or plastic, except that pfc through sergeant wear straight rather than slanted stripes. Several variations of the jump wings in cloth and metal have taken place over the years, illustrated here.

During the war in Vietnam, the South Koreans sent forces to fight against the North Vietnamese, and these included the 2nd ROK Marine Brigade. Known as the 'Blue Dragon' brigade, these Marines wore a distinctive insignia shown in two versions here. The smaller was in metal and was what was known as a 'beer can' insignia. The large badge appeared in cloth and shows the dragon in a slightly different position. On the smaller badge, the scroll above the dragon says '2nd ROK MARBDE' (2nd Republic of Korea Marine Brigade), and the scroll below has 'Vietnam' as one word. The larger version has only the acronym 'ROKMARBDE' at the top and 'Viet-Nam' with a hyphen below.

The Ranger qualification badge is similar to one used by the Army, but has the ROK Marine insignia in the center of the rope circle at top. Two versions of the variety patches worn by Force Recon Marines are shown here, although the one with the skull is unofficial. Both the ROKMC stencil worn on the left breast pocket of fatigue jackets, à la the USMC, and the belt buckle show the Korean words for ROKMC.

The ROKMC patch with the red star is a variety patch not widely worn, and the other two are blazer or shooting jacket patches. The yellow and red patch with the initials for ROKMC in

Korean on either side of the shield is plastic and worn on field clothing.

Indonesia, Korps Marinir Kommando

The Republic of Indonesia's Marine Corps was formed in 1945 under the name 'Korps Marinir', which is the Indonesian spelling of the Dutch Korps Mariniers. The first cap badge carried this name. Although the name showed the Dutch influence, at least a slight U.S. influence was apparent in the design of the badge which featured a foul anchor behind a circle. The name 'Korps Marinir' appeared on this badge, as well as a triangular shoulder patch with a kris above lapping waves. Later the name of the unit was changed to 'Korps Kommando', and this name appeared on the new cap badge along with the kris, the waves and the Indonesian motto 'Jalesu Bhumyam Ca Jayamahe', which means, 'Glory on land and sea'. A variant is also illustrated.

The kris, a dagger-like weapon, is considered both traditional and sacred in Indonesia and is handed down from father to son. The five curves in the kris on the KKO badge represent the five principles on which the Indonesian state was formed. The waves on the badge symbolize the unit's duties on land and sea. The kris also appears in the center of the jump wings which are awarded to those who qualify as parachutists. The sports patch worn informally by sky divers in the KKO is illustrated, although it is not an official patch to be worn on uniforms.

Plate 42 Nationalist China (Taiwan) Marine Corps, Epaulets

The Nationalist Chinese Marine Corps is one more of the Asian Corps whose insignia has been greatly influenced by the USMC. The familiar globe and anchor are there, but the map on this globe is that of mainland China. Above the globe is the sunburst symbol of the Nationalist Chinese. The cap badges come in several styles including wreathed versions mounted on cloth backgrounds for officers and non-commissioned officers and a cloth-backed type for other ranks. Smaller versions in both gold-colored and silver-colored metal are used on sidecaps. Lapel insignia follows the USMC pattern, anchors facing in.

Officers' rank devices are stars for general officers, stylized plum blossoms for staff grade and bars for field grade. There is no rank of brigadier general. One star is the device for major

generals and two stars are worn by lieutenant generals. Enlisted ranks use a system of inverted chevrons, dashes and bars, which gives a rank badge for everyone, including privates, who wear a single chevron.

Few of the world's Marine Corps have their own air support units, but in those that do, the wings worn by pilots are usually Naval pilot badges. The Chinese, however, have unique wings for Marine pilots, and apparently is the only Marine Corps in the world that does. The wings are very similar to the U.S. Naval Aviator's 'wings of gold', but in the center, instead of the shield and vertical anchor, there is the Chinese Marine Corps insignia.

There are also other speciality badges worn by NCMC members, including HALO (high altitude, low opening) specialist badges in bronze and silver and the airborne commando-frogman badge.

Plate 43 Republic of the Philippines Marine Corps; Thailand and Japan

Despite the fact that the Philippine Islands were an American possession for nearly a half century, there is surprisingly little American influence in the insignias of their Marine Corps. The foul anchor and shield with the superimposed sun bears no resemblance to the USMC emblem, although some Asian nations made obvious adaptations of the eagle, globe and anchor emblem. Since the Philippine Marine Corps is an integral part of the Navy, the non-com chevrons are the same as for naval petty officers. Various shoulder and pocket patches are worn in the PMC, most of which incorporate the Corps insignia.

Thailand, Royal Thai Marine Corps

The USMC influence on the Thai insignias are easily seen, with winged garuda figure appearing in two versions on top of the globe with the outline of Thailand on it. The Thai Marines wear naval uniforms and insignia of rank.

Japan, Imperial Japanese Naval Infantry

There is many a veteran of the Pacific campaign during World War II who will swear he fought or saw Japanese 'Imperial Marines'. There was no such organization. The Japanese not only had no Marine Corps, but no specially trained naval landing organization even existed within the Japanese Navy until the late 1920s. Prior to that time, all Japanese seamen were trained in land warfare, along with training in seamanship. When a naval landing party was needed, the temporary unit was formed from within the fleet, then disbanded, and the men returned to regular duties after the operation. This often proved disruptive within the fleet, so an alternative was sought.

This led, in the late 1920s, to the formation of Special Naval Landing Forces – called 'Rikusentai' in Japanese – at four major naval bases: Sasebo, Kure, Maizuru and Yokosuka. They were given numerical designations related to the base where formed, such as Sasebo 2nd Rikusentai, Yokosuka Rikusentai, etc.

The first use of the Naval Landing Forces came in 1932 in the Japanese offensive against China. Once an objective was gained, the Landing Force often remained as the occupying unit. The Landing Forces were used extensively throughout the Pacific during World War II, often spearheading operations for Army troops.

Since members of the Landing Forces were essentially sailors, they wore naval uniforms when not serving in their roles as landing troops. While serving on land, they wore khaki drill uniforms with naval rank insignia. The distinctive Japanese soft peaked cap was worn by both officers and enlisted men with a cloth badge, consisting of a foul anchor, on which a cherry blossom had been superimposed. Variations of this device were also worn on steel and sun helmets. Naval rank insignia was worn on khaki uniforms with yellow or gold devices on dark blue backgrounds. Officers wore one to three silver cherry blossoms on gold stripes of varying widths mounted on dark blue backgrounds to indicate rank. Parachutists' cloth sleeve emblems are illustrated in white and blue versions.

plete picture of what they wore. However, no known picture of a CSMC enlisted man in uniform has been uncovered by researchers.

Surviving records established that the Confederate Corps members followed the Army rank system. The officers' uniforms were patterned after those of the USMC, substituting gray for blue and black for scarlet trim. Officers wore both looped sleeve braids and collar devices to indicate rank. One braid was for lieutenants, two for captains and three for field-grade officers. Gold horizontal bars were worn on the collars for the ranks, second lieutenant through captain – one to three respectively. Majors wore one five-pointed gold star, lieutenant colonels two and the colonel-commandant three.

Shoulder knots without rank devices are attached to Graves' uniform coat. It is believed these were worn on dress occasions and may have contained rank devices for those above second lieutenant. The buttons on Graves' uniform are USMC-pattern, which apparently was the standard of CSMC officers, many of whom were former USMC officers. There is some evidence that a button with the letter 'M' was also used by the CSMC, as on the shoulder knot here.

The belt buckles shown have never been authenticated and are shown simply because they exist and are sold to collectors as replicas. The buckle with the 'CSMC' on it displays the type of crude 'homemade' lettering found on many Confederate belt buckles of the period. The wreathed buckle is the more common of the two and was supposedly manufactured in England during the 1860s. Non-coms wore USMC-style chevrons, which they wore point up like their Union counterparts. It is doubtful if very many had the manufactured look of the USMC stripes. The southern Marine apparently wore gold on black chevrons and probably handmade.

Plates 44 and 45   Confederate States of America   Marine Corps, Collar Rank Insigina, Enlisted Insigina

Although only one known uniform of a Confederate States Marine Corps officer has been preserved – the uniform of Lt Henry Lea Graves, which is displayed at the Atlanta Historical Society – there are enough photographs of other CSMC officers in uniform to give a fairly com-

Plate 46   Imperial German   Marines

Although the officers and men of the See-Bataillon wore Army-style rank insignia, they had many emblems worn by no other organization. The Imperial eagle plate worn on shakos and tropical helmets is a typical example. This appeared in both brass and white-metal versions, and by some accounts, it was painted in a darker shade by Imperial Marines headed for the front at the onset of World War I. The eagle plate had been worn since 1875 when it replaced a plain anchor that had a scroll with the German words for 'With God for King and Country' on it.

A variety of shoulder straps were worn during the history of the unit, which dates back to 1850 and the Prussian Navy, when maroon epaulets were worn. Later, the white shoulder strap with a foul anchor in golden-yellow became standard. Between 1856 and 1867, the Imperial Marines had a Sea Artillery Battalion which wore crossed cannon over a plain anchor in yellow on the white shoulder straps. The decoration on the shoulder straps was changed in 1888 to the Imperial crown above two crossed anchors. Roman numerals to indicate the battalion were added below the anchors. There were several variations in color, the main one being during World War I, when the color of the shoulder straps was changed to field gray for field uniforms. The crowns, anchors and numerals remained yellow, although some that were orange have been discovered.

Members of the field artillery battery in the 3rd See Battalion wore a flaming bomb device over the crossed anchors. Buttons on the shoulder straps were supposed to bear Arabic numerals for the company, although surviving examples indicate that, more often than not, a button with the Imperial crown over an anchor was used.

A number of specialty emblems were used, not all illustrated here. Pioneers wore a circular arm patch with an entrenching tool over a pickaxe. Signalmen wore crossed flags and cannoners wore winged, flaming bombs. Since some mounted contingents were included in the 3rd Battalion, farriers were needed and they wore an emblem of a horseshoe pointed downward. In American lore, this position means luck is running out, and it did for the 3rd, isolated in China and defeated by an Allied force in 1914.

Plate 47 South Vietnam Marine Corps, Rank Insignia

The cap badge of the South Vietnamese Marine Corps seems to have borrowed from both the United States Marine Corps and the British Royal Marines in that it featured an eagle, globe and anchor, plus a wreath. However, in the center of the globe is a raised five-pointed star with an outline of the map of South Vietnam centered. Lapel badges, sometimes also worn on

caps, were of the same design, but lacked the wreath. Both cap and lapel badges were usually in metal, although some embroidered cap badges were used, particularly on berets. The badges followed both the U.S. and British Marine pattern—yellow and white metal for officers and yellow metal for enlisted ranks.

For insignia of rank, the VNMC officers used British Navy style stripes and curls, although Army rank titles were used. Shoulder boards and sleeve stripes were authorized for more formal uniforms, but were seldom seen since the Corps was usually in the field. Officers in field clothing frequently followed the French practice of wearing small rank devices above a button on the front of the jacket. Miniature rank insignia was also worn on field caps, often below the VNMC insignia.

Instead of a warrant officer rank, the Vietnamese had a rank known as 'chuanuy', which, roughly translated, means aspirant, although those holding the rank were not cadets.

Senior NCO grades were established in 1967 covering the ranks of sergeant major, master gunnery sergeant, first sergeant and master sergeant, to give their U.S. Marine Corps corresponding ranks. They did not wear chevrons but straight bars. Sergeants major and master gunnery sergeants wore one broad yellow bar at the top, a single gold bar in the center, and a narrow yellow bar at the bottom. The first and master sergeants wore the one broad and one narrow yellow stripe. Some references show NCO chevrons worn with a curl at the top on shoulder boards, as officers wore, apparently a variation.

NCOs from staff sergeant through lance corporal wore inverted chevrons of a French pattern, usually as miniature devices on the field clothing. Pfcs wore single gold inverted chevrons.

Plate 48 South Vietnam Marine Corps, Unit Patches, Parachutists Badges

Just before the collapse of the South Vietnamese government in the spring of 1975, the VNMC had a strength of ten battalions, although most of them were at least a couple of hundred under the authorized strength of 931 men each.

A variety of pocket and shoulder patches were used by the South Vietnamese Marines, including one for each of the battalions. But even company-sized units sometimes adopted a patch.

The insignias appeared in several forms, the most common being a flimsy cotton patch on which the design had been printed. Some embroidered versions existed, and also some of the miniature-sized metal badges which became popularly known as beer can insignia because of the material used in their manufacture. There were a great many variations, particularly in colors, although that was often in degrees of shading. There is some evidence that so-called 'subdued' versions of some of the patches (olive drab and black) cropped up among some of the Marine units late in the war, although this was usually an Army practice.

The exact number of patches used by South Vietnamese Marine Corps units is anybody's guess anymore. It has been estimated that all South Vietnamese units – Army, Navy, Air Force and Marines – had a total of cloth patches exceeding 2000 by the war's end. Positive identification of some of the smaller units' patches is next-to-impossible. Even 'experts' are at odds on some of the identifications. The patches on this plate are largely presented as examples and are those most commonly seen in collections.

There were several patches that apparently were for members of the South Vietnamese Marine Corps in general, without regard to a specific unit. The most commonly seen was a green shield with the VNMC insignia printed in yellow and red. With a black background this became the patch of Commando-like units known both as Rangers and Raiders. Two other patches for Corps-wide use were round, and both had the motto 'Danh-Du-To-Quoc' (honor and country) at the top. The more elaborate version carried the full cap-badge style insignia, which included the wreath plus a scroll below the circle with the words 'Thuy-Quan Luc Chien', which translates as Vietnamese Marine Corps.

All of the battalion patches carried Vietnamese wording, which usually described the central figure in the patch. The 1st Battalion, which features an owl, has the words 'Quai-Dieu' which, in effect, mean 'monster bird'. The 2nd Battalion, with a stylized wolf carrying a trident, had the words 'Soi Bien', or 'sea wolf'. The 3rd Battalion's symbol was the head of a water buffalo and the words 'Trau Dien' which mean 'crazy buffalo'. It should be pointed out that something is lost in the translation.

The Corps' hard-luck battalion, the 4th, which was virtually wiped out in a battle with the 9th Viet Cong Division 31 December 1964, used a shark symbol and the words, 'Kinhi-N-Gu' which translate literally as 'bulky shark', but is closer to 'great shark' to Vietnamese.

The wording on the 5th Battalion's patch – 'Hac-Long' – means 'black dragon', although the dragon on the patch was usually yellow. The patch of the 6th Battalion had an eagle perched at the top of a vertical anchor, which was piercing the numeral '6', and on a scroll at the bottom, the words 'Than-Ung Cam-Tu', which mean 'sacred bird'. The 7th Battalion patch showed a leaping tiger and the words 'Hum Xam' which means 'gray tiger'. The symbol of the 8th Battalion's patch tells at a glance that it is an 'O-Bien', or 'sea eagle', while the 9th Battalion's patch displays a tiger with fangs exposed and the motto 'Manh-Ho', 'ferocious tiger'.

There were two VNMC Brigades, designated 'A' and 'B'. The 'A' Brigade patch was a blue shield with a red star in the center with the letter 'A'. At the top are the words 'Lu-Doan', which mean brigade, and at the bottom the Vietnamese words for their Marine Corps. These words also appear on the 'B' Brigade patch, which was also named after an ancient Vietnamese knight – Bac Binh-Vuong – pictured on the patch with sword raised, riding a white horse.

The names used on these patches were probably duplicated to some extent on Army patches, since dragons of various colors and birds of various degrees of ferociousness and sanctity were popular names for Vietnamese units.

The VNMC also had its own artillery units which adopted patches, and some other support units did likewise. The patch of the 1st VNMC Artillery Battalion was a black-bordered red and blue-green shield with black centered crossed cannons and the numeral '1' over blue-green surf. (The plate annotations to these three patches should be "1st/2nd/3rd Artillery Battalion".) The 2nd Battery had a green bordered shield halved in red and white with a green feathered red arrow headed for the bull's-eye of a white and red target.

The 3rd Battery's patch features an artillery piece and an eagle. No exact translations of the mottoes were available to the author. For instance, 'Than-Tien', the 2nd Battery motto means something like 'marvelous deity' while the 3rd's 'No-Than' relates to a crosshow.

INDEX

References in *italics* are to illustrations in the text.